BENELUX
An Economic Geography of Belgium, The Netherlands and Luxembourg

BENELUX

An Economic Geography of Belgium, The Netherlands and Luxembourg

By

R. C. RILEY

G. J. ASHWORTH

1975

HOLMES & MEIER PUBLISHERS, INC.

NEW YORK

Published in the United States of America 1975
by Holmes & Meier Publishers, Inc.
101 Fifth Avenue
New York, N.Y. 10003

Library of Congress Catalog Card No. 74-84586

ISBN 0 8419 0174 0

© R. C. Riley and G. J. Ashworth 1975

Printed in Great Britain

CONTENTS

5

MAPS AND DIAGRAMS

7

8   MAPS AND DIAGRAMS

FOREWORD

Despite their proximity to Great Britain and the key position that they hold both in the European Economic Community and in the wider context of Western Europe, the countries of Benelux—Belgium, the Netherlands and Luxembourg—have received scant specific attention from geographical writing in English. Many texts have dealt with the three lands in conjunction with others in Europe, variously defined, and the detail accorded has necessarily been somewhat restricted. Here an attempt is made to remove from Benelux its mantle of a *terra incognita*, focusing on the economic aspects of the three countries in the belief that the principal characteristics of modern West European civilisation may be explained in economic terms. In order to understand the contemporary economic situation it is more useful to resort to a systematic rather than a regional treatment, and therefore the greater part of the book is given over to the consideration of major themes rather than areas. Chapters 3-6, which consider primary, secondary and tertiary activity, including transport, form the core of the book. They are preceded by introductory material which seeks to help explain some of the main economic patterns which follow. Particular attention is paid to social considerations which are often a cause of and a response to economic conditions. Rather than compress a comprehensive regional analysis into a single chapter, a typology of regions, identifying regions by their economic characteristics, has been constructed and a number of regions deemed typical of each category selected for closer examination. Although its aim is to identify regional problems, this chapter serves to highlight the contrasts which do exist between and within the Benelux countries and offers a useful counterpoint to the broader approach employed elsewhere in the book.

Foreign place-names always cause problems, but here the difficulty is compounded by the existence of three languages in the study area. In addition, the better-known towns have anglicised names. A number of conventions have therefore been employed both in the text and in the figures. Firstly, where an anglicised name exists this has been used; rather than Den Haag we have The Hague and instead of Bruxelles or Brussel, Brussels is preferred. Secondly, because many Belgian towns and administrative areas have both Flemish and French names, some bearing little resemblance to each other, viz. Waremme, Flemish Borgworm, the location has been taken as the criterion. Towns and regions in Flemish-speaking districts attract Flemish names, and those in French-speaking areas French names. Thirdly, where a river cuts through two or more language areas, it is referred to by the name given to it in the area concerned. Hence when leaving Wallonie the Meuse becomes the Maas on reaching the Dutch frontier. In Luxembourg the French Moselle becomes the Mosel since the language spoken is German. Friesland is an exception since although Fries names are legal and in use, they are not commonly known outside the Netherlands, and Dutch equivalents have been used. Fourthly, in order to overcome confusion between identical provincial and city names, the former are identified by the introduction of the word 'province'. In this context the term 'Holland' has only been used in the historical section; elsewhere 'the Netherlands' has been used to denote the nation and 'Noord-' and 'Zuid-Holland' to denote the provinces of these names. In the case of 'Flanders', the English form is used for the historical county and for the area occupied by the Flemish-speaking people. The terms 'West-' and 'Oost-Vlaanderen' are reserved for the provinces bearing these names.

The authors have received invaluable help from individuals and institutions too numerous to mention both in all three Benelux countries and in Great Britain, and we are deeply grateful to all those who have answered our questions, replied to letters and supplied us with information during the production of the book and over the much longer period of our acquaintance with Benelux. A special debt of gratitude must be recorded to our colleagues and students who have manfully agreed on many occasions to pursue foreign fieldwork in Belgium and the Netherlands, to Michael Draper of the Portsmouth Polytechnic Cartographic Unit who drew the maps with much patience and even greater skill, and to our wives for providing extended periods of silence and for their support in so many other ways.

Chapter 1

THE PHYSICAL AND HISTORICAL BACKGROUND

A. The Physical Background

1.1 INTRODUCTORY

Any attempt to understand the geography of an area must include a consideration of its physical components, the most important of which are climate, relief, geological structure, soils and drainage. These can be the subject of investigation for their own sake, but they may equally well be examined on account of the part they play in shaping the human geography of particular areas. That Benelux, with the exception of the Ardennes (Fig. 1.1), is part of the north European plain rather than a tropical region, places general restrictions upon agricultural production, and within the countries themselves further restrictions stem from differences in relief, climate, slope, drainage and soil cover. Clearly tropical crops cannot be grown at all, while physical influences within Benelux, such as the harsh climate and poor soils of the Ardenne mountains, are important determinants in the choice of cereals grown. Uplands and infertile heathlands are unattractive to settlement, and unless workable mineral deposits are present, as is the case of the coalmining districts of Kempenland in Belgium, such regions tend to be of small economic importance. It is geological processes, coupled with the early date of exploitations, that have created the population concentration to be found on the Walloon coalfield, and it is possible to argue that the waterlogged nature of the rock above both the Kempen and Zuid Limburg coalfields prevented their development until the 20th century. The Dutch struggle against inundation by the waters of the Rhine and the North Sea has endured for two millenia, and is seen not only in the physical and economic landscape but also in many of the social attributes of the Dutch people. Physical factors may not always be stressed in subsequent chapters, but they are nevertheless of great general significance.

The climate of Benelux is critically affected by three factors which interact to create the broad climatic régime experienced. Firstly the North Atlantic Drift brings warm tropical water into the North Sea, appreciably raising coastal temperatures in winter and lowering them in the summer,

11

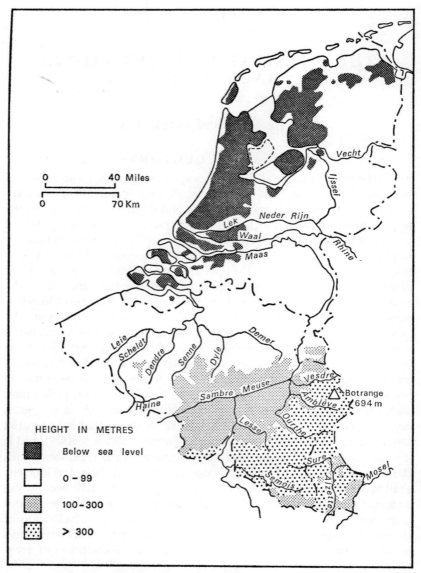

Fig. 1.1 Benelux: relief and drainage

and frequently causing fogs. Secondly the three countries are greatly influenced by the passage of depressions caused by the mixing of polar and tropical air masses, giving rise to unstable weather conditions. Thirdly the presence of anticyclonic airmasses in the continental interior brings hot summer and cold winter conditions to the eastern and southern regions of Benelux. The maritime and continental influences are such that the western half of the Netherlands and north-western Belgium are part of the Flemish Oceanic climatic region, and the remainder of Benelux belongs to the West European continental climatic region. The oceanic region has a mild climate, witness the mean January and July temperatures for Vlissingen of 4°C (40°F) and 17°C (63°F), but the seasonal differentiation becomes progressively more marked towards West Germany. Maastricht records mean temperatures of 2°C (36°F) in January and 20°C (68°F) in July. Maximum summer temperatures for these two stations reflect the differences between them, for at Vlissingen the maximum is 31°C (88°F) while at Maastricht it is 37°C (98°F). The number of days of frost illustrates the same principle; there are 31 such days at Vlissingen, but 79 at Winterswijk in the Dutch province of Gelderland. The severity of the continental régime is greater in the uplands, Arlon in Belgian Lorraine having 103 days of frost. At Bastogne in the Ardennes the first frost occurs in early October, at Brussels the event is experienced in the second week of November and finally at Ostend in the middle of that month.

In the lowland districts rainfall is evenly distributed throughout the year with a slight maximum in the autumn, when cyclonic activity is at its greatest. Only a small increase in altitude is required to raise the total rainfall, so that those areas north of the Sambre-Meuse depression receive between 510 mm (20 in) and 760 mm (30 in), and the hilly region to the south up to 1 270 mm (50 in) per annum. Stavelot in the Hautes Fagnes uplands south of Liège receives 1 120 mm (44 in) a year; Chiny in the western Ardennes above the middle Semois valley receives 1 259 mm (49 in) per annum. As befits an area affected by depressions, the weather is similar to that in Britain—changeable with overcast skies and considerable drizzle in the winter.

Although Benelux belongs essentially to the north European plain, some relief from otherwise monotonous lowland is provided by the Hercynian massif of the Ardennes, which rise to 694 metres at Botrange. These uplands, with the pre-Ardennes to the north and the Lorraine plateau to the south, comprise the whole of the area to the south of the Sambre-Meuse depression, including Luxembourg. Uplift has caused the rejuvenation of the rivers which have cut deep valleys in the peneplained plateau of the Ardennes, emphasising the contrasts between the area of the rest of Benelux. Some of the valleys, such as that of the Meuse between Dinant and Namur, are particularly attractive. On the northern margin of the massif, Carboniferous rocks are exposed and erosional action by the Haine, Sambre and Meuse rivers has created a series of valleys along the line of the coalfield. Undisturbed Cretaceous and Tertiary beds to the north give rise to a series of low limon-capped hills which reach 220 metres near Namur, but for the rest of Benelux low relief prevails. Lowland Benelux largely comprises the composite delta of the Scheldt, Maas and Rhine rivers, an area either directly or marginally affected by the Quaternary ice sheets. The effect of direct glaciation is to be seen in the 'push moraines' of the north-eastern Netherlands; here fluvio-glacial deposits were pushed by the ice into strongly delineated ridges. In some areas glacial sands and gravels have accumulated to form relief features such as the Veluwe and Kempenland, which stand above the level of the lowlands. The dune coast of Benelux, created by tidal currents and winds, creates a line of low hills separating and protecting the low-lying interior plain from the sea. Above all in Belgium, the dunes represent an obstacle for rivers seeking the North Sea.

The term 'Low Countries' is applied advisedly to Belgium and the Netherlands, for not only does lowland comprise the larger part of the land area of the two countries and house the majority of the population, but some 30% of the Dutch land surface is below sea level. No less than 42% of the Netherlands is below the level of the sea or is liable to flooding by rivers. Since the Tertiary period the land has been sinking, and although this has been offset by the large quantities of alluvial material deposited by the Maas, Rhine and their distributaries, the Dutch are nevertheless planning to pump sand from the Dogger Bank to 'fill in' their country as it sinks. The balance between deposition and sinking is very delicate, and when the speed of deposition slows down, or when there is a small rise in the level of the sea, widespread flooding occurs. Between the 4th and 6th centuries AD a great lake, named Lake Flevo by the Romans, was transformed into a gulf of the sea, the Zuider Zee. In 1334 the Friesian sandspit was breached by the sea and became the Friesian archipelago. In 1421 the famous St. Elizabeth's flood inundated a fertile area at the mouths of the Rhine and Maas leaving the reedy marshlands of the Biesbosch as a present-day memorial to its devastation. The great flood of January 1953, when 1 800 lives were lost, is only the latest of a series of events inflicted on the Dutch by their physical environment. In this sense the absence of relief is very much more important than the presence of upland in other regions of Benelux. The protective dykes, drainage ditches and polders characteristic of so much of the Netherlands, and to a lesser extent Belgian Flanders, are man's response to the difficulty of the area, and it is at this point that there is a very thin line between the natural and the man-made landscape.

Benelux does not encompass the entire length of any of its three great rivers, for the Scheldt (Escaut in France) and Maas both rise in France, and the Rhine originates in Switzerland. The Rhine is the largest of the three and such is its size that the Netherlands is effectively its delta. Immediately prior to the last glacial period the Rhine entered the sea via the Zuider Zee, but as a result of the subsequent glacial barrier and an increase in the tidal range southward towards the Straits of Dover, its main outlets have entered the sea progressively farther south. As late as Roman times the main stream of the Rhine reached the North Sea to the west of Leiden, but today the more southerly distributary, the Waal, takes two-thirds of the flow. Although not a distributary of the Rhine, the Maas makes a huge sweeping change of direction below Liège and enters the sea in combination with the Waal. Such a concentration of water serves to emphasise the risk of flooding, but more advantageously creates a large belt of fertile alluvial soil. The Scheldt drains the Flanders plain—only the Ijser and Zwijn escape its clutches—and enters the southern reaches of the Rhine delta at Antwerp. This adds to the problem of water disposal in the Zeeland district of the Netherlands, and it is to avoid major flooding in the area that the Delta project has been inaugurated. This is discussed later in the chapter. Although they bring their problems, the great rivers of Benelux, including the Mosel flowing through Luxembourg, are all navigable and therefore constitute a great saving to the economy. Indeed much of Dutch commercial growth has depended on the navigability of the Rhine and on the access it provides to inland industrial regions.

1.2 PHYSIOGRAPHIC REGIONS

An analysis of the physical components of the geography of Benelux, considered above in general terms, at the regional and local scale, enables a number of clearly defined physiographic regions to be isolated. This is not a sterile exercise, for such a system of regions helps to explain many of the variations in the human geography of the three countries. There is a close relationship between physiographic regions and agriculture, and it is hardly surprising that Belgian agricultural statistics are issued for fourteen agricultural regions, all of which have a physiographic basis. Less obviously, many of the broader aspects of the social and economic geography of Benelux can be related to physiographic regions. It is the relief, soils and climate of the Ardenne uplands that cause them to be a region of difficulty, and the infertile sands and clays of the heathlands in the eastern Netherlands and Kempenland have had the same effect. Unattractive to settlement and possessing scant incentive for immigration, such regions are characterised by rural depopulation, a trend which regional planning policies are trying to halt, and ideally reverse. Also the nature of the dune coastline and the recently reclaimed lands in Zeeland and Ijsselmeer place restrictions on human activity. On the other hand, it is no accident that the areas of densest population, such as the concentration of towns in the western Netherlands, are located on some of the most fertile soils in Benelux. In addition, some of these towns are ports which have grown up on the commerce brought by the Rhine, a major natural feature. The same reasoning may be applied to the Belgian 'growth' axis between Brussels and Antwerp, although this corridor of development does not fit quite so snugly into a single physiographic region as does the Dutch metropolitan area. Here the economic region spans part of four regions, but, with the exception of Kempenland, these regions are hardly inimical to settlement. Finally, while the south Belgian coalfield is but a small sub-region within the Ardennes, the concentration of population, the industries and the problems of this declining area nevertheless have an indisputably geological basis. Thus most of the areas with particular economic characteristics, examined in Chapter 6, also have distinctive physical backgrounds. Benelux may be divided into seven physiographic regions, which are delimited in Fig. 1.2.

1. The vales and scarplands of Belgian Lorraine and Luxembourg Gutland

This region is structurally a northern extension of the scarplands of Lorraine, with the consequence that its southern margin is somewhat nebulous. The northern boundary, however, is quite unambiguous for it is constituted by the Ardenne massif, and the eastern limit, if not geologically clear, is at least naturally defined by the Mosel and its tributary the Sûre. Belgian Lorraine and the western and central area of Gutland comprise Lower Jurassic rock, to the north and east of which in Gutland are older Triassic outcrops. Three important scarps traverse the region from west to east and are the origin of the term Côtes Lorraines, by which Belgian Lorraine is sometimes known. The northern escarpment, the Côte des Grès de Luxembourg, is most well developed and runs the width of the region, rising to a height of 465 metres near Arlon. The central scarp, the Côte des Grès de Habergy, describes an arc between Virton and Bettembourg and is much shorter than the northern scarp. The most southerly scarp, the Côte Calcaire de Longwy, is well defined, with a sharp north face. Comprising Oolitic Limestone, it forms an effective southern boundary to the region for the political frontier approximately follows its line. This escarpment has played a critical part in shaping the economy of Luxembourg and, to a smaller extent, Belgian Lorraine, for it has provided both with valuable deposits of *minette* or lean iron ore, which has led to the establishment of iron and steel plants on the orefields.

Between these ridges in Belgian Lorraine are to be found clay and marl vales through which the head streams of the Semois and Chiers run in an easterly direction. In Gutland the streams flow in the opposite direction to join rivers such as the Alzette and Attert, which eventually join the Mosel. This watershed is the only physical justification for the political division of the region. Central Gutland, lying between the northern and central scarps, consists of an undulating plateau of Liassic Sandstone between 320 and 430 metres in height, punctuated by deep gorges, pinnacles and caves caused by differential erosion and solution. The most spectacular scenery lies in the valley of the Ernz Moire in the north-east. This area, known as the Petite Suisse, has become a tourist attraction, and the 70-metre-deep gorge cut by the Alzette at Luxembourg adds to the charm of the city. Climatically the region has a continental régime, and the incidence of frost at Arlon has already been mentioned. Although the rainfall is not appreciably lower than that in the Ardennes to the north—the southern scarp receives more than 1 000 mm (40 in) per annum—and the winters no milder, the principal difference is the very much higher summer temperatures, especially in the Mosel valley. The term Gutland arises from the fertile soils and warm dry summers experienced in the part of the Duchy compared with the more unpleasant régime of the Oesling in the Ardennes.

2. The Ardennes

The Ardenne upland is an old Hercynian block, the denuded remnant of a former mountainous area. Such has been the work of erosion that there are no upstanding peaks, and the Cambrian and Silurian rocks that constitute the core of the upland form gently rounded summits barely exceeding 650 metres. The Cambrian and Silurian rocks are limited to the north-east and to the Rocroi massif to the south of the Famenne depression in the west. Elsewhere, rocks of the Devonian series prevail, exhibiting the same north-west—south-east trends, creating a plateau with gentle ridges and distinct continuous surfaces at particular heights, for example, at 600, 500 and 430 metres. Rocks of the Carboniferous series have been eroded from the higher areas, and remain only in a 80-km-long strip north of Dinant and in the coal furrow in the Haine and the Sambre-Meuse valleys. The tableland has been deeply cut by rivers such as the Our, Amblève, Ourthe, Semois and Meuse, a process which has been emphasised by successive uplifting. Within the broader region of the Ardennes, a three-fold subdivision is possible.

(i) *The High Ardennes* This is the area above the 350-metre contour, and includes the Oesling or Luxembourg Ardennes. Typical of these higher areas are poor drainage, peat bogs, acid soils, mists and high humidity. Such conditions are exemplified in the Hautes Fagnes in the north-east close to the German border. On the lower, somewhat drier slopes between

B

425 and 600 metres, the *fagnes* give way to heath and woodland, especially conifers, and the area in the south adjacent to the French frontier is heavily wooded. At a lower altitude beech, oak and elm are encountered; the High Ardennes have one-third of the total wooded area of Belgium. Heavy rainfall, 120 days of frost and infertile soils combine to make this an inhospitable environment.

(ii) *The Famenne depression* Following the structural grain of the Ardennes, this lower area runs from Chimay in the south-west to the vicinity of Liège in the north-east. It is largely below 200 métres and is the result of the greater susceptibility to erosion of Devonian schists and shales compared with the sandstones and schists of the High Ardennes. The valleys are well wooded, the climate mild and outcrops of limestone give rise to caverns, the best known of which is the Grottes de Han.

(iii) *The Condroz and the Entre Sambre-et-Meuse* To the north of the Famenne depression are two plateaus between 200 and 350 metres, separated from each other by the Meuse. Both comprise parallel valleys caused by differential erosion, but there is a general decline in elevation from the Condroz in the east to the Entre Sambre-et-Meuse in the west. With greater soil fertility and a less rigorous climate than the High Ardennes, these hill regions are transitional in character between the Ardennes and the low plateau to the north.

The central low plateau

The principal delimiting criterion for this region is relief, for it incorporates those areas north of the Sambre-Meuse depression which are more than 50 metres above sea level, and the Herve plateau south of the Meuse. The highest point is located in the Herve plateau, and although there is a loss of height of 354 metres to the northern boundary, this is achieved gradually, giving rise to a gently undulating landscape, very often without any perceptible fall in height to the north. The underlying rock comprises Palaeozoic and Mesozoic materials such as slates, quartzes, sandstones and chalk, but these are almost everywhere covered by deposits of sand, clay and, more characteristically, limon, a secondary delimiting criterion. The rivers have cut through the limon cover, but in the interfluves it varies from 10 to 20 metres in thickness, creating a highly fertile buff-coloured loam. This low plateau is part of the great north European loess (limon) belt laid down at the foot of the Hercynian mountains. Lying between the difficult Ardennes and the damp, low-lying plain of Flanders, it is not surprising that this fertile plateau, which in no way impedes movement, should not only be densely populated but also have seen the establishment of some of the earliest European cities. 20th century technology can transcend areas of difficulty in a way that medieval man could not, and it was thus the physical advantages of this region which were conducive to its early historical prominence.

Five sub-regions may be recognised, but it should be emphasised that the physiographic differences between them are not large. To the west is the plateau of the provinces of Hainaut and Brabant comprising limon-covered sands and clays straddling the Scheldt tributaries, the Dendre, Senne and Dyle. The Hesbaye plateau, drained by the Gette and the upper Demer, lies to the east. It is higher than Hainaut and Brabant and also differs from them in that in the south its limon is underlain by chalk. The consequence of the latter is a notable absence of surface drainage and thus of dissected surfaces caused by river erosion. The third sub-region is small and lies to the north-east of Hesbaye. Following the Demer valley it represents a transition zone between the *région limoneuse* and the less fertile sands of the Kempenland. Its function is expressed in the name given to it by Belgian geographers, *la région mixte*. The Herve plateau, bounded by the Meuse, the German frontier and the Vesdre valley, is the fourth sub-region. Since it is south of the Meuse and of similar height to the Condroz to the west, it is sometimes treated as part of the Ardennes. However, the surface rocks are younger than those of the Ardennes and comprise chalk capped by a thin layer of limon, which alone would suggest inclusion with the low plateau region. The ridge and valley structure of the Condroz and Entre Sambre-et-Meuse is lacking, and the surface terrain is more in keeping with the Hesbaye. It is the highest part of the plateau region, large areas being above 200 metres and the highest point rising to 354 metres. The final sub-region is that part of the Netherlands which extends southwards between Belgium and West Germany to Maastricht, known as South Limburg, or occasionally as the Dutch 'panhandle'. The underlying rock is largely chalk and, characteristically, is overlain by limon, creating fertile loamy soils. There is considerable evidence of the post-glacial work of the Maas in the form of terraces, but the most important influences upon human geography are provided by the rocks of the Carboniferous series which outcrop in the east and dip to a depth of 650 metres in the west, forming the basis of the South Limburg coalfield. The physiographic contrast between this region and the remainder of the Netherlands, together with the landscape beauty created by the alternating ridges and valleys, have directly contributed to its importance as a tourist district.

Interior Flanders

This is a small, triangular-shaped region represented by the basins of the Leie (Lys), Scheldt and the lower Dender (Dendre). The first two of these originate in France, and in fact the region is part of a larger area which extends west to the Artois hills. The region can be defined as lying between 5 and 50 metres, and as such is higher than the polders on one side and lower than the central plateau on the other. There are some important exceptions to this generalisation, however, for in the interfluves of the Scheldt and Dender there are a number of hills of Pliocene sands standing above the level of the Flanders clay. Two of these hills face each other about Ronse, one, Pottelberg, attaining 157 metres, and a third to the north of Tournai reaches 149 metres. There are also patches of clay to the north, but sands are more important. Because of the slight variations in relief over most of the region, river flow is slow and streams wind their way slowly in a north-easterly direction to the sea through alluvium-filled valleys. In such a régime natural drainage is not easy, and as the polderland is approached it becomes increasingly necessary to provide drainage ditches. The physical advantages of this region do not compare with those of the plateau to the south, but man, by dint of hard and persistent labour, has managed to transform the area into one of intensive agricultural production.

The heathlands of Benelux

In their areal extent, the various heathland sub-regions comprise the largest single physiographic region in Benelux. This is in itself not surprising since large areas of the north European plain consist of heath, and the Netherlands and northern Belgium are part of this plain. Characteristic are infertile, sandy soils which sometimes degenerate into sand with sparse vegetative cover, and areas of moorland between 50 and 100 metres, regarded as monotonous by some but exhilarating by others. The porous nature of the soils results in constant leaching from rain which rapidly percolates downward, removing the nutrients from the soil. In places waterlogging occurs as a consequence of the formation of a hardpan 1 metre below the surface. At one time peat bogs were widespread, but reclamation which has been in train since the 17th century has improved large tracts of land. The study of place-names suggests that woodland was once quite extensive, but having been removed by man and his animals, trees were unable to regenerate in the acid and infertile soils which developed after the removal of the woodland. Here is an unusual, and extensive example of man degrading the physical environment so that it has increased its control over him. The use of these unattractive areas as political frontiers between the Netherlands and both Germany and Belgium underlines their influence, albeit negative, on later human development. The sands and gravels north of the Maas are of glacial and fluvio-glacial origin, while those south of the river in Noord Brabant and Belgian Kempenland were laid down by the Maas in the post-glacial period when the river carried a large volume of such material. This difference in the mode of origin is of small consequence, however, and does not detract from the unity of the larger region. Four sub-regions may be recognised.

(i) *Kempenland* This region is common to both Belgium and the Netherlands. In Belgium it is bounded by the Scheldt in the west, the Maas in the east and the Demer and Dyle on the south. Highest in the east where it abuts the Hesbaye plateau, the region dips north-west in the direction of Antwerp, but it is not only the low-lying areas that are ill-drained, marshy and patterned by drainage ditches, for these are a characteristic of the entire Kempenland. Its barren nature has been immortalised in the paintings of Van Gogh, and this zone of repulsion became a convenient frontier between the two states. In the Netherlands the region is enclosed by the great loop of the Maas. The Peel, an area of extensive peat bogs, is a projection of the plateau to the north-west, but other than this there is a gradual loss of height towards the alluvial plain of the Maas in the north.

(ii) *The Veluwe* The translation of 'veluwe' is 'barren' or 'bad', and is indicative of its difficult nature. It is bounded on the east by the Ijssel, by the Neder Rijn on the south, the Ijsselmeer on the north and by the fertile Geldersche Vallei on the west. Sands predominate, reaching their greatest height (107 metres) in the east, and much of the land is given over to coniferous plantations and to nature conservation. An example of the latter is the Hoge Veluwe National Park. It is the most extensive area of sparse population in the Netherlands and one of the largest areas of continuous open space in North-West Europe.

(iii) *Gooi-Heuvelrug* To the west of the clay vale of the Geldersche Vallei is a ridge of sand rising to a height of 63 metres, stretching from Ijsselmeer to the Neder Rijn. It is known as Het Gooi in the north and the Utrechtse Heuvelrug in the south. Although similar to the Veluwe in its repulsion of settlement and hindrance to communications, its smaller size and greater proximity to the densely populated areas of the province of Zuid-Holland have recently made it more attractive to settlement.

(iv) *The heathlands of the northern and eastern Netherlands* These lands extend for 130 km between the polderlands of the Friesian and Groningen coast in the north to beyond Winterswijk in eastern Gelderland. They are highest in the east, and in the provinces of Overijssel and Gelderland the sandy hills rise above 70 metres in the vicinity of the West German border. Most of the former peat bogs have been reclaimed, but this has not encouraged immigration, nor has soil fertility reached that of the alluvial valleys and older polders. Unquestionably the physical environment has greatly influenced the relatively backward nature of economic activity, cultural separation and social deprivation that is traditional to this region. The worst affected areas are the Twente region of Overijssel and the eastern part of the province of Drenthe, but the plight of the heathlands as a whole has led the Dutch planners to designate them as a problem area.

The valleys of the Rhine and Maas in the Netherlands

This area of river alluvium comprises the valleys of the Maas and the Rhine and its distributaries, the Ijssel, Neder Rijn, Lek and Waal, from the point at which they flow into the Netherlands to their entry into polderland. The gradients of the river valleys are gentle, and coupled with the small tidal range in the North Sea off Zeeland, the rate of the deposition of sediment is high. Mention has been made of the changes in the direction of the lower Rhine after the last glacial period, and as a consequence large quantities of clay and sand have been deposited over the whole of this region. Flooding has helped the process. The Maas has cut three river terraces in its valley between Maastricht and Maasbracht, but beyond the latter point the valley broadens and similarity to the Rhine increases. Both rivers thus shape the pattern of man's activities, for his principal concern is flood control, and it was not until after the Second World War that serious attention was paid to the problem of cultivating the wet soils of the region. The danger of flooding, the sour soils and the isolation induced by the scarcity of communications have all caused the population to be sparse on many of the intra-riverine lands. These are the areas of economic difficulty known as the *kompgrondgebieden* which receive special government assistance as a result of their physical background. Only in a few favoured areas, such as the Betuwe or 'good land' between Nijmegen and Arnhem, where the heavy land is lightened by alluvial gravels, is the environment less inimical to man.

The polderlands

The polderlands face the North Sea from the French frontier near Adinkerke in Belgium to the West German frontier in the Dollart, protected in some areas by a dune coastal belt. The term polder may be defined as an area which is completely drained and whose water table is regulated. The Dutch polders are almost wholly below sea level, but those in Belgium are now above this height. In contrast to the other physiographic regions of Benelux, the polderlands are the result of man's efforts to protect existing areas and to reclaim land from the sea. Rather than allow the sea and low-lying land to inhibit him, man has overcome his environment to such a degree that he has been constantly adding to the area of the Netherlands over the last two millenia. The Dutch polderlands, comprising the provinces of Zeeland, Noord and Zuid-Holland, parts of Friesland, Groningen and Noord-Brabant, in addition to the Ijssel Lake polders, represent two-fifths of the area of the country, and are a real tribute to Dutch ingenuity. In the post-glacial period a sand bar developed along the coast of Flanders, continuing northwards and ending in what are now the Friesian Islands. Behind the sand dunes extensive layers of peat were laid down, especially in Friesland and Noord-Holland where the *laagveen*, or low peat fen, reaches a thickness of 15 metres in the vicinity of Amsterdam. The sand bar off the coast of Flanders was later destroyed, but the dunes between Den Helder and The Hague extended seawards and now form an extremely valuable defence against the incursions of the sea. However, the gradual rise in the level of the sea in respect of that of the land, amounting to between 10 to 15 cm each century, has resulted in the flooding of many areas, for instance Zeeland and Groningen, and the deposition of layers of marine clay, which the Dutch term *jonge zeeklei*. Thus there are three principal types of soil in the polders: the sands of the dune coast, the peaty areas to the east and the 'older' areas of Friesland and Groningen, and the recent marine clays of maritime Flanders, Zeeland, the Ijssel polders, coastal Friesland and Groningen and the north of Noord-Holland. Agriculture is influenced to some extent by these differences, but an interesting influence of soils upon human activity is to be seen in the Ijssel polders, for here planners have designated the most infertile sandy tracts as recreational areas, rather than as relatively high-cost farmland.

1.3   THE 'PAYS' CONCEPT

The application of local names to distinct physiographic regions and sub-regions is established practice in Belgium, especially in the French-speaking district to the south. Each area is said to be a *pays* which derives its individuality essentially from physical characteristics such as geology and relief. The peat bogs of the High Ardennes are reflected in the *pays*-names of Hautes Fagnes and Fagnes. The rivers that form two of the boundaries of the Entre Sambre-et-Meuse appear in the name of the *pays*, while other *pays* simply take the name of the geographical locality, for example Pays de Herve, Waasland (Pays de Waes), Pays Gaumais, Condroz and Meuse. In some cases former administrative areas such as Brabant, Hesbaye and Flanders form the derivation of the *pays*-name. However, the principal reason for the survival of these old names is that they apply to regions which are geographical units, and the impact of the physical environment has been such as to create distinctive human activities, above all with respect to agriculture. The official Belgian agricultural statistical returns are based on the *pays*, but with very few exceptions in no other way are they administrative units. The *pays* of Belgium are shown in Fig. 1.3.

Occasionally the *pays*-name take on a sociological significance when the inhabitants strongly identify themselves with the sub-region. The Borinage, a coalmining area, is such an example. The name springs from a physical source in the sense that the term *borin* was used to describe someone who used to hawk coal for sale, carrying it in panniers on his back. Thus the Borinage is the land of the *borains*, who until the 1960s were traditionally coal miners. The *borains* formed a tightly knit community, possessing their own folklore, customs, religious beliefs and, to a lesser extent, their own dialect. Essentially rural in outlook they held intellectuals, commercial interests and urban dwellers in very low esteem. The Borinage is distinctive sociologically, but it is also a recognised economic unit for it comprises the western part of the South Belgian coalfield.

Comparison of Figs. 1.2 and 1.3 indicates that there is a remarkable similarity between the *pays* and the physiographic regions of Belgium. For this reason the *pays* are of use to the regional geographer for they comprise accurate geographical regions. However, it is necessary to question the present-day importance of the *pays* and the geographical regions they represent, for although they are valid agricultural, and in some instances sociological regions, they have little relevance to the greater part of human activity at the present time. The idea of the *pays* has become a fossilised concept which, in the modern political and socio-economic environment, cannot really be justified in terms of regional unity. The development of inter-regional trade, of improved means of transport and of newspapers and television has broken down areal independence and has eroded the validity of the *pays* concept. It is because of the small size of many of the *pays* that they are frequently ignored by planners when regional policies are being devised. Thus the problems of all the *pays* south of the Sambre-Meuse valley are similar and very little is to be gained by considering each *pays* individually. For this reason Chapter 6, which is concerned with regional economic differences, makes no reference to *pays* as such.

1.4 LAND RECLAMATION IN THE NETHERLANDS

An account of the physical background of Benelux would not be complete without a detailed examination of the efforts the Dutch have made to control their natural environment. This is not to say that the Belgians have not been involved in winning land from the sea. For example, the town of Ostend is sited adjacent to Sint Katharinapolder, drained in 1744. However, the extent of these activities has been much more restricted than in the Netherlands where so much land has been won from the sea and rivers, as Fig. 1.4 suggests.

In Roman times settlement was largely restricted to small islands, known as *wierden* or *terpen*, constructed by the Friesians from mud

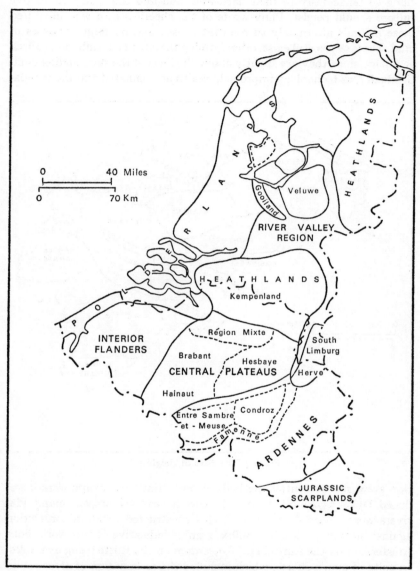

Fig. 1.2 The physiographic regions of Benelux

recovered from the immediate locality. Small wonder that these people clung so tenaciously to their hard-won land and that their distinctive culture should persist. Pliny wrote of the cheerless race who inhabited these mounds alternately surrounded by sea and by large expanses of mud. These *terpen* still exist, often forming the site of a farmhouse, church or village since they are slightly above the level of the surrounding land. Gradually, as technology improved, wealth accumulated and the popula-

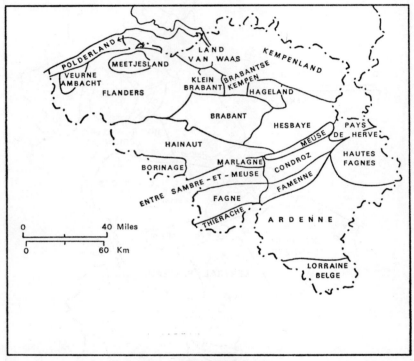

Fig. 1.3 The *pays* of Belgium

tion grew, more scientific methods of protecting settlements were introduced. Dykes were built about AD 1000 as the sea level rose, and many tidal rivers were dammed and sluice gates constructed to afford protection against incoming tides. The suffix 'dam' is indicative of this work, both Amsterdam on the Amstel and Rotterdam on the Rotte being examples. In spite of man's efforts, which included the reclamation of areas round the shore of Lake Flevo, the sea increasingly encroached on the land, and the combination of high spring tides and gale-force winds frequently caused dykes to be breached and many years' work to be destroyed in a few hours. The dune coast north of Den Helder was pierced by the sea in

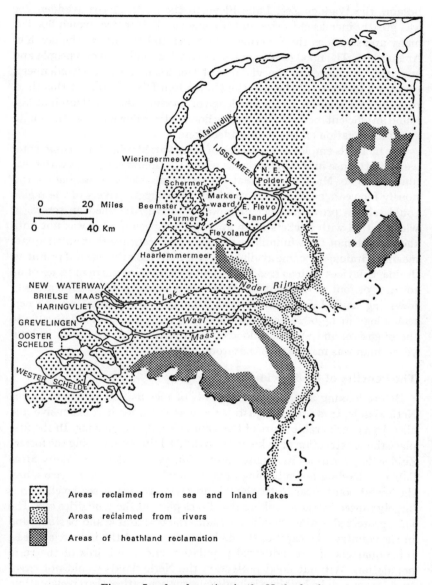

Fig. 1.4 Land reclamation in the Netherlands

1334, forming the present Friesian Islands, and the marshes to the east became the Wadden Zee. Lake Flevo to the south of the Wadden Zee was greatly increased in size and became the Zuider Zee, which flooded many areas such as the Schermer, Beemster and Purmer to the north of Amsterdam. The flood of November 1421, which killed 10 000 people and engulfed 72 villages in the vicinity of Dordrecht and Geertruidenberg, created a new arm of the sea, the Hollandsch Diep. It was at this time, possibly as a response to the challenge of flooding, that the Dutch at last found an efficient method of removing floodwater, allowing more thorough-going reclamation efforts to be undertaken.

The methods employed in regions of more varied relief for raising water were of little use in the Netherlands where the volume of excess water was quite massive. Machines of great capacity, capable of operating contin-uously for years on end, were required. The sluggish rivers of the region could seldom provide sufficient power to drive Archimedean screws or wheels fitted with buckets at an appropriate speed, and it was not until the invention of the windmill in the early 15th century that an adequate means of drainage became available. These mills took the place of primitive drainage devices such as treadmills, and by arranging them in series of up to three or four at different levels, it was possible to drain large areas of low-lying land. Limmenmeer, near Alkmaar, was drained by the new technology in 1430. Henceforth the Dutch moved from the defensive to the offensive, and although floods were by no means unknown in later years, man was master of his environment.

The benefits of land reclamation

Before looking at the different kinds of reclamation practised in the Netherlands, it is useful to justify the operation, for it is expensive and absorbs a considerable share of the country's national income. In the first place the construction of dykes such as the Afsluitdijk enclosing the former Zuider Zee, forms an invaluable protection against flooding. Many areas liable to flooding are subsiding approximately 2 cm every 10 years, and the lowest point, near Rotterdam, is now 6 metres below sea level. This is largely caused by the shrinking that takes place as the land dries out. The land protected against flooding includes the best arable and pasture land in the country, the capital, the major port, most of the industrial areas, three-quarters of the industrial population and two-thirds of the rural population. Without flood protection the Netherlands would not exist. In this sense, dyke building is land conservation rather than reclamation. Secondly, the construction of dykes is usually followed by the drainage of land behind them, and this land then becomes available for agriculture, settlement and recreation. The Ijssel Lake polders will add 10% to the land area of the country, which is the most densely populated in Western Europe. Thirdly, by improving control over the movement of salt water, which is constantly penetrating the low-lying areas through rivers, locks and canals, agricultural production will be assisted. Salt water is heavier than fresh water, and at the ebb tide the latter runs out to sea while the salt water remains. Salt water has now penetrated 13 km east of Rotterdam. An important result of the Ijsselmeer project and the Delta Plan will be the widening of the 'fresh water isthmus' from its 1930 position between Rotterdam and the southern shore of the Zuider Zee, to a line between Walcheren and the Ijsselmeer *afsluitdijk*. Fourthly, because strict control over the water table is possible, agricultural production is endowed with a degree of flexibility not often found outside the polderlands. By raising the water table the growth of grass is encouraged, allowing dairy farming to take place. Should arable farming be regarded as more profitable, the water table is simply lowered. Rainfall is thus not a critical consideration. Fifthly, the creation of freshwater lakes such as Ijsselmeer ease the problem of drinking water supply. It is perhaps ironic that there should be a drinking water shortage in a country whose principal problem is that of water disposal, but this is the case. The lakes can also be used for recreational purposes. Sixthly, the disposal of surplus water can be effected more rationally in areas where canalised rivers, drainage ditches and the regulation of water tables form a basic part of the infrastructure. Finally, dykes may be used for new transport routes, opening up formerly isolated regions and providing shorter links between existing settlements.

Categories of land reclamation in the Netherlands

(i) *Small-scale coastal reclamation* Early dyke building was carried out for protective reasons, but gradually dykes came to be built for both protection and for the acquisition of new land. Two or more dykes behind each other are better protection than one, and at the same time new land becomes available. The process is helped by the accretion of land by marine deposition. The northern coast of Groningen is an excellent example of this method. To the north of Uithuizen there are three lines of dykes beyond the original shoreline, those inland now performing no protective function. It is noticeable that both the regularity and the size of fields increase progressively towards the present shoreline, representing a visual comment on the development of agricultural techniques since mid-19th century. To the south of Uithuizen are a large number of *terpen*, now largely unoccupied. Further west, the Lauwerzee is being reclaimed by the construction of settling basins or *bezinkvelden* which accelerate the deposition of marine silt. In contrast to the linear growth of dykes is the poly-

nuclear development that occurred on the islands of Goeree and Overflakkee, eventually resulting in their amalgamation. A traverse from the
oldest part of Goeree to the core of Overflakkee passes through land im-
poldered in 1591, 1611, 1653, 1769, 1780, 1760, 1705 and 1408, indicating
that the two finally met in 1780. This kind of small and gradual expansion
is typical of the delta. An interesting cultural pattern has followed the
reclamation of the Hollandsch Diep, the joint estuary of the Waal and the
Maas. The inhabitants of the heathlands to the south of the estuary were
Catholic, but the polders reclaimed from the estuary shore were established
by immigrant Protestants from the north. Although it is now somewhat
modified, this correlation between land use and religion still exists.

(ii) *Reclamation of inland lakes* The invasion by the sea of large areas of
Noord-Holland created a number of inland lakes whose presence constituted a danger to the surrounding land. Thus in order to conserve existing
areas, it was necessary to reclaim others from the sea. Although it was
technically possible to drain quite large areas from the early 15th century
onwards, scarcity of capital effectively prevented large-scale operations
until the 17th century, although one inland lake west of Alkmaar was
drained in 1564. Merchants who had amassed fortunes from the lucrative
colonial trade came to regard the creation and sale of polders as a suitable
outlet for investment capital, and a spate of reclamation followed the
draining of the Beemster in 1612. This was achieved by the building of an
enclosing ring-dyke, outside which was a peripheral canal or *ringvaart* into
which the surplus water from the polder was pumped by 40 windmills.
Other projects completed in this period included the creation of Purmer
polder in 1622, Wormer polder in 1626 and Schermer polder in 1635. The
scale of these schemes, shown on Fig. 1.4, was considerable. Beemster
polder covered 7 174 hectares and Schermer polder 4 824 hectares and
their completion must have involved technical skills of the highest order.
Each year between 1591 and 1665 Dutch engineers reclaimed at least
1 200 hectares, and between 1616 and 1640 the average was 1 783 hectares
annually. Small wonder that Dutchmen were employed to canalise rivers
in Britain at this time. Even with the use of steam pumps in place of windmills in the 19th century, drainage projects seldom exceeded those
of the 17th century in scope. For example one of the largest 19th-
century schemes was the draining of the Ij polder, 4 823 hectares, in
1877. The most ambitious scheme was undertaken after extensive flooding
of Amsterdam and Leiden by water from Harlemmermeer in 1836. The
ringvaart of the Harlemmermeer polder is 60 km long and 45 metres wide,
and it took three steam engines driving 27 pumps five years to drain the
18 500 hectares, a task completed in 1852. This polder proved to be particularly fertile, although the changing evaluation of resources has caused the

north-eastern corner to be used for Amsterdam's Schiphol airport. As an augury for what was to follow, the Harlemmermeer project was financed by the government, for the costs were almost twice the sum that could be realised from the sale of the land, and private capital was not forthcoming. It was to meet situations such as this, and the need for integration between drainage schemes, that the Dutch *Waterstaat* had been set up in 1798. Hitherto the local coordinating organisations, the *waterschappen*, had been adequate, but the increasing size of drainage works brought the need for a central administrative body.

The most far reaching project to date has been the reclamation of the Zuider Zee. Although this was a gulf of the sea it became a lake with the completion of the enclosing dam in 1932. Once again the principal justification was reclamation as the best means of conservation, for the risks and costs of maintaining 300 km of dykes along the shores of the Zuider Zee would be reduced to the 30 km of the *afsluitdijk* if the plan proceeded. The scheme was first mooted in the golden age of Dutch water engineering, the 17th century, and again in the 1840s and in 1890. Legislation authorising work to begin was enacted in 1918, the details of the project being essentially those of the 1890 plan drawn up by Cornelius Lely. An enclosing dyke was to be built between Noord-Holland and Friesland, and five large polders were to be reclaimed from the resulting freshwater lake, the Ijsselmeer. Drainage channels were to be retained to facilitate the discharge of rivers, such as the Ijssel, which flowed into Ijsselmeer. The new lake, representing 40% of the area of the Zuider Zee, would provide freshwater supplies for the neighbouring provinces, and help in the maintenance of the water table in the polders.

Reclamation of Wieringermeer, in the north-east corner of Noord-Holland, began in 1927 and was completed three years later, adding 20 400 hectares to the Netherlands. The *afsluitdijk*, with a main road, two sets of barge locks and provision for a double track railway, was finished in 1932 so that the four later polders were reclaimed from an inland lake. The North-East polder (49 000 ha) was drained between 1937 and 1942 and East Flevoland (54 000 ha) between 1950 and 1957. The construction of the ring-dykes of the other two polders, South Flevoland (44 000 ha) and Markerwaard (62 000 ha) is progressing and drainage will be completed during the late 1970s. The benefits of reclamation have been discussed above, but it is worth noting that there has been a slight shift in the emphasis placed upon land uses since Wieringermeer was completed. At that time 23% of the Dutch working population were farmers, and new land made available by reclamation almost automatically became farmland. The subsequent improvement of agricultural techniques has reduced the area of land required to produce a fixed output of crops. At the same time the process of urbanisation has been continuing, causing land in the vicinity of towns to be in short supply. Thus East Flevoland and the two polders to be reclaimed will make an important contribution to the supply of land for the population and industrial activities of Amsterdam and other towns in the crowded provinces of Noord and Zuid-Holland. Satellite towns, industrial estates and recreation areas will flourish beside the farms of the later Ijssel Lake polders.

   (iii) *Major coastal works* The *afsluitdijk* having greatly improved the security of the lands bounding the former Zuider Zee, the remaining area at risk was Zeeland, the province comprising the islands and channels of the Rhine-Maas delta. Apart from the possibility of storm tides attacking the dykes, many of the channels were deep and the ebb flow constantly scoured the base of the dykes, eventually undercutting the masonry. The obvious, and most expensive solution to reduce the danger of flooding was to raise the height of the 1 000 km of dykes about 2 metres. The second solution was to throw huge enclosing dykes across the main entrances to the delta, thus reducing the length of the coastline subject to attack by the North Sea and offering the possibility of controlling the action of the tidal scour on the inland dykes. The calamitous floods of February 1953, which inundated 156 000 hectares and breached the dykes in 67 places, provided the final incentive for the Delta Plan. This envisages the construction of four major and four minor dykes linking the islands of the delta with the mainland, leaving Rotterdam's tidal sea canal, the New Waterway, open to the North Sea (see Fig. 1.4). In a similar fashion the Scheldt estuary will not be closed. The coastline of the Netherlands will be reduced by 700 km, and although the scheme will cost £200-300 millions, its true value may be judged against the £100 million losses incurred as a result of the 1953 flood alone. Other benefits arise from the use of the Zeeuwse Meer behind the dams as a freshwater reservoir into which floodwater from the New Waterway and the Lek can be directed when necessary, the control of the incursion of salt water inland, the provision of a roadway between the Netherlands and Belgium and the use of the Zeeuwse Meer as a recreational area. Since it is the intention to develop a limited area of polderland, amounting to only 13 540 hectares, in association with this scheme, conservation may be regarded as more important than reclamation. By 1972 the dams at each end of the Haringvliet, the Veerse Gat and the Grevelingen had been completed together with the dam at the inland end of the Ooster Schelde. The dam across the western end of the Ooster Schelde is scheduled for completion in 1978.

   A plan to link the Friesian Islands and reclaim the Wadden Zee has been mooted, giving the Netherlands an entirely smooth coastline and further reducing the risk of flooding. Although it is desirable, this scheme lacks the urgency of the Delta Plan and is unlikely to be launched during this century.

(iv) *River dykes* The deposition of sand and clay by the rivers of the Rhine-Maas delta has resulted in the land being lower than the rivers, a process greatly assisted by the way in which land sinks when it is drained. Dykes were thus built to preserve reclaimed land and to regularise the flow of the rivers, frequently enabling more land to be drained. The distributaries of the Rhine are almost everywhere dyked, but especially elaborate precautions have had to be effected in the Land van Maas en Waal where these two great rivers are separated by a very thin strip of land about 300 metres wide. Because of flooding this inter-riverine region was gradually transformed from an area of fertile to one of poor soils, and it was not until 1939 that a scheme of dyke construction and water control permitted the region to be reclaimed and for its former fertility to be re-established.

(v) *Heathland reclamation* Although it is less spectacular and less critical to the nation than dyke building and the reclamation of land from the sea, heathland reclamation is an important issue in the Netherlands. The work of improving the infertile soils of these areas has been proceeding since the 12th century, and land improvement has followed the same centrifugal pattern found on Goeree, Overflakee and other islands. Gradually the neighbouring common heathlands, called *marken* in the northeast, were colonised and improved by the use of animal manure and garbage from towns and villages, and by the introduction of primitive irrigation canals where a river was near at hand. Many such *veenkolonien* were established in the 17th century, although the 40-km *Stadskanaal* built in the early 19th century between the town of Groningen and the German frontier for the movement of peat and fertilisers, resulted in a rash of new settlement. Sometimes the *veenkolonien* were created by a company rather than by the efforts of several farmers; an example is that set up in the Peel in 1853 by the van de Griendt brothers. However, the common enemy, the sea, which resulted in communal action in the west, was absent in the east, and private interests transcended efforts by the central government to speed the process of improvement. Major progress was not made until the second half of the 19th century, but cooperatives such as the Dutch Heath Society, founded in 1888, played an important part in redressing the balance. The cooperatives, which received assistance from the government, could organise reclamation projects, arrange leases, offer advice and carry out research work. The supply of cheap fertilisers from Germany also helped as did the invention of deep ploughing techniques which turn the top 2 metres of soil, break up the hardpan and allow a mixture of fertilisers, marls and river clays to be applied. In particularly sandy areas pines are planted to prevent soil erosion and the Dutch Forestry Commission has been involved in this work since its foundation in 1899.

Recently, a change in the evaluation of heathland has taken place. Areas previously devoid of settlement because of their unsuitability for agriculture are now seen as valuable open spaces in an otherwise crowded country. Increasingly the heathlands are being used for residential development, as in the Gooi and the Kempenland to the north-east of Antwerp, military training, as in the Heuvelrug and the Kempenland, and recreation, as in the proposals for a Drenthe National Park which will extend over most of the province.

B. The Historical Background

The way in which the physical environment is capable of shaping man's activities has been demonstrated above, but an understanding of the present day socio-economic structure of Benelux is not completely possible without a glance at its historical evolution. Throughout historical time physiography has played an important part in the development of the three countries, but equally their geographical position in respect of other nations and international trading routes has been a critical consideration. The complex machinations of politicians and rulers have had a powerful influence on evolution, for apart from brief periods in the 16th and 19th centuries, Benelux has never possessed political unity and has been continually subjected to the grand designs of other European states. Such political action has had its effect upon economic activity, particularly in the sphere of international trade. At the same time some of the components of the area's cultural geography, for instance the division of the Netherlands into a Protestant north and Catholic south and the existence of Flemish culture in northern Belgium and Walloon culture in the south, stem from events in the early centuries of Christendom.

1.5 EARLY HISTORY

The Rhine-Maas delta, by virtue of its marshy terrain which impeded movement, represented the effective northern limit of Roman colonisation. To the north lay difficult, infertile territories while for the Romans the Baltic lands were barbarous and unattractive. Even the towns established by the Romans do not seem to have enjoyed much commercial prosperity. Rather they were outposts of an empire, sited at strategic positions on routeways. The Roman name for Utrecht was Trajectum, a

passage. The Germanic tribes to the north of the Rhine were thus left
largely undisturbed and were never subjected to the Romanising influence.
Among these tribes were the industrious Frisii who inhabited the coastal
marshlands between the Rhine delta and the estuary of the Ems. Their
environment, as we have seen, was conducive to maritime activities such
as fishing, and this led to the growth of trade, albeit of a very simple nature.
They formed a strong, cohesive unit, and coupled with the harsh nature of
their lands, it is not surprising that the Germanic tribe known as the Salian
Franks avoided the bleak littoral studded with *terpen* in their westward
movement in the 3rd century AD.

The Franks hailed from the Rhinelands and their expansion took them
into the area between the River Ijssel and the lower Maas. They crossed
the Waal, but in spite of their defeat by the Emperor Julian in AD 358,
they were allowed to settle in what is now Noord-Brabant. Naturally
expansionist, and driven on by the difficult nature of the Kempen, the
Franks gradually infiltrated into more favoured regions, and by AD 450
had colonised virtually the whole of Belgian and French Flanders. They
ignored Flemish polderland and avoided the then forested low plateau
of Brabant, in part because of its physiography and in part because it
was organised as a Roman frontier zone. The Franks thus took the main
Roman road linking Boulogne and Cologne by way of Arras, Bavai and
Tongeren as their southern boundary in Belgium. There then existed the
basis of the current tripartite cultural division of the Netherlands and
Belgium. The Friesians held sway north of the Rhine delta, the Franks
occupied the southern Netherlands and Belgian Flanders, imposing a
degree of linguistic uniformity in the shape of Netherlandish upon the area,
and the Roman influence remained south of the Sambre-Meuse valley,
where French was spoken.

While the Franks were pursuing their territorial expansion, the Friesians
were building up an impressive trading empire which extended into the
Baltic and the Irish Sea. They had trade representatives and possibly
trading establishments in towns as separate as Mainz, London and Bjorko,
near Vyborg on the Gulf of Finland. The chief port was Dorestadt on the
Waal, a location suggestive of the way in which the Friesians had extended
their domain. Like the Dutch today on land and at sea, the Friesians were
great commercial carriers of merchandise, initially augmenting and benefiting from the movement of goods between regions. They were skilled
shipbuilders, even though much of the timber had to be brought from the
Baltic lands, and they pioneered the construction of flat-bottomed vessels
without keels which could navigate the shallow waters and shoal-filled
channels of their land. It was inevitable that Friesian prosperity should
become a target for the Frankish Empire. Relations between the two were

far from friendly, and eventually the Franks succeeded in overcoming the Friesians at the Battle of Dorestadt in 689, although it was not until 785 that they were finally subdued by Charlemange and absorbed into his empire.

The death of Charlemange in 814 was followed by the break-up of his territories. Until 870 the Low Countries formed part of the Middle Kingdom or Lotharingia, but they were subsequently partitioned between Carolingia to the west and the German realm to the east. The line of the partition was approximately north-south and cut across the linguistic boundary. The Low Countries became border lands between two kingdoms and with the development of feudalism they formed a number of separate units, each with a considerable degree of independence. The Duchies of Brabant, Luxembourg and Limburg and the Counties of Flanders, Hainaut, Namur, Gelders, Holland and Zeeland, although owing allegiance to the Holy Roman Empire, were effectively sovereign territories. A main result of this political independence was a quite remarkable economic prosperity in the Middle Ages.

1.6 THE MIDDLE AGES

The geographical position of the Low Countries astride the lower reaches of the Scheldt, Maas and Rhine enabled them to benefit from the resurgence of economic life that took place in the 11th and 12th centuries. They found themselves at the focus of routes between France, England and the Baltic and of the landward continuation of these routes into Europe, by both road and river. No longer did the Low Countries occupy a terminal position as they had done in the Roman period, for they, and above all Flanders, were now at the hub of economic activity in Western Europe. Rich markets were available in the feudal estates, bishoprics and monastic centres. Many of the smaller rivers such as the Leie, Dender and Senne in Flanders, as well as those in the Rhine delta itself, were navigable far inland by ocean-going craft, allowing the growth of inland ports. This was an important consideration when water transport was much more rapid than movement by road. In addition to commerce there was a traditional industrial activity which received great impetus. The metallurgical industry of the Meuse valley, with important centres like Liège and Huy, and the Flemish cloth industry, a survival from Gallo-Roman times, made an important contribution to the upsurge of activity.

Out of these events came the rise of the town. Prior to this towns had been built to perform military, administrative and ecclesiastic functions. The growth of commercial activity threw up a merchant class who established themselves outside the walls of the towns to take advantage of the protection afforded by such a situation. They also benefited from the nodality of many of the towns. With the merchants came craftsmen and eventually the townspeople were able to set up autonomous municipal corporations which further assisted growth. By the 13th century Flanders had become the leading commercial and industrial area in North-West Europe, and so unusual was the density of its towns that it was regarded as a 'continuous town'. The medieval cloth halls and civic buildings of towns such as Ieper, Bruges, Ghent, Tournai, Leuven, Mechelen, Antwerp and Brussels are testimony to the prosperity of the period. Various estimates place the population of Bruges, Ghent and Ieper at between 40 000 and 80 000 inhabitants, that is, larger than London, in mid-14th century. Whatever its size, Bruges came to be the most important trading centre in Western Europe. It boasted branches of the great Italian banks, its merchant colony included Italians, Spaniards, Portuguese and Germans, it possessed a formidable fleet of ships and the first European wet dock was constructed there in 1234. Unfortunately the River Zwijn on which Bruges stood was incapable of scouring its bed and the port gradually silted up. The outport of Damme was built about 1200, large ocean-going vessels did not venture beyond the later outport of Sluis on the estuary of the Zwijn after 1350, and by 1490 the silting was complete, leaving Bruges 20 km inland. Ironically enough, as a result of a particularly fierce storm in 1405 which helped to accelerate the closure of the Zwijn, the entrance to the Scheldt was improved, enabling Antwerp to capture much of Bruges' former traffic.

Important though these physical impediments were, they were not the only cause of the decline in the fortunes of Bruges and the other Flemish textile towns. The rapid growth of the textile industry necessitated the import of English wool, but the development of cloth making in England resulted in supplies from this source being cut off. Further, the English were able to undercut the prices of Flemish cloth. Guild restrictions led to a migration to rural areas in order to take advantage of low labour costs, and for this reason the 13th and 14th centuries saw the rise of Armentières and Tourcoing in French Flanders and Verviers in the Vesdre valley south-east of Liège. Moreover, if the sea had given Antwerp a navigational advantage, so the absence of tight oligarchic control and the policy of encouraging international trade by every means possible also stimulated commercial activity in the port. The merchants of the Hanseatic League, a commercial organisation linking German cities set up in 1260-1265, finally abandoned Bruges for Antwerp in 1545. Notwithstanding, the fine buildings remaining in many Flemish towns are eloquent testimony to their early prosperity.

The political independence of the principalities comprising the Low Countries engendered the development of trade, but in order to encourage this trade and the wealth it brought, a number of treaties and commercial agreements were enacted in the 14th century. Links were forged between Brabant, Hainaut and Holland in 1328, and an important commercial treaty between Flanders, Brabant, Hainaut, Holland and Zeeland was signed in 1339. These events represented the beginning of the long process of unification of the Low Countries which resulted in the formation of Benelux in 1948. The gradual domination of the House of Burgundy in the 14th and 15th centuries worked in the same direction. Under Philip the Good (1419-1467) the County of Namur and the Duchies of Brabant and Limburg were acquired in 1430, the Counties of Holland, Hainaut and Zeeland in 1433 and the Duchy of Luxembourg in 1443. The Duchy of Gelderland fell into the hands of his successor Charles the Bold (1467-1477) in 1473. Although a central administrative organisation existed, much authority was vested in the principalities themselves, and thus it was possible for the Low Countries to emerge within the Burgundian State and remain free of the influence of France and Germany.

1.7 THE SIXTEENTH CENTURY

The work of Philip the Good and Charles the Bold was continued in the 16th century by Charles V (1506-1555). In the space of two decades he added Friesland (1524), Utrecht (1527), Overijssel (1528), Groningen and Drenthe (1536) and Gelderland (1543) to the Burgundian territories. There were 17 provinces in the resulting geographical unit, now known as the Netherlands, for only the autonomous bishoprics of Liège and Stavelot detracted from its unity. Fig. 1.5 shows the 17 provinces at the end of the reign of Charles V. Save for the inclusion of Artois, Cambrai, parts of Flanders and Hainaut now in France and a greatly enlarged Luxembourg, the year 1543 saw the existence of a single political unit consistent with the present extent of Benelux. Each province was represented in a 'circle' or council, originally set up in 1512, so that although the provinces were not obliged to conform rigidly to the desires of the monarch, at least they shared common elements of statehood, a powerful cohesive influence. Political independence gathered additional impetus in 1548 when the Netherlands were declared free of the Holy Roman Empire. Despite the east-west linguistic division into Netherlandish in the north and French in the south, the inclusion of the conquered northern provinces and the existence of strong provincial feeling, there seems to have been a considerable identification with the Netherlands by the population. There was certainly nothing in 1550 to suggest the eventual division along an east-west axis.

Political unity encouraged, and was encouraged by economic prosperity and it was the city of Antwerp that became the focus of commercial

Fig. 1.5 The 17 provinces at the end of the reign of Charles V in 1555

activity. It was a gradual process for the silting up of the Zwijn at Bruges took time, and the sheer impetus generated by the success of the merchants of the town ensured that Bruges did not collapse with any suddenness. But the absence of medieval restriction, the encouragement of the dukes of Burgundy and the admirable estuary and harbour provided by the Scheldt were important factors in the rise of Antwerp to a position of real eminence in the 16th century. As the commercial centre of the Hapsburg Empire it benefited enormously from the shipment by the Spanish of rich cargoes from the New World. On a more mundane level, there was an important cloth trade, and an enquiry of 1550 showed that 20 000 people in the town earned their living from the English cloth trade alone. It was logical that such activity should include banking, and the city became the chief money market of the time. Apart from the industries associated with the trade of the port, manufacturing in the Antwerp region included the highly skilled linen and tapestry industries which to some extent offset the decline of wool textiles. In 1560 the city had 100 000 inhabitants.

The political events of the second half of the 16th century were critical for the Low Countries, for shortly after its conclusion, in 1609, Belgium and the Netherlands, as they exist today, became separate units. This situation was formally recognised at the Treaty of Westphalia in 1648, but the separation sprang from developments in the previous century. Philip II succeeded his father in 1555, and even before his departure for Spain in 1559 (the Low Countries had become the Spanish Netherlands in 1516) there were indications of the difficulties ahead. The presence of Imperial troops, even though they were largely Walloons, was greatly resented by the Dutch, as was the administration of the Netherlands by foreigners. Additionally the minority religion of Protestantism in the shape of Lutheranism and Calvinism provoked the Spaniards into repressive measures to remove such heresy. Resistance was organised by William of Orange and the revolt gained much popular support when the 'sea-beggars' from the north took the Spanish-held ports of Brielle and Vlissingen in 1572. However, for the very reasons that had prevented the Romans from colonising the lands north of the Rhine and Maas, it was only in Holland, Zeeland, Utrecht and Friesland that this resistance proved effective. The Catholic aristocracy of the south was cultivated by the Spanish, and this served to harden the attitude of the northern or United Provinces who came together in the Union of Utrecht and declared their independence from Spain in 1581. The United Provinces then became quite separate from the royal provinces to the south. The declaration also represented the birth of the first modern nation state based on capitalism rather than feudalism, although the state did not receive full recognition until 1648.

Under Maurice of Nassau, William's son, Groningen and the eastern parts of Overijssel and Gelderland were recovered from the Spanish between 1590 and 1607. Taken in conjunction with their sea power, the United Provinces were in a very strong position to secure a favourable peace treaty. By this means in 1609 they obtained complete independence from Spain, and they gained possession of the northern parts of Brabant and Flanders and a small part of Limburg, which came to be known as the Generality Lands or *Generaliteitslanden*. They also secured the closure of the Scheldt to all but Dutch shipping. Henceforth the United Provinces, now the United Netherlands, popularly called Holland after their most powerful member, could advance. The southern provinces, on the other hand, could only decline as long as they remained under Spanish rule.

If the 1609 settlement explains the political division of the Netherlands and Belgium, it does nothing to explain the cultural pluralism that exists today. The new political boundary was not a linguistic one, and indeed many southern provinces included both Flemings and Walloons. Nor was it a religious division for there were Catholics in the north (Groningen even joined the Spanish in 1580) and Protestants in the south. The basis of the Netherlands, then, was only in part religion; more important was nationalism and capitalism, coupled with the strength that William and his son derived from the protective nature of the rivers and lakes of the northern provinces, and from their mastery of the sea.

1.8   THE SEVENTEENTH CENTURY

The political separation of 1609 seemed to set in motion a number of divisive events which accentuated the differences between the Spanish and the United Netherlands. During the 17th century the religious differences which had been present in a muted form crystallised out to give a predominantly Protestant United Netherlands and a Catholic Spanish Netherlands. The Generality Lands were also Catholic, which explains the present dominance of the religion in the Dutch province of Noord-Brabant. The Calvinist north was shielded from the influence of the Counter Reformation, but this did not prevent great pressure being placed on the Catholic population, who were numerically still very strong. In the south the Catholic church was assisted by the Jesuits and by the strength of the Counter Reformation.

Economically, the wars which spanned the period 1572-1648 left the southern provinces in a state of depression, and they were prevented from rapid recovery by the sheer prosperity of the Dutch, the loss of the Generality Lands to the United Netherlands in 1648 and the closure of their great port Antwerp until the end of the 18th century. The Thirty Years War, concluded in 1648, reduced the prosperity of the German cities and high protective tariffs effectively removed the possibility of selling goods in France. It is to be expected, therefore, that manufacturing should decline in favour of agriculture, and it was at this time that the intensive cultivation of Flanders was begun. The United Netherlands were a cohesive and independent political unit, but not only were the Spanish Netherlands ruled by a foreign power, but during the 17th century they were very much a buffer state between the Netherlands, France and Spain. As a result of the wars fought on her soil, the Spanish Netherlands lost the whole of Artois and Cambrai and large parts of Flanders and Hainaut to the French, and the southern shore of the Scheldt to the Dutch. Luxembourg, the largest province, suffered territorial losses to the French along the length of her southern boundary. As though these disruptions were not sufficient, at the Treaty of Utrecht in 1713 the southern provinces passed to Austria and for the next century became the Austrian Netherlands.

By contrast the 17th century saw the United Netherlands reach its zenith. It was 'de goldene eeuw', or golden century. The country became the most powerful maritime nation in Europe, and as such, in the world. Her merchants accumulated vast fortunes, Amsterdam became a powerful financial centre and port and the techniques of land drainage and reclamation were mastered. The war of independence waged against the Spanish had greatly strengthened the mercantile marine, and even before 1609 Dutch vessels had usurped the position of Spain and Portugal as 'the wagoners of the world'. The struggle against the Spanish caused the Pope to forbid the Portuguese to trade with the Dutch, making the latter intensify their efforts to create a colonial empire. The union of Spain and Portugal in 1580 gave the Dutch the excuse they needed for attacking the scattered colonies of Portugal as well as those of Spain in south-east Asia and elsewhere, and they came into the possession of territories in the West Indies, South Africa, Ceylon and the East Indies. The Dutch East India Company was established in 1602 and in 1670 it was able to declare a dividend of 40%. The Dutch West India Company was less successful but settlements were effected in Brazil, Guiana, on the eastern seaboard of North America (New York or New Amsterdam was founded by the Dutch), and in the West Indies.

Important though this colonial trade was to the Netherlands, of greater significance was maritime commerce in Europe, and above all in the Baltic lands. In 1594 the Dutch could claim a 34% share of the import trade of Finland, and between 1580 and 1589, half the ships passing through the Sound between Denmark and Sweden each year were Dutch. The goal of this trade was material for shipbuilding, for naval stores, as they were called, were as vital to sea power in the 17th century as coal and iron were to industry in the 19th. Lacking in materials themselves, the

Dutch found it relatively easy to develop their economy by relying on imported goods and they benefited greatly from the simple fact that different regions in the world have particular advantages for the production of certain commodities. This international regional specialisation is in fact the basis of world trade. Imports included cereals, flax, coal, iron, copper, diamonds, wine, wool, herrings upon whose bones Amsterdam was said to have been built, whale oil, cotton, spices, cocoa, coffee, sugar, rum and tobacco. The processing of these goods formed an important activity, as did the re-export of the finished products up the Rhine and Maas and across the North Sea. The nearest approach to large-scale industry was provided by the most fundamental activity of all, shipbuilding. Zaandam, north-west of Amsterdam, became the largest European yard, incorporating such innovations as wind-powered saws, and her ships were sold throughout Europe.

1.9 THE EIGHTEENTH CENTURY AND AFTER

The Netherlands participated in the War of the Spanish Succession (1702-1713) on the side of the English in the defeat of the French, and there is no doubt that the struggle weakened her economic position. She retained her colonial possssions, and her economic base, laid with such glittering panache the century before, sustained her to some extent, but after 1730 she failed to improve her commercial position. France and England, however, with their larger size, greater population and better provision of natural resources, moved confidently forward leaving the Netherlands a spent force. Other nations developed their mercantile marine and their ports, and goods previously carried by the Dutch were shipped by vessels flying a variety of national flags. The silting of her rivers and ports, coupled with increases in the size of vessel, placed the Dutch at a disadvantage. At the same time the Dutch were not able to replace their mercantile activities with alternative methods of earning money. The Dutch East India Company collapsed in the 1780s and with it the Bank of Amsterdam. Even the inventive genius of the Dutch water engineers seemed to wane and no dazzling schemes were completed. The absence of coal and iron were great handicaps to industrialisation in the 19th century, but the commercial framework laid in the 17th century, the possession of some colonies and great agricultural skills ensured that the Netherlands played an important, if secondary, part in the economic events of the 19th century.

The 18th century in the Austrian Netherlands was a period of gradual economic advance. Assisted by protective tariffs, there was a revival of the textile industry in Flanders and Brabant, particularly in Brussels and Antwerp where quality silks and laces were manufactured. The Liège

44   BENELUX

gunmakers flourished and coalmining began to establish itself as an important if small-scale activity between Mons and Liège. Copper manufacture at Namur was large enough to allow exports. In short the century witnessed the rumblings which later were translated into the industrial revolution based on coal, iron and steam. There were also political rumblings, manifested in 1790 by the declaration of independence by the provinces under the name of the United States of Belgium. Before such nationalistic gestures could lead to anything, the revolutionary army of France invaded the country, which then passed into the French Republic. Once again the paths of the northern and southern provinces met, for the United Netherlands were also conquered by France. By simplifying the ancient provincial constitutions and legal systems in both countries, the French aided the trend towards effective unification in both states. The process was halted by the temporary (1813-1830) union of the Netherlands and Belgium following the defeat of Napoleon.

The union was not a success. The two countries had existed quite separately since 1609, and while the Netherlands believed in free trade as the best means of encouraging commerce, Belgium was wedded to tariff protection for her developing industries. They were separated by religion for the Catholic Flemings and Walloons resented their Calvinist, Dutch King William. The administration was very largely in the hands of Dutchmen and it was inevitable that nationalist feeling should lead to the separation of 1830, and the creation of an independent Belgian state. At the Treaty of London in 1831 the Duchy of Limburg was ceded to the Dutch and the western part of the Duchy of Luxembourg, which had become a member of the German Confederation of the Rhine in 1815, passed to Belgium. The Scheldt was declared open to ships of all nations, but subject to a toll, and it was not until 1863 that the dues levied by the Dutch were finally abolished.

The Grand Duchy of Luxembourg now became an independent state after having been an integral part of the southern provinces, with the exception of the years 1815-1830, for so long. Once the largest of these provinces, it achieved statehood with an area less than that of many of the Belgian provinces, including Belgian Luxembourg. The three constituents of French Luxembourg were lost in 1659; the Orchimont district went to France in 1697; territories on the eastern side of the province became Prussian Luxembourg in 1815 and the Belgians received an area larger than the Duchy in 1831. It was inevitable that such a small nation should wish for close ties with a more powerful country, although the Belgo-Luxembourg Economic Union was not established until 1922 and the Benelux Customs Union some twenty-six years later.

The year 1831 saw the creation of the three Benelux states as they exist today, and it is therefore unnecessary to trace their historical development beyond this point. Present-day cultural aspects of Benelux are explored further in Chapter 2, and economic growth during the 19th century is referred to in Chapters 3, 4 and 5.

Further Reading

Naval Intelligence Division, Geographical Handbook Series, *Belgium, Netherlands* and *Luxembourg* (three volumes), 1944.

F. J. Monkhouse, *A Regional Geography of Western Europe* (Longmans, London), 1959.

J. Van Veen, *Dredge, Drain, Reclaim: The Art of a Nation* (Nijhoff, The Hague), 5th edition, 1962.

Paul Wagret, *Polderlands* (Methuen, London), 1968.

M. H. M. Van Hulten, 'Plan and Reality in the Ijsselmeer Polders', *Tijdschrift voor Economische en Sociale Geografie*, 1969, pp. 67-76.

A. K. Constandse, 'The Ijsselmeerpolders: an old project with new functions', *Tijdschrift voor Economische en Sociale Geografie*, 1972, pp. 200-210.

M. Snijdelaar, 'Water Management of the Netherlands: the struggle for Water', *Tijdschrift voor Economische en Sociale Geografie*, 1972, pp. 211-225.

W. G. East, *An Historical Geography of Europe* (Methuen, London), 1956.

Audrey M. Lambert, *The Making of the Dutch Landscape. An Historical Geography of the Netherlands* (Seminar Press, London), 1971.

C. T. Smith, *An Historical Geography of Europe before 1800* (Longmans, London), 1967, Chapters 7-10.

G. L. Burke, *The Making of Dutch Towns* (Cleaver-Hume Press, London), 1956.

P. Geyl, *History of the Low Countries* (Macmillan, London), 1964.

J. C. Boyer, 'La notion de "Région" aux Pays-Bas', *Annales de Géographie*, 77, 1968, pp. 323-335.

Chapter 2

THE SOCIAL GEOGRAPHY OF BENELUX AND THE STRUCTURE OF THE ECONOMY

A. The Social Geography of Benelux as a Background to the Economy

A consideration of such aspects of social geography as the distribution of population, migration, language, religion and political considerations is essential to the understanding of the geography of a country, for these areas are important parts of human behaviour and influence men's actions, not least in the economic sphere. Thus the growth of population in particular regions both encourages further increments of economic activity and at the same time is encouraged by economic growth. In turn an increasing population requires housing, retail facilities and other amenities, and in an area so short of space as Benelux, resources may be strained. Mention has already been made of the Dutch solution of using the Ijsselmeer polders for urban development, but the Belgians are obliged to combat the problem by more conventional means. The classic division of Belgium between the Flemings and Walloons has an all-pervading effect upon the operation of the economy of the country, and with the increase in government support for a wide range of development projects, both factions jealously guard their interests more tenaciously than ever. The existence of areas of moderate economic health is often partly assisted by the attitude of the population, and equally the prosperity of other regions can to some extent be attributed to the dynamism of the inhabitants.

2.1 DEMOGRAPHIC STRUCTURE
Population density, growth and structure

The density of population in the Netherlands and Belgium is high even by West European standards, as Table 2.1 indicates. The Netherlands has one of the highest figures for any nation in the world, and the province of Zuid-Holland has a density of 1 037 people per square kilometre. Although a large part of Luxembourg comprises the difficult terrain of the Ardenne mountains, its population density is nevertheless greater than

that of France. This dense population is an indication of the high level of
economic development characteristic of the three countries, but the
distribution of population within Benelux is far from uniform, emphasising that employment opportunities are not everywhere equal. Industrial
activity both requires and results in a highly urbanised population, but
since industry tends to concentrate into a few areas, population acts
similarly. The population density map of Benelux (Fig. 2.1) is thus a useful
background to the geography of the economy, for although it says nothing
about the kind of activity being pursued, it isolates the manufacturing
and other areas where people cluster together, and prompts questions
about the reasons for the distribution pattern.

TABLE 2.1

Population Characteristics of Benelux and selected countries 1970

	Population '000	Population density per km²	Birth rate per 1 000	Death rate per 1 000	Annual population increase 1963-70 %	Senility index
Belgium	9 676	317	14·7	12·4	0·6	51
Netherlands	13 019	319	18·4	8·4	1·2	28
Luxembourg	340	131	13·0	12·2	0·7	50
W. Germany	59 554	240	13·3	11·6	1·0	49
France	50 775	93	16·7	10·6	0·9	50
Italy	53 667	178	16·8	9·7	0·8	38
UK	55 711	228	16·2	11·8	0·5	50

Industrial activity based upon local natural resources can be identified
along the length of the Walloon coalfield stretching from Liège in the east
to the French boundary in the west, and the population cluster in the
southern extremity of Luxembourg is the result of iron mining and iron
smelting. The port areas of Antwerp, Rotterdam and Amsterdam, having
become industrial areas in their own right in the 20th century, are important centres of population, and in the Netherlands their prosperity has
spread to neighbouring towns to form the Dutch ring-city or Randstad.
Neither port nor source of raw materials, Brussels has grown because of its
function as the Belgian capital, and the proximity of Antwerp in the north
and Charleroi in the south has encouraged the development of a major
population axis linking all three. In contrast with these areas of high population density are areas such as the north-eastern Netherlands, Kempenland and the Ardennes, large parts of which support less than 150 persons
per square kilometre. The regions mentioned are peripheral to Benelux

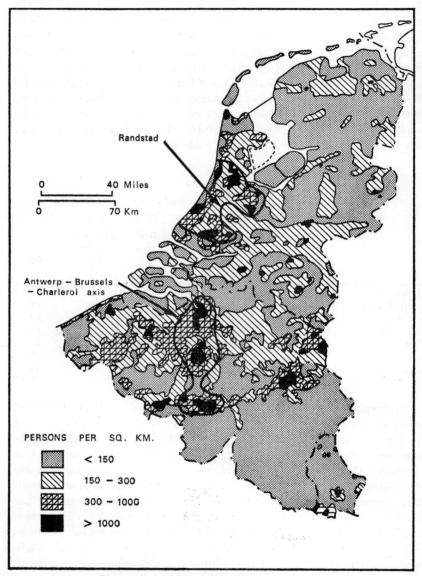

Randstad

0   40 Miles

0   70 Km

Antwerp — Brussels
 — Charleroi axis

PERSONS   PER   SQ. KM.

< 150

150 — 300

300 — 1000

> 1000

Fig. 2.1 The density of population in Benelux

and they have suffered from the distance separating them from the areas
of rapid expansion, and it is government policy to stem the outflow of resources from these regions. Between the two extremes lie areas of medium
population density, for example Belgian Flanders, the regions peripheral to
Dutch Randstad, especially the river-valley region, which practise intensive agriculture and which have taken an important share of new
industrial growth since the Second World War.

In all three countries the population continues to grow, the greatest
increases being recorded in the Netherlands. Between 1947 and 1969 the
Dutch population increased by one-quarter, emphasising the problems of
finding living space in such a small country. Over the same period the increases in Belgium and Luxembourg were more modest — 12% and 14%
respectively. The Dutch birth rate is the highest of those countries appear-
ing in Table 2.1, and her death rate is substantially below that of the
countries shown, comparing especially favourably with Belgium and
Luxembourg. The very low Dutch death rate is greatly assisted by the
country's excellent record in respect of infant mortality. These differences
between the Netherlands and her Benelux partners can be attributed to a
whole range of factors, such as the absence from the Netherlands of the
poor housing conditions to be found in the Belgian Walloon coalfield,
where the average house is 70 years old, and the recent expansion of new
economic activity and continued acceptance of the large family in the
Netherlands. These population trends are expected to continue, and it is
anticipated that the Dutch population will increase from 13 millions in
1970 to almost 20 millions by 2000. It is thought that the Belgian and
Luxembourg populations will increase from 9·7 and 0·3 millions to 14·0
and 0·5 millions respectively over the same period. These increases are
of the order of 36%, 31% and 40% respectively, suggesting a spread of the
existing areas of great population density.

It is to be anticipated that the largest population increases will be
experienced in the most prosperous areas, and Fig. 2.2, a population
growth map for the years 1947-1969, helps to test this hypothesis. The
data for each province show the extent to which the population has increased compared with the national average, so that in some cases a
negative value is obtained, although in absolute terms all provinces
registered an increase. The proposition works tolerably well for Belgium.
Here the areas of recent economic growth, Antwerp and Brabant, have
experienced greater than average increases in population, and the Walloon
coalfield, with its declining industries, the Ardennes and Flanders have
grown more slowly than the country as a whole. The greatest increase, of
17% more than the mean, took place in Limburg, not an area of outstanding economic health, but where the numbers involved are small and where

D

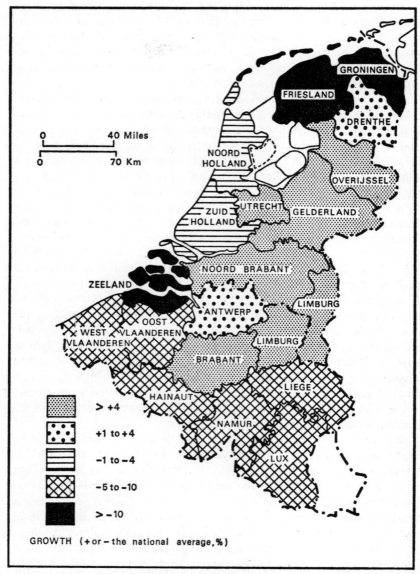

Fig. 2.2 Population growth in Belgium and in the Netherlands, 1947-1969

a predominantly young and fertile population is associated with the coal-mines of the Kempen.

A slightly different position exists in the Netherlands, for the two provinces at the centre of Dutch economic life, Noord- and Zuid-Holland, grew more slowly than the national average. The population of Zuid-Holland increased by two-thirds of a million, more than the total inhabitants of many Dutch provinces, but even this has not been sufficient to match the growth experienced by the provinces to the east of Randstad. Noord-Brabant, Limburg, Gelderland, Utrecht and Overijssel all increased their population at a rate more than 4% above the mean, although these provinces have only medium population densities. This may represent a reaction to the high densities to be found in Randstad and it certainly suggests the development of a new zone of prosperity extending eastwards from the core of the country. By comparison with the national figure, the peripheral provinces of Friesland, Groningen and Zeeland grew very slowly indeed, more slowly than Belgian Luxembourg which had the worst record in Belgium, although differences in the national rates of growth have to be borne in mind.

It follows from her high birth rate and low infant mortality rate that the population of the Netherlands is particularly youthful. This is a basic characteristic of her population structure, and is brought out in Fig. 2.3 which shows age pyramids for Belgium and the Netherlands. Belgium has a much more steep-sided pyramid than the Netherlands, indicative of the greater importance of the young age groups, up to the age of 25, in the Dutch population. A further indication of the youthfulness of the Dutch population can be obtained by comparing the national coefficients of senility, that is, the number of persons over 65 as a percentage of those under 15. The Netherlands has the lowest coefficient in Western Europe at 28 (Table 2.1). This expanding, young population gives a feeling of buoyant optimism and vigour, and this is reflected in the current dynamism of both Dutch labour and management.

Migration

During the 19th century the balance of migration was traditionally outward. As a result 0·8% and 0·4% of the population of the USA is of Dutch and Belgian descent respectively. Since 1945 this trend has altered dramatically with the arrival in the Netherlands and Belgium of migrants from the Dutch East Indies after 1948 and from the Belgian Congo after 1960, following the independence of these former colonies. These migrants created problems both by their quantity and by the difficulties of cultural assimilation. However, the Dutch in particular appear to have been

successful in absorbing immigrant groups, although the Ambonese have
presented difficulties.

Short-term migration has become important in all the Benelux countries
since 1945, when the conclusion of hostilities found the advanced countries
of Western Europe extremely short of labour, especially in industries
such as coal and iron mining. Workers from countries with low *per capita*
incomes such as ·Jugoslavia, Greece, Turkey, Spain and Italy, entered
Benelux to find work at what for them were high wages. These migrants
were naturally to be found in industrial districts such as the Walloon

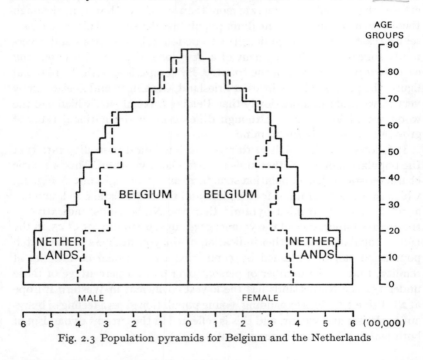

AGE
GROUPS

Fig. 2.3 Population pyramids for Belgium and the Netherlands

coalfield, where 10% of workers are foreign. In 1969 some 29 000 foreign
workers were employed in the Luxembourg iron and steel industry,
and they comprise an important part of the labour force at the Dutch iron
and steel plant at Ijmuiden. Half the Luxembourg manual labour force
consists of foreigners, and in the case of the construction industry the proportion is above 90%. Particular nationalities often congregate at selected
points; some coal mines in the western Borinage in Belgium in the early
1960s were virtually colonised by Italian labour which comprised 65% of
the work force at some of the pits there. Students both from former colonies
and elsewhere attending universities or specialist institutions, such as the

Common Market College at Bruges or the Agricultural University at Wageningen, may be regarded as short-term migrants, as may the Eurocrats of Brussels and Luxembourg City.

Internal migration within the Benelux nations has three main components. Firstly, there is a movement of population from the regions of poor economic health towards more prosperous areas. Randstad Holland and the Brussels-Antwerp axis offer excellent employment opportunities compared with the situation in the agricultural areas of northern and south-western Netherlands and the old established Walloon coalfield. Between 1967 and 1970 the three Belgian coalfield *arrondissements* of Charleroi, Mons and Liège experienced unfavourable net migration balances of 2 924, 1 959 and 1 676 respectively in respect of Brussels-Capital, and this has been a continuing trend for the last two decades. Unfortunately for the poorer regions, migrants are normally the more youthful and dynamic elements in the population, leaving the declining areas with a relatively old population, which is itself unattractive to industry.

The second component of internal migration is rural depopulation. Despite the long history of urbanisation in Benelux, the drift to the towns has been accentuated in the 20th century, and the Dutch planning service is now of the opinion that villages as such no longer exist in the Netherlands. Rural areas have unfavourable migration balances with the nearest towns, irrespective of whether they are in a declining area or not. This is exemplified by the flows from the Ardennes to the Walloon coalfield. The counterpart of this process is the growth of towns to form urban agglomerations, such as Ijmond along the Dutch North Sea Canal, Rijnmond along the New Waterway west of Rotterdam and Greater Brussels itself.

Thirdly, the growth of city regions has been accompanied by a centrifugal movement of population away from the city centre, sometimes leading to an absolute decline in the number of inhabitants of the central area, despite immigration from rural districts and declining areas. Fig. 2.4 illustrates this situation in the case of the official agglomerations of Brussels and Antwerp during the period 1947-1969. In both cities the ancient cores record population losses in excess of 10%, and equally the areas of greatest gain lie on the periphery. The three peripheral *communes* of Edegem (+145%) in south Antwerp, Ganshoren (+123%) in north-west Brussels and Woluwe St. Pierre (+113%) in east Brussels, more than doubled their population between 1947 and 1969. The outer suburbs of Brussels, not shown on the map, experienced even greater growth, and some of the flows from the central area to neighbouring *arrondissements* are quite substantial. Between 1967 and 1969 the *arrondissement* of Brussels-

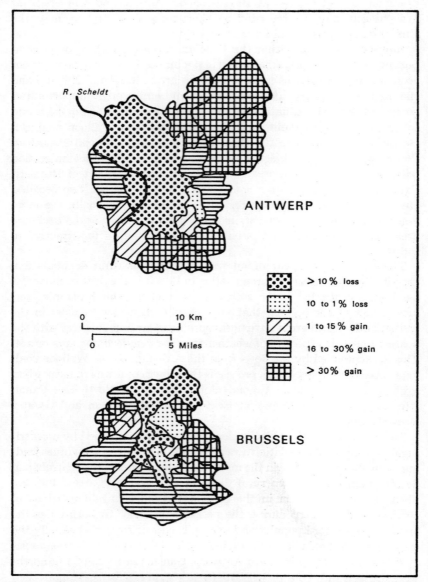

Fig. 2.4 Population changes in the agglomerations of Antwerp and Brussels, 1947-1969. The official Brussels agglomeration is restricted to the 19 central *communes* and excludes many of the present-day suburbs

Capital returned negative net migration balances of 10 534, 8 074 3 709 with the suburban *arrondissements* of Halle-Vilvoorde, Nivelles and the Brussels *arrondissement* respectively. Peripheral growth such as this often develops contiguously along lines of communication, such as the Zaanstreek of Amsterdam, Ijsselmonde south of Rotterdam, or Merksem north-east of Antwerp, or in areas detached from the city but within commuting distance of it. Such satellite towns began in the Netherlands in the inter-war period with the *tuindorpen* of Amsterdam, and today are seen in The Hague overspill town of Zoetermeer. These developments are taking place simultaneously with private colonisation of convenient rural districts. Examples are Het Gooi and Kennermerland for Amsterdam, the Heuvelrug for Utrecht, and Waasland and south Kempen for Antwerp.

2.2 SOCIAL DIFFERENTIATION

In an area as small, on a world scale, as Benelux, it is not unreasonable to expect a relatively high degree of cultural and social uniformity. Yet despite the emergence of the means of mass communication, making for national and even international modes of living, there are present in Benelux certain divisive factors which emphasise regional differences and create regional problems.

Religion

The long-standing conflict between Catholicism and Protestantism, dating from the religious wars of the 16th century, has been of such importance in Benelux that religion has come to influence social and political life. Thus the religious frontier, shown in Fig. 2.5, running from the vicinity of Steenbergen on the coast of Noord-Brabant to the German border at s'Heerenberg in Gelderland, represents a real division in the human geography of the Netherlands. The frontier is remarkably sharply defined. Villages within a few kilometres of each other are often overwhelmingly committed to one belief. The frontier is also characterised by great stability, for no major changes have taken place since the early 17th century. The Dutch provinces south of the frontier, Noord-Brabant and Limburg, with 80% and 85% of their population belonging to the Catholic Church respectively, have been separated from the mainstream of Dutch life. They were regarded merely as conquered territories or 'generality lands' rather than provinces until well into the 19th century, causing the growth of regional consciousness among the inhabitants who resented their position. The seven original provinces, including the economically and politically powerful province of Holland, were able to stamp a Protestant ethos on the country at the expense of the Catholics in the south. However, even within Protestantism, there is a distinction between the official

Erastian Church and the *gereformde* or Nonconformist Church. The latter
is especially strong in the northern areas of the provinces of Friesland and
Groningen and in parts of Zeeland (Fig. 2.5), and is a cause, and perhaps a
result, of the cultural isolation of the northern provinces of the Netherlands.

Belgium and Luxembourg found themselves within the Catholic sphere
of influence after the religious wars, and are thus free from the social
problems of religious divisions. Nevertheless there is a clear distinction
between Flemish Catholicism, which is Spanish in the intensity of its
expression, and the anti-clerical Catholicism of Wallonie, French in its
casual attitude to formal religion. This religious difference is one of the
many contributory factors to the very real friction that exists between the
Flemings and the Walloons. In the Netherlands the strength of regional
religious divisions is dwindling following the migration of Catholics from
the south to Randstad, and the increase in numbers professing no religious
adherence to all (17% of the Dutch population). In Belgium, on the other
hand, although 19% of the population profess no religious beliefs at all,
there is less opportunity for the two religious groups to intermingle because
of the linguistic and other differences separating them.

Language

Five linguistic regions, mapped in Fig. 2.5, may be identified in Benelux.
Fries is still spoken in the larger part of the province of Friesland, but is
subject to severe pressure from the mass media. The Luxembourgers
speak Letzeburgesch, a German dialect liberally sprinkled with French
expressions, even though the official language is French. The German-
speaking region extends north into the eastern part of the province of
Liège to include that area ceded to Belgium from Germany at the Treaty
of Versailles in 1919. Its presence within Belgium is officially recognised
on the same basis as the Flemish and Walloon communities. Dutch is
spoken in the Netherlands and Belgian Flanders, French is the language
of the Walloons in south Belgium, and Brussels is officially bi-lingual
although French is usually preferred to Dutch.

There is no doubt that the linguistic division between the Flemings and
the Walloons is of the greatest significance, for its existence has important
economic, social and political repercussions. The Belgian constitution of
1830 included a declaration of linguistic equality, but since most politicians, officials and bourgeoisie were French-speaking, French came to be
the official language in practice. Further, industrialisation in the 19th
century took place largely on the Walloon coalfield, and the wealth
generated was almost wholly in the hands of Walloon entrepreneurs and
financiers. Flemish remained a working-class dialect, and among many

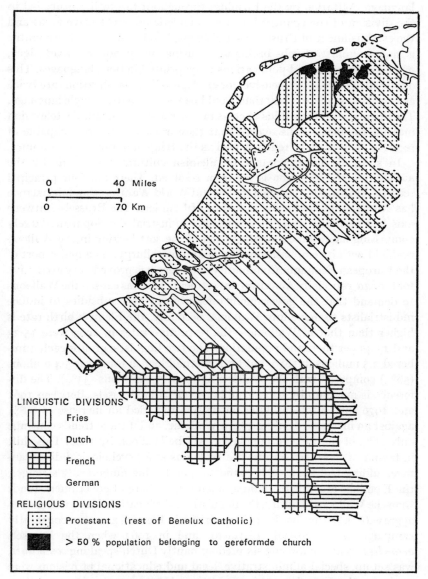

LINGUISTIC DIVISIONS
- Fries
- Dutch
- French
- German

RELIGIOUS DIVISIONS
- Protestant   (rest of Benelux Catholic)
- > 50 % population belonging to gereformde church

0 — 40 Miles

0 — 70 Km

Fig. 2.5 The religious and linguistic divisions of Benelux

middle- and upper-class Flemings there was a stigma attached to the language. Agitation by the Flemings throughout the 19th century led to the division of the country into two linguistic administrative areas and the establishment of Brussels as a bi-lingual capital in 1921. The country is now administratively bi-lingual, causing many notices, road signs, official documents and publications to be printed in both languages. This duplication is clearly expensive; for example official publications are twice as lengthy and more costly than would be the case with a single language. The linguistic problem adds to costs in other ways, for example, television manufacturers have discovered that they must provide sets capable of receiving Dutch and French as well as the Belgian national programmes.

In spite of the acceptance of Flemish cultural aspirations by the authorities, the situation is far from resolved. There are four principal reasons for this. Firstly, since the Second World War the economic balance has swung quite drastically in favour of Flanders. The Brussels-Antwerp axis has been the scene of remarkable industrial development, largely comprising neotechnic manufacturing of the sort lacking in the Walloon coalfield with its emphasis on mining and metallurgy. As a major port of the European Economic Community, Antwerp has proved very attractive for foreign, especially American, investment. This has caused the Walloons to demand that the government offer even greater subsidies to induce industrialists to move into Wallonie. Secondly, the Flemish birth rate is higher than that in Wallonie—the respective rates in 1969 were 15·23 and 13·45 per thousand population. The two linguistic groups each numbered 2·5 millions in 1880, but by 1970 the Flemish total was 5·4 millions (56%) compared with the Walloon figure of 3·1 millions (33%). The difference is made up by the 1·1 millions (11%) in Brussels. Between 1961 and 1970 the Dutch-speaking population recorded an increase of 6·8% against an increase of only 2·5% in Wallonie, and if these trends continue only 28% of the Belgian population will be Walloon by 1980. This shift in favour of the Flemish puts the Walloons at a psychological disadvantage, adding to Flemish self-confidence, and being numerically stronger, the Flemings are able to claim a much larger share of government funds than the Walloons. Thirdly, the linguistic and educational laws themselves aggravate the situation. French minorities in Flemish areas are constantly campaigning for special treatment, and in 1963 when the Brussels *arrondissement*, comprising six predominantly Dutch-speaking *communes*, was set up, special administrative, legal and educational provisions were made for the French-speaking minority. More recently the *arrondissement* of Mouscron was created to safeguard the interests of French-speaking areas formerly just north of the linguistic frontier. The riots and demonstrations that followed the Flemish demands in 1966 for the use of Flemish as the sole medium of teaching at the University of Leuven, located in Flanders, are symptomatic of the friction that exists. The French-speaking part of the University has since moved 18 km south to Louvain-la-Neuve at Ottignies, but this has been achieved at some cost to academic efficiency and one of the finest libraries in Western Europe has been split.

The fourth disruptive factor is the long-felt resentment by the Flemings of the dominating presence of Brussels within Flanders as a Walloon exclave, for French-speakers account for 80% of the population of the capital. However, the boundary reforms of 1963 were an important victory for the Flemings. The old Brussels *arrondissement* was contiguous with the Walloon *arrondissement* of Nivelles in the south, so that the southward expansion of the city was gradually causing it to become a northern extension of Wallonie. In 1963 three *arrondissements* were formed from the Brussels *arrondissement*. Brussels-Capital comprised the 19 French-speaking *communes* of the core of the city, and this was completely encircled by the two Flemish *arrondissements* of Halle-Vilvoorde and Brussels. By restricting the French-speaking population of the city to the central area, the boundary reforms have slowed down the movement of Walloons to the southern suburbs of Brussels. The Flemish controlled areas encircling Brussels-Capital have come to be known as the 'iron collar', and they represent an unusual restricting influence on the expansion of a city. The situation before and after the boundary reforms is mapped in Fig. 2.6.

The linguistic problem has several specifically economic consequences, quite apart from the energy and money spent on it. Members of both groups are prepared to work in the other's territory, but to live there is anathema. This causes well-developed commuter patterns to evolve. During the 1950s Flemings would commute into the Walloon coalfield from as far afield as Ostend, Bruges, Ghent and Antwerp, spending two to three hours on the journey. Fleets of special buses were used to convey miners to and from the pits. Now the trend is reversed, and it is the Walloons who work in Flanders. Mutual antagonism has certainly reduced permanent migration across the linguistic frontier. In the mid-1950s the ECSC tried to move unemployed Walloon miners to the Kempen field, but they either preferred to remain without work, thereby exacerbating regional unemployment, or to commute on a daily basis. Despite the rapid economic growth of Antwerp, immigration to the area from Wallonie is unimportant, and the Walloons move to the Brussels end of the growth corridor so that they may remain with their French-speaking fellows. Equally Flemings are loath to move to nearby Walloon towns, but prefer to migrate to Antwerp. The allocation of government funds is a major problem, for decisions on the establishment of industrial estates,

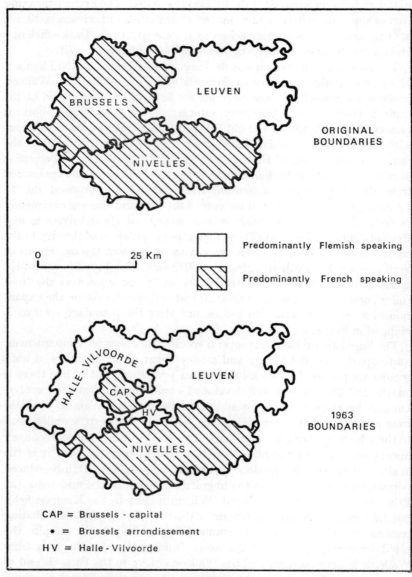

Fig. 2.6 The 1963 boundary reforms as they affected Brussels

new manufacturing plant, new transport provision or aid to the regions must take account of both cultural pluralism and economics. Thus the regional development grants initiated in 1966 were intended to help areas dependent on coalmining, but they had to be extended to include other industry in order not to appear to help principally the Walloon coalfield. Similarly the decision to build a new iron and steelworks north of Ghent was used as the basis of a campaign for more financial support for the traditional metallurgical districts of Charleroi and Liège, and the establishment of an oil refinery at Féluy in Wallonie was used by the Flemings as a lever to force the government to drop their opposition to the Rotterdam-Antwerp oil pipeline. The Walloons have stated their preference for the French port of Dunkirk rather than Flemish facilities, a comment stimulated by the government's decision to undertake the expansion of Zeebrugge to enable it to handle 125 000 dwt. vessels. Eventually the government was obliged to agree that for every franc spent on the Zeebrugge project in excess of the original estimate, a similar sum would be invested in Wallonie.

The problems besetting the government resulted in 1971 in the creation of two Ministries of Regional Economy to allay criticism of partiality, although regional economic councils already existed. A third Ministry for Greater Brussels was originally envisaged, but it has proved impossible satisfactorily to define the region. A meaningful planning region would encompass Brussels-Capital, the Brussels *arrondissement* and parts of Halle-Vilvoorde, but cooperation between Fleming and Walloon is required, and this has not been forthcoming. The two communities seem to be moving away from each other and the 1971 constitutional reforms granted them considerable cultural autonomy in respect of such matters as education, television and radio services, sport and the arts. However, it may well be that economic factors will prevent these divisive factors from destroying the Belgian state. Most Belgians would agree that a free Flanders or a free Wallonie would not be economically viable, and the obvious advantages not only of the Benelux Union, but also of the EEC make such small economic units seem wholly unrealistic.

Politics

Traditionally, rural areas are conservative and urban areas socialist. Benelux is no exception. The areas with more than 50% socialist voters are, with the exception of the north-eastern Netherlands, urban-industrial areas. The oldest industrial area, and therefore the region with the greatest problems of reshaping its economic infrastructure, the Walloon coalfield, is most fiercely socialist, and some areas move towards communism. Indeed, before their pits closed, the miners of Quaregnon in the

Borinage regarded their town as a communist cell second only to Moscow. The Dutch rural provinces of Zeeland, Drenthe and Overijssel are predictably conservative, but Groningen, because of its isolation, rural poverty and a desire for self-identification, has a strong communist vote. The direct effect of religion upon politics is exemplified in the support for the Christian Democrats (KVP) in the Catholic provinces of Noord-Brabant and Limburg. The effect of language upon politics is seen as a particularly divisive factor in Belgium. Here the militant Flemings have created the Volksunie, whose commandos wear leather shorts and boots with neo-Nazi overtones. They were behind the riots in the Kempen coalfield at Zwartberg in 1966, and persuaded redundant Flemish miners that the Walloon lobby in parliament was instrumental in closing their mine. Two miners were killed and 100 wounded in the ensuing fracas. Some 32 members (15%) of the present Chamber of Representatives belong to linguistically based parties.

Provincial rivalry

The historical origins of the Benelux countries are bound up with the development of towns such as Bruges, Ghent, Brussels, Antwerp, Amsterdam and Rotterdam, each of which came to be identified with a particular province or burgher republic. Each town developed independently and established its own identity. The original Netherlands were a federal union of independent provinces, and the creation of Belgium and the Netherlands has involved the surrender of much authority to a central government. What independence remains is often reflected in inter-city rivalry and needless competition, both a waste of scarce resources. Nevertheless economic planners are obliged to accept these rivalries if they are not to be met with a lack of cooperation.

Despite the divisive elements discussed above, Benelux is in many respects a cohesive unit. The Dutch provinces of Noord-Brabant and Limburg are connected by religion, language, historical association and custom with the Belgian provinces of Limburg and Antwerp. Luxembourg endeavoured to join Belgium in 1830, and since 1922 has been part of the Belgo-Luxembourg Economic Union. The extension of the latter to form Benelux in 1948 and the decision to remove tariffs on goods moving between member countries suggests at least a common desire for economic unity. Each state pursues social democratic policies, each is a monarchy and their small size and history of international contacts have assisted the creation of an open-minded attitude to foreign influences. For these latter reasons there is a readiness to surrender national sovereignty to international and supranational institutions. There is a long-standing readiness to accept community action, possibly as a result of the need for collective rather than individual action in the fight against the sea in the Netherlands and in Flanders. The experience of a long series of wars and invasions by stronger neighbours has had the same effect.

B. The Structure of the Benelux Economies

2.3 GENERAL CHARACTERISTICS OF THE ECONOMIES

The most obvious attribute of the Benelux economies is their prosperity. Table 2.2, showing *per capita* shares of the gross national product in selected countries, indicates that the Benelux countries are among that group of states that enjoy the material benefits of the western way of life. Using the *per capita* gross national product as the criterion, the Netherlands, Belgium and Luxembourg occupy 13th, 11th and 8th places in the world ranking list respectively. The distribution of the national income is as equitable as would be expected in a social democracy, with a redistributive system of taxation and well-developed welfare services.

TABLE 2.2

Per capita gross national product, 1969

		World rank
Luxembourg	$2 580	8
Belgium	$2 372	11
Netherlands	$2 196	13
USA	$4 664	1
France	$2 783	6
West Germany	$2 512	9
UK	$1 976	15
Italy	$1 548	22
India	$84	117

Relative poverty does exist, particularly among immigrants in the towns and agricultural workers in such areas as the Belgian Ardennes, but the distribution of income about the mean compares favourably with other advanced countries. Improvements in technology in all sectors of the Benelux economy have made great advances in real income possible in the last two decades. Between 1958 and 1968 real incomes in Belgium and Luxembourg very nearly doubled, while in the Netherlands they increased two and a half times.

The result of the growth of affluence is a gradual increase in disposable income, that is, income available for the purchase of luxury goods. Some

57% of the Dutch, 60% of the Belgian and 65% of the Luxembourg national income is spent on consumption. An index of prosperity is always the extent of car ownership. Between 1958 and 1970 car ownership in Belgium more than doubled, while in the Netherlands it increased three and a half times. There are more cars per head in Luxembourg than in the United Kingdom, West Germany or France, as Table 2.3 illustrates, although this may reflect the presence of many EEC offices in Luxembourg City. Television ownership is relatively well developed, although not to the same extent as in the United Kingdom or West Germany. Expenditure on consumption has in turn strengthened the manufacturing and service industries. The manufacture of consumer durables, especially of household appliances and pharmaceuticals, has developed particularly rapidly, as have consumer services such as entertainment, recreation and travel. The

TABLE 2.3

Consumer goods in Benelux and other countries, 1970
(per 1 000 population)

	Cars	Television sets	Telephones
Belgium	198	210	190
Netherlands	180	220	232
Luxembourg	250	180	304
West Germany	210	260	201
France	235	205	160
UK	205	280	253

old established industrial areas have failed to attract these new activities, so the geographical consequence of affluence is a shift of prosperity to newly established manufacturing regions. Their very success has resulted in what Gunnar Myrdal calls a 'backwash effect' on the less fortunate regions, for the latter find it increasingly difficult to compete with the growth areas, and decline even further. The high wages paid in the Benelux countries provide incentive towards greater mechanisation of production, implying a reduction in craft skills. Industry is consequently becoming more footloose, and this allows governments to divert some of it towards the declining areas in order to restructure the economies of these areas.

The ownership of capital is much less equitably distributed than that of income. Commercial banks and financial institutions provide much of the capital invested in industry, and they participate to a greater extent in the management of private industry than is the case in Britain. In Belgium in particular, the involvement of the large finance houses, such as the Société Générale de Belgique, in various sectors of the economy has led to concern about the concentration of economic power. The Société

Générale now owns some 80% of Belgian industrial capital. As in most advanced countries, the rates of taxation are high. A large proportion of the tax revenue is raised from personal incomes. This is offset by high levels of public expenditure, partly in the provision of welfare services, which account for 19% of the gross national product in Luxembourg, 18·5% in the Netherlands and 15% in Belgium, and partly in public works programmes. There does appear, in the Netherlands in particular, to be a greater readiness to accept income in the form of public expenditure, for example in the form of imposing public buildings and well-stocked museums or large-scale reclamation projects, than is the case in Britain, where private affluence and public squalor can too often coexist.

2.4 THE COMPOSITION OF THE NATIONAL PRODUCT

The relative importance of the various sectors of production within the three countries can be seen in Table 2.4. The table illustrates two methods of establishing the significance of each sector, that is by using employment data and by using the contribution to the gross national product. Since all three countries are advanced industrial nations, we would expect broadly

TABLE 2.4

Employment by sector and contribution to the gross national product, 1970

	Belgium	Netherlands	Luxembourg
A. *Employment*			
Agriculture and extractive	6·2%	6·8%	11·1%
Manufacturing	34·9%	37·1%	46·5%
Services	58·9%	56·1%	42·4%
B. *Contribution to the GNP*			
Agriculture and extractive	5·7%	7·2%	7·8%
Manufacturing	40·9%	42·4%	49·3%
Services	54·5%	50·4%	42·8%

similar statistics for each country, and this indeed is the case. It is customary to recognise three principal sectors: the primary sector comprising agriculture, forestry, fisheries and extractive industries, the secondary or manufacturing sector, and the tertiary or service sector.

The primary sector

This is the least important of the three sectors, for the three countries have found it more profitable to develop their manufacturing and service sectors and to rely heavily on imported foods and minerals. Agriculture

E

is the largest constituent of the primary sector, but even so the activity accounts for only 4·9%, 6·4% and 9·7% of the working population of Belgium, the Netherlands and Luxembourg respectively. The agricultural labour force has declined rapidly since the end of the war, and it is anticipated by the EEC that an employment situation similar to that in British agriculture, which employs 3% of the working population, will be reached by the 1980s. The flight from the land is a result of increased mechanisation, the tendency to concentrate agricultural resources on the most profitable areas and products, and the abandonment of marginal farms in areas of difficulty such as Luxembourg Oesling, the Ardennes and northeastern Netherlands. These changes have been accompanied by increases in the size of farm, although the average size of farm in Benelux is well below the 25 hectares (ha) which is regarded as being the minimum viable size. Dutch farms average 10·7 ha and those in Belgium 10·2 ha, but it must be remembered that intensive agricultural production such as bulb grow-

TABLE 2.5

Agricultural productivity

		A. Wheat yields, '000 kilogrammes per ha,				
Netherlands	Belgium	Luxembourg	Denmark	W. Germany	France	Spain
4 430	4 130	2 700	4 650	4 100	3 650	1 380
		B. Milk, kilogrammes per cow,				
4 239	3 673	3 556	3 959	3 771	3 490	ha

ing and glasshouse culture is viable at much smaller farm sizes. The Dutch have made great strides in farm consolidation which will increase the size of farm and further improve productivity. By 1970, of a total area of 2 636 000 ha, 323 000 ha had been consolidated, 531 000 ha were undergoing reorganisation and plans for a further 1 782 000 ha had been drawn up. Table 2 5 shows that Belgian and Dutch agricultural productivity compares well with that in other West European countries. The same cannot be said for arable farming in Luxembourg.

Agriculture makes a substantial contribution to export earnings. In 1968 some 28·0% of Dutch exports by value were agricultural products, while the figure for Belgium and Luxembourg together was 8·6%. The share of agricultural products in Belgo-Luxembourg exports is actually rising; the average for 1955-1959 was 5·4% and for 1960-1964, 6·5%. Dutch cut flowers, bulbs and cheese, Belgian market garden produce and Luxembourg wines are obvious components in this trade. It is only in Luxembourg that agriculture does not make a contribution to the economy in excess of the factors of production it utilises. As Table 2.4 indicates,

Luxembourg's primary sector contributes only 7·8% of the gross national product but employs 11·1% of the labour force.

The extractive industries provide a contrast between the Benelux countries. In the Netherlands the absence of easily mined raw materials was a retarding factor in the development of industry. Additionally, the raw materials that were used had to be imported, causing the coastal location of much heavy industry. Even road and dyke construction materials are largely imported, for only sand, peat, gravel and limestone are available within the country. With advances in technology it became possible to work the concealed coalfield in south Limburg after 1895, and the area of the province of Limburg between Geleen and Sittard is the only part of the Netherlands where extractive industry forms the basis for the regional economy. However, by 1973 this will no longer be the case, for it is planned to cease coal production in the area by this date. The exploitation of the natural gas and oilfields of Groningen, Drenthe and Zuid-Holland has accelerated the shift away from coal and lowered energy costs, but in total only 1·5% of the labour force is employed and the significance of the extractive industry to the economy is slight.

Belgium was fortunate in her possession of easily worked coal and to a lesser extent iron and non-ferrous metal deposits such as zinc, for these largely formed the basis of her 19th-century industrialisation. At present 1·2% of the working population is engaged in the extractive sector, which contributes 0·8% of the national product. At the regional level, however, the Belgian extractive sector is of great significance, for the Walloon coalfield is one of the great problem areas in Benelux, while in the Ardennes quarrying is an important economic activity.

Luxembourg can be said to owe its economic viability and even its political survival to the exploitation of the lean *minette* iron ores in the south of the country. Some 1·4% of the national labour force is engaged in this sector, all, with the exception of the Oesling road stone quarries, being involved in the mining of 4·5 million tons of iron ore per annum. The importance of this industry lies not in the small contribution to the balance of payments by the export of 1·5 million tons of ore each year to Belgium, but in its historical role in the establishment of the Luxembourg iron and steel industry.

The secondary sector

Manufacturing is the most fundamental of the three sectors, for industry transforms primary goods into consumer goods, and in the process supports the tertiary sector which provides services both to industry and to the community which is dependent on industry. There is a considerable similarity between the proportions employed in manufacturing in the three countries (Table 2.4) and there is only a small variation in the contribution of manufacturing to the gross national product. However, these similarities mask real differences between the three economies, and as can be seen by reference to Table 2.6, the most obvious dissimilarity is the enormous importance of primary metals to Luxembourg. In value terms, iron and steel accounts for 70% of the country's exports and between 1967 and 1971 an average of 16 tons of steel were produced per inhabitant, a world record. Moreover, output largely comprises standard steels with little or no diversification into special steels or the production of tubes, tinplate or wire. Metal fabrication, although it is the third most important activity, is of smaller importance than in either the Netherlands or Belgium, for much of the steel made is exported rather than being

TABLE 2.6

Industrial sectors in Benelux by value of production, 1964

Belgium		Netherlands		Luxembourg	
Primary metals	14·4%	Food	13·9%	Primary metals	68·7%
Textiles	8·5%	Electrical		Food	5·0%
Food	8·5%	engineering	10·7%	Metal fabrication	3·9%
Transport		Chemicals	10·2%	Non-metallic	
equipment	6·8%	Transport		minerals	3·8%
Chemicals	6·7%	equipment	9·7%	Transport	
Non-metallic		Metal fabrication	6·6%	equipment	3·0%
minerals	6·5%	Mechanical			
Electrical		engineering	6·3%		
engineering	5·9%	Textiles	6·1%		
Metal fabrication	5·8%	Shoes/clothing	5·1%		
Mechanical		Primary metals	4·9%		
engineering	5·3%				

transformed into goods of higher value within the country itself. Such great dependence on one manufacturing sector is a powerful argument for economic and political union with the steel consuming countries. Luxembourg steel output in 1971 was 5·2 million tons compared with 12·4 and 5·1 million tons in Belgium and the Netherlands respectively.

The data in Table 2.6 suggest that the traditional comparison of industrial Belgium with the agricultural and commercial Netherlands is no longer tenable. Both countries have diversified during the 20th century, Belgium having broadened her industrial base, and the Netherlands having reduced her dependence on agriculture and developed industrial activity. Indicative of the latter is the reduction in the value of Dutch agricultural exports of recent years. Thus between 1955 and 1959 such exports represented 33·6% of total exports, but by 1970 this had fallen to 22%. Food processing is still the most important activity in the Nether-

lands, but there is much evidence of the growth of other forms of manufacturing. Since this is a relatively recent development, new technological
industries have been established, contrasting with the situation in Belgium
with its older industrial base. Typical of the process is the relative importance of electrical engineering in both countries. Led by the Philips
organisation with its main plant at Eindhoven, this activity is the second
most important industry in the Netherlands, but in Belgium it lies in
seventh place behind more traditional activities. Chemicals, particularly
petrochemicals, have become important in the Netherlands, especially
along the Rotterdam-Europoort axis, and now lie in third place. Chemical
production is important in Belgium, but here the older carbochemical
industry is better developed than petrochemicals, although this situation
is changing rapidly. The establishment of new shipbuilding yards at
Rotterdam and Amsterdam, capable of launching vessels of 100 000 tons,
and the growth of vehicle manufacture at Eindhoven and Born, north of
Maastricht, have assisted the rise of the transport equipment industry in
the Netherlands. Metal fabrication and mechanical engineering are now of
greater importance in the Netherlands than Belgium, and are testimony to
the extent of industrialisation in the former country.

Belgium was the first continental country to experience the industrial
revolution, and it is not therefore surprising to find that primary metal
production is the most important sector. The Walloon coalfield is still the
major producing centre and it was only in 1966 that the Sidmar iron and
steelworks on the Terneuzen-Ghent canal at Zelzate was opened. Another
great staple of the industrial revolution, textiles, in particular Flemish
cotton and Verviers woollen manufacture, are in second place. Although
the manufacture of transport equipment is not so well developed as in the
Netherlands, there has been considerable diversification into automobile
production in Belgium. In 1970 the country was the world's leading automobile assembler among countries possessing only final assembly plants.
A total of 770 000 cars were assembled from imported parts. Ford, General
Motors and British Leyland have assembly plants in the country. Petrochemical production at Antwerp has added to the importance of the
chemical industry, while there has been some growth in the electronic
products industry in Flanders as a diversification of the heavy electrical
engineering industry of Charleroi. That the Belgian economy is changing
may be seen from the lowly positions held by the formerly very important
metal fabricating and mechanical engineering industries.

The tertiary sector

It is a characteristic of advanced countries that the service sector is
more important than manufacturing in both numbers employed and in

respect of its contribution to the gross national product. The secondary
sector may be fundamental to industrial economies, but it is transport,
advertising, retailing, commerce and the provision of professional services
that are expanding the most rapidly. This is true even of Luxembourg
with its undiversified economy.

The historical importance of trade and the associated growth of the
financial and transport sectors, described in the first part of this chapter,
coupled with the strategic position that Benelux holds in Western Europe,
help to explain the significance of institutions servicing international trade.
The commodity, stock, money and insurance markets of Amsterdam,
Antwerp and Brussels, while not on the same scale as those of New York
or London, are nevertheless important employers of labour. The use of
Benelux-owned transport media for the transit of freight through Benelux
neither originating nor terminating in Benelux can be traced back to the
carrying trade of the 17th century. Today, however, international rail
routes and road haulage companies have replaced the sailing ship. Some
40% of inter-EEC road freight is carried by Dutch firms, and both Belgian
and Dutch barges carry large tonnages of German, Swiss and French
cargoes on inland waterways.

The recreation industry is one of the fastest growing economic activities
in Benelux. Demand has been stimulated by rising incomes, the larger
time available for leisure activities and improved personal mobility, both
within Benelux and in neighbouring states that make use of Benelux
facilities. In terms of land-use, labour employed and contribution to the
national product, this industry ranks as one of the most important in all
three states, and one which will continue to grow in the foreseeable future.
If none of the Benelux states can be considered to be 'tourist countries'
in the same sense as Austria or Switzerland, Luxembourg nevertheless is
able to exploit both its position and curiosity value as a small state, and
Belgium and the Netherlands have managed to capture a portion of the
newly prosperous West European mass tourist market. Although all
three states have an increasing deficit on the foreign tourist account, the
importance of the industry to such areas as the Dutch coast, with its large
German clientèle, or the Belgian coast, with its French and British visitors,
is considerable.

The governmental and administrative sectors have been augmented by
the growing role of the state in the planning and operation of the economy,
and by the international status that has been conferred on Benelux cities.
The housing of the EEC secretariat at Brussels, the headquarters of
SHAPE at Casteau, the headquarters of NATO at Evere and the Secretariat of the European Parliament at Luxembourg City have given very
considerable stimulus to the local construction and service industries. A

political decision which has considerable economic repercussion through Benelux is active membership of NATO. In order to meet their contribution to European defence the three states are forced to rely on conscription, and labour shortages are consequently exacerbated.

2.5 THE OPERATION OF THE ECONOMY

Many of the characteristic features of the Benelux economies can be attributed to the constraints imposed by high labour costs, the need to import most raw materials and sources of energy and the small size of national markets. High labour costs are largely offset by the attention given to achieving high yields per man, by a relatively high level of capital investment per operative and by the emphasis that has recently been placed on the high value-adding processing industries. Imported energy and raw materials form a small part of the finished value of manufactured goods and great use is made of indigenous human resources in the shape of technical skill and 'know-how'. National markets are small and a considerable proportion of manufactured goods must be sold outside Benelux in neighbouring states. So intimate have these trading relations become over the last century that it is difficult to consider any aspect of the Benelux economies without some reference to Germany, France or Britain. Benelux has developed as an essential part of this great complex of industrial nations. One of the most powerful reasons for the creation of Benelux itself was the need to build up wider markets for the output of the three nations, and there was a similar incentive behind membership of first the ECSC and later the EEC.

The balance between the role of private capital and the intervention of the state has been evolved as a response to conflicting pressure groups over a long period of time. The early necessity for coordination in the economy gave the national and provincial governments the responsibility for the creation of economic policy. Despite this intervention the size of the directly state-owned sector is small in all three states, and is largely confined to transport and public utilities. Within the private sector two seemingly contradictory situations may be noted. There are a large number of very small enterprises (some 19·5% of the Belgian labour force is self-employed) and the small firm remains significant in many commercial and industrial activities, as well as in the more usual agricultural and retailing undertakings. A contrast to this is the continued growth of the large firm, usually with international connections, serving an international market. In the *Time-Life* list of largest firms outside the USA, Dutch companies occupy the first three places (Shell, Unilever and Philips), and the rôle in the Benelux countries of the risk-taking entrepreneur in the style of Cockerill, Van de Bergh and Plesman, is still considerable.

The fostering of an attractive climate for private investment by deliberate government incentive has encouraged the movement of foreign capital into Benelux. French and German capital has long been accustomed to seek profits in the region, but more recently United States, British, Canadian and Scandinavian enterprises have found that the establishment of branch plants, or the take-over of existing Benelux firms, provides a means of entry through the tariff wall of the EEC into the expanding Community market. Oil refining, chemicals, motor vehicle assembly, paper and brewing have proved among the most attractive sectors to foreign investment. It is estimated that some 30% of Belgian private industry is foreign-owned, with a rather smaller percentage in the Netherlands.

2.6 PLANNING

The objectives of state involvement in the planning of the economy may vary from complete control to a mere insurance that free competition can operate. The Benelux countries stand mid-way between these two extremes, with the state undertaking responsibility for outlining economic policy, integrating the various sectors of the economy so that these policies can be executed and ameliorating the results of regional imbalances. All three states are essentially 'mixed economies' in which there is a measure of both public and private economic activity.

The nature of the planning institutions makes it necessary to consider this topic under national headings, although the increasing impracticability of conducting planning entirely within national limits, especially in an area as small and as mutually interdependent as Benelux, has led to the growing integration of planning within the three states. This coordination operates at two levels. At the national level, under the auspices of the Benelux Union, it ensures that contradictory policies are not adopted nor national interests threatened by the actions of Benelux partners. An example here is the problem of trans-frontier freight traffic. In addition the planning of regions which are dissected by international frontiers, but which possess similar problems and need a comprehensive solution, is undertaken on the local scale by coordinating committees. Examples are the Semois valley scheme between Belgium and Luxembourg, and the Scheldt estuary development between Belgium and the Netherlands. Such joint planning projects can even involve non-Benelux states; West Germany and the Netherlands are cooperating in the Rhine-Ems-Ijssel development project. Planning at the national level is particularly well developed in the Netherlands, and serves as a useful example of the general principles involved.

It has been claimed that the origins of Dutch planning can be traced to the essentially communal effort necessary in water control. Indeed, the first planning institution was the *Hollands Waterstaat* of 1282. Modern planning is, however, a response to the economic realities of the survival of a small state in a competitive world, and many of the institutions owe their creation to the period of strong central government during the German occupation of 1940-1945.

Dutch planning is fairly rigidly divided between two sets of institutions dealing with economic and physical planning, but basic to both is the collection of statistics by the Central Bureau for Statistics. Economic planning is the responsibility of the Ministry for Economic Affairs, whose Central Planning Bureau publishes reports of the past performance of sectors of the economy and suggests goals to be achieved in the medium term future of between 5 and 10 years. Physical planning is the responsibility of the State Planning Service which has, to date, published two national structure plans in 1962 and 1966, outlining present land occupance and suggesting a desirable pattern for the following 20 to 30 years.

Planning operates at four distinct levels. The main lines of the future economy are prepared at the national level. At the regional level these national proposals are considered by the planning departments of the 11 provinces and the governing authority of the southern Ijsselmeer polders. The provincial authorities both implement the national proposals on the regional scale and feed back recommendations to the central authority. At the third level there is the *gemeente*, a unit of local government that may consist of a great city like Amsterdam, or a group of villages of a few hundred inhabitants. Groups of *gemeenten* are sometimes brought together in *streek* or district plans prepared by the province, and this can be regarded as a fourth planning tier. In special cases a regional planning authority, comprising groups of *gemeenten*, is set up, as in the case of the Rijnmond authority concerned with the planning of the Rotterdam-Europoort complex.

The comprehensiveness of Dutch planning is obvious, but problems nevertheless exist. Coordination between institutions at different levels, or between national institutions with different responsibilities, is complicated by the multiplicity of authorities. Thus there is considerable room for disagreement by the province concerning the rôle allocated to it under national plans, and for the *gemeente* to contradict the province. Even at the national level there are, for example, more than 20 institutions having an interest in the planning of recreation areas. There is also an apparent lack of correspondence between what is stated in planning documents and what is actually occurring on the ground. For example, the clear intention of preserving the so-called 'open heart' of the Randstad is contradicted by the rapid rise in population, and also by the recent establishment of manufacturing plants in the area. Finally, the large number of often very small *gemeenten*, the necessity for inter-provincial planning authorities and the realisation that the province is too small a unit for many modern purposes, are raising the issue of the most suitable size of planning unit.

Further Reading

R. E. Dickinson, 'The Geography of Commuting in the Netherlands and Belgium', *Geographical Review*, 1957, pp. 521-538.

E. C. Vollans, 'Urban Development in Belgium since 1830', in R. P. Beckinsale and J. M. Houston (Eds.), *Urbanization and its Problems* (Basil Blackwell, Oxford, 1968), pp. 171-198.

S. Leiker, 'Friesland: Preserving a Minority Culture in a mass Communication Age', *Progress*, No. 293, 1967, pp. 75-82.

Vernon Mallinson, *Belgium* (Ernest Benn, London, 1970), especially Chapter 13.

G. V. Stephenson, 'Cultural Regionalism and the Unitary State Idea in Belgium', *Geographical Review*, 62, 1972, pp. 501-523.

C. Bagley, 'Holland Unites', *New Society*, London, 7th March 1968.

F. Huggett, *The Modern Netherlands* (Pall Mall Press, London), 1971.

Government Printing Office, *The Kingdom of the Netherlands, Facts and Figures, No. 21, Aspects of Economic Development*, The Hague, 1971.

W. Steigenga, 'Recent Planning Problems of the Netherlands', *Regional Studies*, 2, 1968, pp. 105-113.

R. H. Buchanan, 'Towards the Netherlands 2000: the Dutch National Plan', *Economic Geography*, 45, 1969, pp. 258-274.

Chapter 3

THE PRIMARY INDUSTRIES OF BENELUX

A. Agriculture

3.1 INTRODUCTORY

It is a main characteristic of agricultural production that it is difficult to effect thoroughgoing modernisation programmes, because for many farmers agriculture is a way of life rather than a means of earning a livelihood. Farmers in many countries have been encouraged to maintain the status quo by government action to protect them from foreign competition, with the consequence that their efficiency is less than in those countries which do compete on the world market. In Benelux, Belgium and Luxembourg have adopted the protectionist approach and the Netherlands has chosen to improve her productivity in order to export agricultural produce. The reasons are not difficult to trace. By mid-19th century Belgium was the leading industrial nation on the continent, importing foodstuffs to supplement home production and exporting manufactured goods. This pattern was repeated in Luxembourg towards the end of the century, but the Netherlands lacked the basis of early industrialisation and had to rely upon agricultural exports for foreign exchange. She was able to pursue this path because of the demand for foodstuffs from neighbouring industrial nations, the competitive prices of her products, and because she was able to switch to dairy products in the 1880s when Canadian and American grain prices began to fall below Dutch prices at European ports.

In order to maintain their position as low cost producers, Dutch farmers were obliged to follow manufacturing industry and develop economies of large-scale production. Since the agricultural sector is made up of a large number of small farms, it is difficult to do this, but by the cooperative form of organisation scale economies can be achieved. The Dutch began to develop cooperatives in the 1880s and three broad categories emerged: supply cooperatives, engaged in the bulk purchase of seed, fertilisers and farm machinery; production cooperatives, in which farmers come together to form creameries, bacon-curing factories and egg-packing stations of their own; marketing cooperatives, selling on behalf of production co-

75

operatives. Agricultural cooperatives were introduced in Belgium and Luxembourg, where tiny *comices agricoles* were set up as early as 1875, but they were not established on a large scale until the inter-war period. The initiative did not solely rest with the Dutch farmers, for their government early accepted the need to foster this vital sector of the economy. By the provision of technical institutes, advisory services (there is one information officer per 160 holdings in the Netherlands compared with one per 525 holdings in Belgium) and support for land consolidation schemes, production became increasingly efficient. However, equally important was the institution of Commodity Boards controlled by the government whose task it was to control prices, production, imports and exports in the best interests of the nation. Thus levies could be made on the production of one crop and subsidies paid to another; in this way export subsidies were paid to bacon producers in the 1950s. Commodity Boards govern a wide range of products including cereals, potatoes, sugar, milk and dairy products, feedstuffs, livestock and meat and horticultural produce. Individual farmers could continue to exist in a system whose organisational units — local, regional and national cooperatives and national Commodity Boards — were very large indeed. In principle the farmer came to occupy the position of an operative in a large factory whose production costs were very low.

By contrast agriculture in Belgium and Luxembourg was inward-looking. Without the need to be competitive in the world market, farmers were protected from efficient producers by the imposition of import tariffs designed to keep prices high enough not to embarrass domestic producers. Revenue from tariffs was not put into agriculture but was regarded as national revenue. In some cases processers such as flour millers were obliged to use indigenous produce, and in others, growers such as the Belgian tobacco and the Luxembourg wine farmers, received considerable subsidies. Coupled with the slow growth of cooperatives and the absence of government measures to improve efficiency, at least until the 1950s, it is to be expected that real differences should exist between agriculture in the Netherlands and in the other two countries. The Common Agricultural Policy (CAP) of the European Economic Community (EEC) has not substantially changed the situation, for the protectionist members such as France and Belgium have managed to ensure that prices remain high and that rationalisation induced by low prices does not take place. A 'target price' is established and should the market price fall more than a small percentage (7% in the case of wheat) below this to the 'intervention price', the member countries buy in, causing the price to rise. Imports are subject to tariffs to bring the landed prices up to the 'threshold price' which is high enough not to undercut domestic producers. The 1968

Mansholt Plan has suggested methods of resolving the problems of EEC agriculture, and more recently M. Lardinois, the EEC farming commissioner, has hinted that the high guaranteed price mechanism will have to be altered, but it will be some time before substantial changes can be effected in Belgium and Luxembourg.

Important though the economic-historical background may be, it does not explain the distribution of agricultural production within Benelux. In large measure agriculture is correlated with physiography so that agricultural regions are similar to physiographic regions, but man can and does exercise an influence. In densely populated areas the competition for land is much greater than in rural districts, and this means that if a farmer is going to continue he must be able to obtain as much income from his land as would be yielded were the land in some other use. Land on the periphery of towns is valuable as building and recreational land, and in general only intensive farming such as market gardening and horticulture will be profitable. Thus the heavily populated provinces of Noord- and Zuid-Holland and the city regions of Brussels and Antwerp are the principal intensive farming regions of Benelux. More extensive production, yielding less income per hectare, is carried on in peripheral regions where land-use competition is small. Before the development of efficient transport, the perishable nature of market-garden produce reinforced this pattern. There are exceptions to this general rule, and these can often be explained by the nature of the land itself. Thus the Wieringermeer polder in Noord-Holland is predominantly an arable rather than a market-gardening region, largely as a result of soil conditions.

3.2   THE AGRICULTURAL REGIONS OF BENELUX

Since there are thirteen official agricultural regions in Belgium and six in the Netherlands, a consideration of each in turn would be tedious, but by classifying regions according to the system of production employed this problem may be overcome. Four categories can be recognised. Firstly, regions of pastoral farming, where grass exceeds 60% of the cultivated area. Secondly, arable regions in which arable land exceeds 60% of the cultivated area. Thirdly, mixed farming regions in which neither grass nor arable accounts for more than 60% of the agricultural land. Fourthly, regions of intensive farming in which market gardening and horticulture account for more than 9% of the cultivated area. Table 3.1 lists the areas included in each of the four categories. Dutch provinces rather than the official agricultural regions are used owing to the greater availability of data. The regions are mapped in Figs. 3.1 and 3.2. The Belgian intensive farming region does not fit into any of the statistical areas, but its outline is indicated on the map.

The pastoral regions

Greater profits can be made per hectare from livestock than from grain production, and there is an increasing shift to pastoral from arable farming. The tendency is much more marked in the Netherlands than in Belgium and Luxembourg, for the trend has received great emphasis following Dutch specialisation in dairy farming. At present 61% of the cultivated surface of the Netherlands consists of permanent pasture, compared with 51% in Belgium and 47% in Luxembourg. At the same time the production of animal feedgrains and fodder crops such as beet and turnips has increased in importance. Inevitably areas especially

TABLE 3.1

The agricultural regions of Benelux
% of area of region devoted to the activity shown

Pastoral regions		Arable regions		Mixed farming regions			Intensive regions	
					pastoral	arable		
Haute		Ijssel		N. Brabant	58%	34%	Z. Holland	13%
Ardenne	93%	polders	78%	Drenthe	56%	43%	N. Holland	11%
Friesland	92%	Zeeland	75%	Gutland	56%	44%	Limburg	11%
Utrecht	91%	Loam		Condroz	52%	46%	Belgian	
Fagne	89%	region	66%	Sand region	50%	42%	market-	
Liège	89%	Groningen	62%	Oesling	41%	58%	gardening	
Overijssel	85%			Polder/			region	?
Gelderland	75%			Dunes	40%	57%		
Famenne	74%			Sand-Loam	38%	55%		
Jurassic	73%							
Kempen	73%							
Ardenne	69%							

suited to pastoral farming have specialised in the activity. Fig. 3.1 indicates that these regions form a ring round the Ijsselmeer and constitute almost the whole of upland Belgium. The Dutch districts have a damp, mild climate and heavy peaty and clay soils, highly conducive to the growth of grass, and population pressure is not such that intensive farming is the rule. The raison d'etre of the Belgian pastoral regions rests on the unsuitability of the uplands for arable and intensive farming. The environment is hardly ideally suited to livestock production, but there are few alternatives to this activity. There are three kinds of pastoral region: those specialising in dairy cattle, those specialising in beef cattle and those undertaking both.

(i) *Dairy farming regions* The four Dutch pastoral farming regions, Friesland, Utrecht, Overijssel and Gelderland are specialist dairy cattle

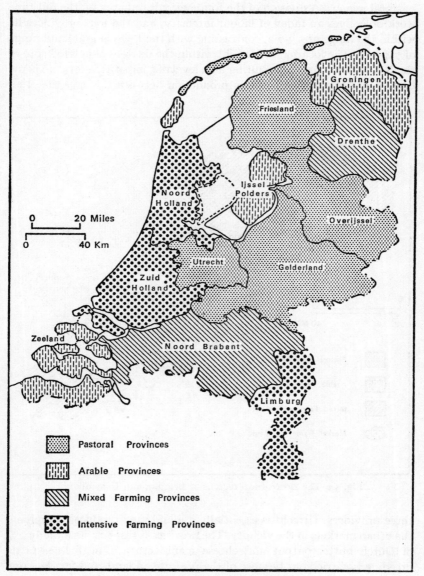

Fig. 3.1 The agricultural regions of the Netherlands

districts. All are intensive users of labour compared with the Belgian
pastoral regions. A division of the total agricultural area by the full-time
workforce gives an index of labour intensity, and the four provinces lie
within the range of 5·3-7·2, contrasting with the Belgian grassland range
of 7·4-18·7. The location of Utrecht within the densely populated core of
the Netherlands and the resulting high level of competition for land is the
basic cause of the differences in production between this and the other

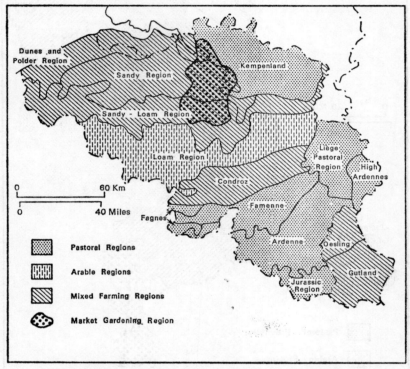

Fig. 3.2 The agricultural regions of Belgium and Luxembourg

three provinces. Utrecht is essentially a liquid milk producer, supplying
the urban markets in the vicinity. The province is responsible for only 2%
of Dutch butter output and cheese manufacture is negligible. Little
breeding is carried out because of the pressure on land, and for the same
reason fodder crops are unimportant. Orchards, however, can be justified
and one-sixth of the Dutch apple crop originates in the province. In the
absence of large urban markets in the other three provinces there is no
great local demand for liquid milk, and there is thus great incentive to

manufacture dairy products which do not deteriorate and can stand the costs of being transported to markets within Benelux and Western Europe. Friesland, Overijssel and Gelderland together make 51% of Dutch butter and 69% of Dutch cheese. Friesland alone makes one-third of the national output of cheese, producing special cheeses such as Friesian Kanter, Friesian clove cheese and Leyden cheese in addition to the standard Edams and Goudas. The province has more than 100 creameries producing butter, cheese, powdered and condensed milk. Because land-use competition is less than in Utrecht, grain and fodder crops are more important than in the latter province. Cattle breeding is well developed, especially in Friesland and Overijssel, the most common breed being the black and white Friesian. Although the application of fertilisers has aided the growth of grass in sandy areas such as the Veluwe and in the heathlands of Overijssel, the most favourable environment is found in the older polders of Friesland. Indeed, apart from the recently reclaimed coastal district, more than 80% of farm labour is on grassland farms, representing one of the best examples of specialisation in Benelux.

Of the four dairying provinces, Gelderland is the least specialist, as its smaller area of permanent grass would suggest. The sandy soils of the Veluwe and in the east of the province have been usefully employed by poultry farmers who are responsible for one-third of Dutch production. Originally a sideline of dairy farmers, this activity now exists in its own right, with a well-developed export trade, in particular to West Germany. Of recent there has been a switch from an emphasis on eggs to broilers because of the rising price of meat. Of particular interest is the growth of duck-keeping around Harderwijk, Ermelo and Barnevelde in the Geldersche Vallei where farmers raise Pekin ducks for meat. There are no special locational advantages in the area, and as is often the case with small-scale regional specialisation, the cause of localisation must be attributed to the success of a few farmers inspiring others in the locality to follow their example. A further specialisation is fruit growing in the particularly fertile Betuwe between Arnhem and Nijmegen; that Gelderland produces 36% of Dutch apples and 30% of Dutch stone fruit is a result of the existence of this small but intensively farmed district.

It is clear that in order to be able to export two-thirds of cheese output, half of butter output and to be the world's leading exporter of condensed milk, the Netherlands must be able to quote low prices. This is achieved by paying close attention to technological advances in cattle food production, the diffusion of information being coordinated by the Central Livestock Feeding Bureau, and to improved methods of grass production. Thus in 1940 a hectare of grass would support 1 cow, but the figure is now 1·3 cows. Selective breeding has assisted productivity and the milk yield of

F

4 250 kg per annum is the highest in the EEC. Also important are economies of large-scale production, and the Dutch dairy farmers have a good
record here for 74% of their cows are in herds of more than 10, compared
with 66% in Denmark and only 30% in Belgium. At the manufacturing
and marketing stages scale economies are derived from cooperatives.
There are 320 cooperative dairies which handle 84% of milk, 88% of
cheese, 84% of butter, 79% of milk powder and 60% of condensed milk
production.

(ii) *Beef farming regions* With the exception of the Belgian Kempenland,
the rearing of cattle for meat rather than for milk is confined to the Ardenne
uplands of Benelux, including the agricultural regions of the High
Ardennes, Fagne, Famenne, Ardenne, and the Jurassic region. In the
absence of the need to export dairy produce because of the strength of the
industrial sector, the Belgian pastoral regions have never moved into
dairying to the extent of their Dutch counterparts. Only 31%-37% of the
cattle in the Fagne, Famenne, Ardenne and the Jurassic region are cows,
the remainder being beef cattle. Predictably the Kempenland has a slightly
higher proportion (40%), following the presence of the large liquid milk
market provided by Brussels and Antwerp to the west. The High Ardennes
has the largest proportion (48%) of dairy cattle in the regional total,
largely a result of the importance of the Amblève valley as a dairy cattle
rearing area. Although beef cattle farming is the principal activity of the
upland regions, it must be observed that beef cattle are more numerous in
the mixed farming regions in Flanders where the Sandy-Loam region
alone has more beef cattle than the combined total of the upland regions.
The Kempenland is distinctive among the Belgian pastoral regions in that
pig farming is important. Pig farming in Benelux is a characteristic of the
intensive farming regions, and its importance in Kempenland is a function
of the location of the region in respect of urban markets.

Arable farming in the beef districts is very largely concerned with the
production of cattle feed. Hence both oats and barley are more important
than wheat, and only in the High Ardennes and the Jurassic region are
oats allocated more hectares than barley, the most nutritious feed. The
Ardenne region is quite prolific in its output, growing 10% of Belgian
oats, 7% of Belgian barley and 13% of green fodder crops such as clover,
lucerne and green maize. The sandy soils of the Kempenland give rise to
a different pattern of grain production, for they are conducive to the
growth of rye, and the region produces one-third of the Belgian crop.

The importance of both dairying and pig farming in the Kempenland
has been noted, and to these poultry farming must be added. The region is
the leading Belgian producer, with one-third of total output. The region
is obviously somewhat different from the upland districts which are not

nearly so well diversified, and in some respects it is similar to the mixed farming regions of Flanders. The average size of holding, 5·2 ha, is very nearly the lowest in Belgium and the index of labour intensity is 7·4, only slightly higher than the index of 6·8 scored by the Sandy and the Sandy-Loam regions. The indices for the upland regions are for the most part very much higher and they have a mean score of 14·0.

There occurs in the Ardenne region a good example of the cultivation of a crop which falls outside the typical pattern of production. Tobacco growing is practised in the Semois valley, and although it occupies only 76 ha, it is the second largest producing region in Belgium, responsible for 13% of the national output. Productivity is much lower than in the Sandy-Loam region, the leading district, but the lower land values help to offset this; the Flemish district grows 3·2 against 2 tons per hectare in the Semois valley. The output comes from small specialised holdings on the alluvial floor and lower slopes of the valley where the *toubatière* system of continuous cropping is employed, each plant yielding for up to 10 years. The specialisation is assisted by the sheltered nature of the valley, but the initial location was a result of chance factors, namely the decision of a local farmer, Joseph Pierret, to grow Kentucky tobacco seeds in 1856, and the acceptance of this practice by his neighbours.

(iii) *Mixed dairy and beef cattle farming regions* This category comprises a single region, the Liège pastoral region, in which dairy cattle just out-number beef cattle. The urban market provided by the Liège industrial region causes liquid milk production to be important, and for the same reason pigs are more numerous than in any of the Belgian pastoral regions with the exception of the Kempenland. The favourable climatic régime causes more wheat than any other cereal to be grown, an unusual situation in a pastoral region, but output is small. The second most important land-use is not arable but fruit growing, an activity concentrated in the Pays de Herve, encouraged by summer warmth, loamy soils and to some extent the neighbouring market.

The arable regions

This category comprises four regions, the Ijsselmeer polders including Wieringermeer, Zeeland, the Belgian Loam region and Groningen. The distribution of all four correlates closely with certain soils. The three Dutch regions fit almost exactly the official *zeekleigebieden* or marine clay areas and the Belgian arable district consists of *limon* or loam. Belgian polderland is a notable absentee from this category, and in view of the use to which the Dutch put their polders, this requires an explanation. The root cause is the age of the Belgian polder region, coupled with the tradi-tional intensive pattern of crop production in lowland Belgium. Recently

reclaimed polders are best suited to arable farming and it is thus no
accident that Oost-Flevoland is the most specialised arable area in Benelux,
with more than 80% of its workforce involved in this branch of agriculture.
The polders reclaimed prior to the 20th century provide farmers with a
much wider choice of production, and mixed farming is the rule, especially
in Belgium where the central low plateau has long been used for intensive
arable farming, reducing the opportunities for arable farming in polderland.

Since the Dutch arable areas are largely a function of soils and the
Belgian arable region a result of historical and economic pressures, differences between the two are to be expected, but the basic pattern of
cropping is remarkably similar. Both are the most important cereal growing areas in their respective countries and the crops grown are almost
identical. The largest areas are devoted to wheat, followed by barley and
oats, but an integral part of the régime is the production of root crops.
The Dutch regions grow 67% of the national output of sugar beet and 68%
of food potato output, while the Loam region alone is responsible for 55%
of Belgian sugar beet production. The similarity of production systems
even extends to purely industrial crops, for each is a specialist producer
of flax. The *zeekleigebieden* grow virtually the entire Dutch output and the
Loam region is the first Belgian producer. Close parallels can also be drawn
in respect of productivity, for the specialist arable areas are not only the
most efficient producers in their respective countries but output per
hectare in all four regions shows remarkably little variation.

Common to the arable areas are large processing factories. Potatoes
grown as a source of starch are cultivated in eastern Groningen, where the
province includes some of the peaty heathland soils and processing is
effected at large factories, the first of which was established as early as
1841. Similar economies of large-scale production can be seen in the
refining of sugar from beet, and some plants can manufacture up to 1 000
tons of refined sugar per day. One of the largest is at Tienen, south-east of
Brussels, producing two-thirds of the total Belgian refined sugar output.
Beet sugar refineries are associated with the beet producing areas because
the average sugar content of the crop is only 16%, and there is every incentive to locate at the source of the material to keep transport costs to a
minimum.

The dissimilarities between the three Dutch provinces and the Loam
region are to be found in the greater importance placed on cattle rearing
and market gardening in the Loam region. The latter area is responsible
for one-third of Belgian market-garden produce and grows a similar proportion of the country's fruit, the bulk of the fruit coming from the
Hesbaye area in the east where there are also canning and fruit juice

factories. Market gardening does attain some importance in Zeeland, where the island of Zuid Beveland is a specialist producer of redcurrants and blackcurrants. Indeed, market gardening covers some 90% of the agricultural area of the province, almost qualifying the region for inclusion among the intensive farming regions. Apart from western Groningen where the Friesland dairying district impinges upon the province, dairying is quite unimportant in the Dutch arable regions. On the other hand, the Loam region is the third largest dairying and second most important beef cattle district in Belgium. It is also the third producer of pigs, suggesting, with the importance of dairying, that the presence of urban markets has modified the nature of farming in this region.

Although the Loam region has an important market-gardening sector, the index of labour intensity shows that more intensive farming is the rule in both Zeeland (6·4) and Groningen (7·1) than the Loam region (11·5). The Ijssel polders have a score of 19·7, reflecting the trend towards extensive agriculture based on mechanised production in these new lands. The standard parcel of land in Wieringermeer was 21 ha, but when land came to be allocated in the Noord-Oost Polder, the standard parcel was increased to 25 ha. For Oost-Flevoland the parcel is 31 ha and the maximum sized holding 125 ha, compared with 45 ha deemed to be the upper limit for Wieringermeer. Despite the economic pressures at work, soil conditions are still a powerful influence upon the location of production. In the Noord-Oost Polder the light soils of the western margin have been designated for mixed farming, the clays of the bulk of the area have been assigned to arable farming, and the very best soils east of Marknesse and Luttelgeest and south of Kraggenburg have been reserved for fruit growing and market gardening.

Mixed farming regions

The two categories of regions so far considered exhibit specialisation in either pastoral or arable farming. Mixed farming places an emphasis on diversification, which may be the result of physical conditions as much as economic factors. In some cases regions of mixed farming are transitional in character between pastoral and arable regions, and in others the proximity to urban markets and population pressure greatly assist the variety of output.

(i) *Transitional regions* Three regions in particular, Noord-Brabant, Drenthe and the Condroz fit the simple model of the mixed farming region as one which lies between pastoral and arable regions. Noord-Brabant includes part of the *zeekleigebieden* in the delta area, with its emphasis on arable farming, part of the dairying district which spills over from Utrecht and Zuid-Holland, and the pastoral farming heathlands spreading northwards from Kempenland. Consequently on the one hand the province produces one-seventh of Dutch milk, and on the other is the leading supplier of barley and the third producer of sugar beet in the Netherlands. As so often occurs in agriculture, there is regional specialisation around particular points within the region, especially in the west. Breda is the most important cane fruit growing area in the Netherlands with 43% of the national output, market gardening, with Breda as its centre, accounts for 6% of the cultivated surface, and the growing of trees and shrubs is better developed than in any other province, the centres being Oudenbosch and Zundert.

The province of Drenthe lies between the predominantly arable Groningen to the north and the permanent pasture lands of Friesland and Overijssel to the west and south. Grass is more important than arable, but Drenthe is by far the most prolific potato growing province in the country. Here, as in the neighbouring part of Groningen, the special varieties of potatoes required by the starch mills are grown on reclaimed peaty soils, or *dalgronden*. Milk, butter and cheese production is of moderate importance in this province which so admirably reflects the agricultural régimes of the neighbouring areas. The Condroz is a neat linear transitional zone between the pastoral uplands and the arable Loam region to the north, and even more than in Drenthe the two activities intermingle. Wheat and barley are grown over wider areas than in the uplands, and the region is the second largest producer of green fodder crops in Belgium. At the same time market gardening creeps in and the region is the southern limit of the sugar beet which grows in such large quantities in the Loam region to the north.

There are three mixed farming regions which, although they do not lie between arable and pastoral regions, are nevertheless transitional. The Polders and Dunes region lies between the newer polderlands of Zeeland and the mixed farming regions to the south. It reflects the polderlands in its high proportion (57%) of arable land, and its cattle rearing and pig farming are suggestive of the mixed farming regions. However it lacks the market gardening activities of the more heavily populated areas to the south. The second region, Luxembourg Gutland, is an eastward extension of the Belgian Jurassic region, an area of pastoral farming, and the suitability of Gutland for cattle farming is seen in the high proportion of permanent grass (56%). Demand from urban markets is helping to increase the area devoted to animal farming, and earnings from this activity account for 88% of the total farm income excluding viticulture. Dairy farming is especially important. The most important specialisation is viticulture in the Mosel valley, the only area in Benelux where grapes are grown out of doors. Substantial physical advantages such as calcareous soils, steeply sloping valley sides and a sunny south-eastern aspect help to explain the localisation of the activity, and indeed the warmest parts of the valley south of Remich are the most productive. Monoculture is rare in the Mosel valley and the average size of holding producing grapes is only 31 ha. However, economies of scale are obtained consequent upon the existence of six cooperatives which control three-quarters of the output. In 1966 five of the cooperatives grouped themselves into a single unit under the name of Vinsmoselle for both production and marketing purposes.

Although Luxembourg Oesling is part of the Ardenne massif, it lacks the concentration on animal farming that typifies the Belgian uplands. For such a physical environment it has a high proportion (58%) of arable land, yet at the same time the region has half the country's cattle and pigs. Physically a part of the uplands, Oesling is nevertheless on their periphery and this transitional position is reflected in its agriculture.

TABLE 3.2

Agriculture in the Sandy and Sandy-Loam regions, 1970

| | | | Percentage of Belgian | | | |
Region	Index of labour intensity	Av. size of holding ha	part-time labour	green-houses	beef cattle	cows
Sandy	6·8	4·9	20	54	16	17
Sandy-Loam	6·8	6·1	29	37	18	18

(ii) *Regions of population pressure* The Flemish Sandy and Sandy-Loam regions have been characterised by intensive agriculture since the later medieval period as a means of providing both employment and sufficient food for these populous regions. Additional incentives were the growth of towns such as Bruges, Ghent, Antwerp and Brussels and the expansion of the textile industry, especially in the 19th century. The early development of a commercial and acquisitive spirit unusual in agriculture aided diversification which has resulted in the cultivation of such industrial crops as tobacco, chicory for coffee, flax and hops. These crops are especially labour intensive and are attractive and profitable for smallholders with large families who have built up specialised marketing channels that discourage cultivators in other regions from entering the field. The two largest urban markets in Belgium, Brussels and Antwerp, are included in these regions, and inevitably market gardening is well developed. Table 3·2 gives some indication of the characteristics of the two regions.

From what has been said it might appear that the two regions could be described as intensive arable areas, but although they are certainly intensive, only 5% of the cultivated surface of both regions is given over to market gardening. Further, pasture is more important than arable land

in the Sandy region, and both areas have more cattle than any other in
Belgium. In spite of their extensive nature sheep are kept, particularly
in the Sandy-Loam region where there are twice the number that exist in
the upland pastoral regions. In short the two regions are truly mixed
farming districts and have for centuries supplied Belgium with a wide
range of produce.

An important influence upon the diversity of agriculture has been the
existence of part-time farming, which is better developed here than anywhere else in Western Europe. In the Sandy region part-time farmers are
nearly as numerous as full-time farmers, the respective figures in 1970
being 24 000 and 29 000. The situation is not fundamentally different in
the Sandy-Loam region, where the figures are 33 000 and 45 000 respectively. Part-timers clearly affect not only the size of holdings and methods
of production, but also the type of crops grown. Their numbers certainly
encourage diversity and the retention of patterns of production rejected
by the more commercially minded full-time farmers. This is best illustrated
from livestock production. On part-time farms sheep, goats and rabbits
are more important than on fully commercial farms where pigs, poultry
and cattle are regarded as being more profitable. Some 62% of holdings
are less than 1 ha in area, and at this scale mechanisation is uneconomic,
with the consequence that income is low. But since by definition part-time
farmers have a second job, low farm returns do not necessarily cause them
to change their system of production and the old cropping patterns are
retained. Additional inertia stems from the fact that half the part-time
farmers own their own buildings and land, whereas only 15% of the full-
time farmers do so. The initial causes of part-time agriculture include the
traditional Flemish attachment to the rural way of life coupled with a
desire to increase income by taking an urban job, and the need for an
income in case of redundancy from the urban job. The system was given
great impetus by the institution in 1870 of cheap workers' returns on
Belgian railways, but there are signs that the security of employment in
manufacturing is causing a sharp decline in part-time farming. Between
1961 and 1970 the number of part-time farmers in the Sandy region and
the Sandy-Loam region fell 45% and 53% respectively.

Within the two regions there is some regional specialisation caused by
differences in soils, by the presence of large markets and by chance factors.
The sandy soils of the northern region cause rye to be grown, and the area
produces more than half the national output. For the same reason potatoes
are also an important crop. The heavier soils in the Sandy-Loam region are
conducive to chicory, flax and tobacco, but the localisation of these crops
into the western district round Kortrijk and Roeselare is at least as much
due to economic factors such as population pressure, the extent of indus-

trialisation and the presence of linen manufacture, as to physical considerations. The alluvial soils of Waasland are especially fertile but the local fruit and vegetable cultivation is heavily influenced by markets in both Ghent and Antwerp. The bulb and cut flower industry of Ghent, responsible for three-quarters of Belgian output, is the result of chance specialisation rather than a particularly suitable environment. The Aalst hop growing region, which produces 90% of Belgian output, fits into the same category. Other localised production, clearly influenced by consumer demand, is the cultivation of fruit and vegetables under glass round Ghent, Antwerp and Brussels. Within the fruit and vegetable areas peripheral to the large towns there are some good examples of specialisation. One is the Hoeilaart grape district to the south of Brussels where 33 000 greenhouses produce 12 000 tons of grapes a year. Another is the *pays de witloof*, or chicory region to the north-east of the capital. Some three-fifths of national output originates from this district and some *communes* such as Evere grow little else. The location of the crop is an interesting case of diffusion, for it was originally grown in the Botanic Gardens and was introduced to the adjacent suburbs by gardeners who worked in the Gardens, and was then taken up by the part-time farmers in the locality.

Intensive farming regions

In the absence of statistics for the Belgian market-gardening region, this category is limited to the provinces of Noord- and Zuid-Holland and Limburg. In many ways Noord- and Zuid-Holland are similar to the Sandy and Sandy-Loam regions of Belgium, for agriculture is diversified, population pressure causes land to be intensively used and there are examples of specialisation about particular points. The differences lie in the greater importance attached to dairy farming, and consequently to permanent pasture, the small importance of part-time farming and the sheer efficiency of production. There is also a difference in the intensity of production, for Noord- and Zuid-Holland have indices of labour intensity of 4·0 and 3·0 respectively, much lower than the figure of 6·8 recorded for the two Belgian regions. Zuid-Holland stands in a class on its own for alone it accounts for one-fifth of the agricultural contribution to the Dutch national income. The figure for Noord-Holland is 12%.

Although the polders of Noord- and Zuid-Holland are extremely efficient producers of grass, and as such are very attractive to dairy farming, such is the competition for land that dairying is not always the most profitable land-use. Both provinces thus produce only half the milk output of Friesland, and it is Noord-Holland, where markets for liquid milk are not as large, that is the larger butter and cheese producer. Even so, Friesland produces three times as much cheese as Noord-Holland. However

there are specialist dairying regions in the polders between Alkmaar and
Amsterdam and in Alblasserwaard, east of Rotterdam in Zuid-Holland.
Fodder crops are not well developed, since it is more economic to grow them
elsewhere, and although sugar beet is of greater importance than in the
pastoral provinces, it is horticulture in which the two provinces specialise.
Vegetable growing is the most important branch, and there is remarkable
localisation which brings external economies of scale. In Westland, between The Hague, Rotterdam and Hoek van Holland, there are 4 000 ha
devoted to vegetables, 1 400 ha of which are under glass, the chimneys of
the heating plants and the sea of greenhouses creating a most distinctive
landscape. A second, smaller area to the north, Kring, has 1 000 ha under
glass; and here there is specialisation of product for only cucumbers,
lettuce and tomatoes are grown. Other concentrations of vegetable production are Zwijndrecht, west of Dordrecht, Venen near Leiden and the
Langedijk district of Noord-Holland. Soft fruits, especially strawberries,
are grown in Venen and Bangert in Noord-Holland, grapes are localised in
Westland and bulb growing is a feature of both provinces between
Haarlem and Leiden, although it is much more important in Noord- than
Zuid-Holland. A greater area is devoted to flowers under glass than to those
grown in the open, and they fetch a higher price as a result. Indeed, prices
are such that flowers can stand the cost of air transport and the proximity
of Schiphol international airport is of great value for export purposes.
Specialist centres include Aalsmeer near Amsterdam, Westland, Venen
and Rijnsburg near Leiden. Shrubs are cultivated in particular in
Boskoop, an area north of Gouda in Zuid-Holland.

The third intensive farming region, Limburg, is unusual in that it is
not subject to the great population pressure that exists in Noord- and
Zuid-Holland, nor is labour so intensively used as in these provinces;
its index of labour intensity is 5·3. Were it not for its especially well-
developed horticultural sector in relation to its agricultural area, the province would be a mixed farming region, for the difference between the
proportions of pastoral and arable land (46% and 43% respectively) is the
smallest of any of the Benelux regions. Much of the region's intensive
farming is a result of the fertile loam of which the province south of
Sittard consists, and which also causes fruit growing to the west in Hesbaye
and to the south in the Pays de Herve. Added to this is river alluvium
from the Maas extending to the northern extremity of the province,
allowing intensive agriculture to take place beyond the loam area. Hence
the district round Venlo is one of the largest concentrations of vegetable
production in the Netherlands, the reason for the precise location being
the proximity of the Ruhr industrial district (Krefeld is only 25 km to the
east). Local growers specialise in asparagus and runner beans. Limburg

is the leading Dutch mushroom producing region, with an experimental station at Horst and a cooperative fertiliser factory at Ottersum; almost half the output of 15 000 tons is exported, largely to West Germany. Stone fruits, apples and pears are concentrated into the loam district, redcurrants are grown in large areas round Venlo and one-fifth of Dutch shrubs are cultivated in the same district. Taking advantage of the attractions of the province as a tourist area, Limburg farmers are able to supplement their incomes by offering accommodation in the summer months. Some 23% of the farmers in the province are engaged in this activity, but as with the Flemish part-time farmers, this additional source of income often serves to reduce the use of more efficient techniques, and in this sense is an unfortunate development.

3.3 LAND CONSOLIDATION IN BENELUX

For many farmers agriculture is a way of life and it is thus very difficult to effect changes to improve productivity. Apart from this, the arduous nature of the occupation and the possibility of high wages in the towns causing young people to be reluctant to remain on the farm, result in shortages of labour and the need to pay higher wages to retain the workers that remain. Between 1966 and 1970 the wages paid to Dutch farm workers rose by one-third and those paid to Belgian workers rose one-fifth. Since increased affluence normally leads to greater outlays on consumer durables than on food, farmers cannot benefit fully from the rise in demand for goods, nor can they afford to pay high wages. The present EEC agricultural policy assists farmers by keeping up prices, but as Mansholt points out, the problem of farmers' income will not be solved by increased prices but by reducing the number of marginal producers and improving the efficiency, and profits, of those who remain. To encourage farmers to retire early, there is now provision for those over 60 to give up their land and to receive an annuity of £350 in order that their holdings may be amalgamated with others. Large farms are normally more efficient than small farms, and the Mansholt Plan suggests that arable and grain farms should be at least 80 ha, or possess at least 40 cattle or 10 000 laying hens. To achieve economies of large-scale production it is necessary not only to increase the size of farm but completely to rationalise the shape of the fields, the location of farm buildings, roads and drainage systems and to cut out plots separate from the main holding. This process is known as land consolidation and the effect it has had on the field pattern in the vicinity of the village of Gelselaar, east of Zutphen in Gelderland, is mapped in Figs. 3.3 and 3.4.

Following the traditional Belgian policy of protection and the low level of agricultural exports, coupled with the importance of part-time farming, there are a very large number of economically marginal farms in Belgium. Three-quarters of the holdings south of the Meuse, occupying half the cultivated area, are thought to be marginal. Between 70% and 80% of the agricultural area of Kempenland is held by uneconomic farms, and the eastern areas of the Sandy and Sandy-Loam regions have one-third of their farms in the marginal category. In some areas the fragmentation of holdings is particularly acute and the High Ardennes, eastern Hesbaye and the Jurassic region all have many farms comprising more than 7 plots of

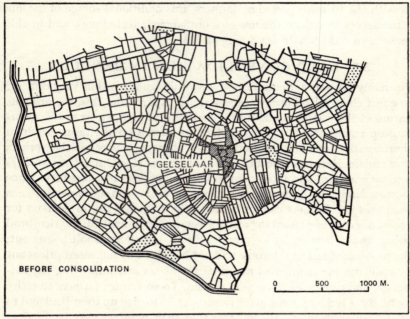

BEFORE CONSOLIDATION

0   500   1000 M.

Fig. 3.3 Field patterns at Gelselaar before consolidation

less than 1 ha each. The problem is hardly less grave in the Loam region between Tournai and Namur. The first effective legislation to further land consolidation was enacted in 1956, although a law of 1869 had laid the basis for the voluntary exchange of land. The work is carried out by the *Société Nationale de la Petite Propriété Terrienne*, 60% of the cost being met by the state, 20%-30% by the local and provincial governments, leaving only 10%-20% to be found by the farmer. It is not surprising that the more enterprising farmers were quick to participate and 84 schemes covering 89 000 ha have been completed or are in progress for the Sandy, Sandy-Loam and Loam regions. There have been rapid developments in the vicinity of Momalle near Liège, Tongeren, Gentinnes, Perwez and Ath in the Loam region. It would seem to represent an interesting example of diffusion from a few innovating centres, with farmers cooperating when visible results are at hand in their locality. In one 780-ha scheme, near Vlijtingen, 3·1 km of new roads were laid and the average size of holding increased from 23 ha to 96 ha at a total cost of £2 million. The scheme took seven years to complete. In the 1950s it was thought that 600 000 ha required consolidating in Belgium, but as the optimum size of farm is continually rising, this estimate has been brought up to 1 million ha, that

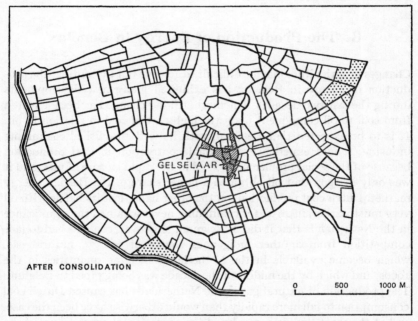

Fig. 3.4 Field patterns at Gelselaar after consolidation

is, two-thirds of the total agricultural area. It certainly seems that the early schemes will themselves shortly consist of marginally sized farms.

With efficiency being of much greater significance to the Dutch, land consolidation legislation dates from the inter-war period in the Netherlands. The first act was passed in 1924 and amendments were made in 1938 and 1954. Plans are prepared by the Government Service for Land and Water Use and are effected by the Royal Netherlands Reclamation Society. Since the intensive agricultural areas are highly efficient, they have received least attention, and only five schemes covering 2 306 ha have been effected in Zuid-Holland out of a national total of 322 729 ha. Overijssel has been the scene of 42 schemes, but Zeeland, with 115 schemes covering 67 000 ha has had the largest area of land consolidated. Noord-Brabant has both the largest number of schemes and the largest area in the process of consolidation and at the planning stage, and when the work is complete the entire province will have been reorganised. For the country as a whole schemes have been drawn up for 1·8 million ha, just short of three-quarters of the total agricultural area, and although 50 000 ha are consolidated each year at a cost of £32 million, it is clear that at this rate of progress the early schemes will here too be of doubtful viability long before all the work is complete.

B. The Production of Energy in Benelux

Changes in agriculture may be difficult to achieve but by contrast the production of energy in Benelux has exhibited many new developments during the last two decades. The most striking change has been a switch from coal to oil consequent upon the high cost of coal in relation to oil. It is to be expected that Belgium, with its well-established coalmining industry, should experience a gradual contraction in coal production because of the social problems involved in the rapid closure of pits, and it was only in 1967 that oil obtained a larger share of the Belgian energy market. Dutch coal production, on the other hand, lost its battle with oil very much earlier, in 1959, for coalmining never attained the significance in the Netherlands that it did in Belgium. Moreover, coal has had to face competition from another indigenous source of energy, natural gas, which became available in the Netherlands in large quantities in the 1960s, and which by the middle of the decade was being piped to Belgium. The production of natural gas in the Netherlands has caused Dutch coal consumption to fall more rapidly than would otherwise have been the case, and at the same time it has reduced the scope for oil, whose share of the Dutch market for energy has actually declined since 1966. Natural gas has had only a recent impact upon Belgium, but as the Belgian coalmining industry slowly declines it is likely that natural gas rather than oil will take the place of coal. The situation in Luxembourg is unusual, for coal retains two-thirds of the market in a country without a coalfield. This is a commentary on the domination of the iron and steel industry, for metallurgical coke is still required as the major blast furnace fuel, providing oil with limited chance of expansion. Table 3.3 sets out the way in which the energy market is shared between the main sources of energy. The table emphasises the unimportance of hydro-electric power, and the part played by nuclear power is even less significant, not justifying inclusion in the table.

TABLE 3.3

Energy consumption in Benelux, 1962-1970

	Coal		Oil		Natural gas		Hydro-electric power	
	1962	1970	1962	1970	1962	1970	1962	1970
Belgium	66%	41%	34%	48%	—	11%	—	—
Netherlands	46%	11%	52%	52%	2%	37%	—	—
Luxembourg	86%	65%	11%	33%	1%	—	2%	2%

3.4 THE COALMINING INDUSTRY

The Belgian and Dutch coalfields form part of the Carboniferous System which extends from the French *départements* of Pas de Calais and Nord eastwards as far as the Ruhr. The principal field follows the line of the Haine, Sambre and Meuse valleys in central Belgium, and is often referred to as the Haine-Sambre-Meuse coal furrow. It has four sectors, from west to east the Borinage, the Centre, the Charleroi and the Liège fields, although the first two are now administered as a single unit. The two other districts, the Kempen and the Zuid-Limburg fields in Belgium and the Netherlands respectively, are simply different parts of the same field which runs north-west-south-east through the Belgian Kempenland and the southern part of the Dutch province of Limburg. The relative location of the fields can be seen in the inset to Fig. 3.5. The Walloon field was developed first because the seams outcropped at a large number of places throughout its length, and because of the early date of the forces giving rise to industrialisation in Belgium. Although the Zuid-Limburg field outcropped close to the German border, it could not be easily worked owing to the aquiferous nature of the surrounding strata, and it was not until the development of the shaft-freezing process at the end of the 19th century that progress could be made.

Some of the important differences between the Walloon and the more northerly fields are a direct consequence of their different dates of exploitation. The Walloon fields were the largest in continental Europe until the 1870s, when they were overtaken by the Ruhr and later by the Pas de Calais mines. Since they were established so early they were small in scale and large in number, and lacked the economies of large-scale production which have always characterised the Kempen and Zuid-Limburg fields. In 1850 there were 408 pits in Wallonie, producing an average of 14 000 tons each, but the pits in the northern fields, sunk in the 20th century, were planned to mine at least half a million tons a year, giving rise to economies of maintenance, handling and marketing. In Wallonie the concessions were often badly organised for profitable working, for example one area in the

Borinage had 14 concessions arranged one beneath the other, but in the Kempen and Zuid-Limburg the state participated in the drawing up of the concessions, with more satisfactory results. The first Dutch concession was granted in 1895 to the Domaniale company at Kerkrade, and by 1927 when the Oranje IV pit opened there were eight private mines in operation, all at the eastern end of the field where the seams were close to the surface. Through an act passed in 1901 the Dutch government reserved the larger part of the coalfield to itself, at the same time forming the publicly owned Nederlandse Staatsmijnen. With the exception of the first pit, Wilhelmina

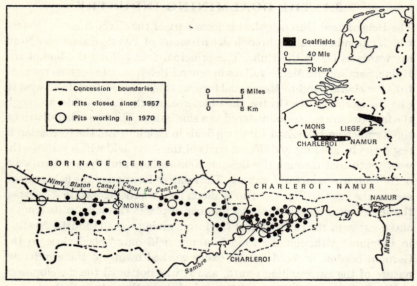

Fig. 3.5 The Borinage-Centre and Charleroi-Namur coalfields

(1906), the four state mines were sunk in the central or western parts of the field, and in the absence of other pits they could work very large areas indeed. The westernmost pit, Maurits (1923) came to be the largest in Western Europe with an output of 2·8 million tons in 1950. The Kempen field was developed even later, and the first coal was not brought to the surface until 1917 at Winterslag. The Beringen, Eisden, Waterschei and Zwartberg pits were brought into operation during the 1920s, and Helchteren-Zolder and Houthalen belong to that small number of pits in Western Europe developed in the 1930s. The differences in scale between the northern and southern fields are well illustrated by Figs. 3.5 and 3.6 in which the crowded pits of the older areas contrast strongly with those in the newer fields.

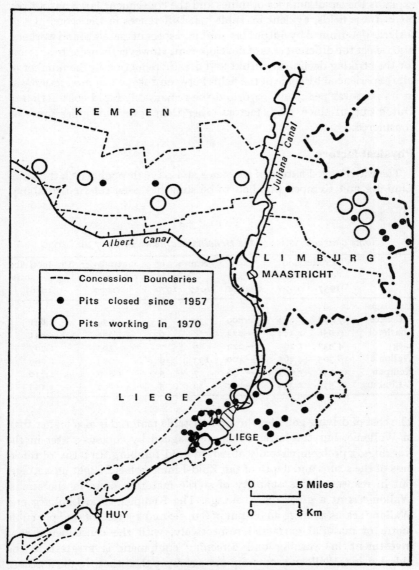

Fig. 3.6 The Liége, Kempen and Zuid-Limburg coalfields

The late date of the opening up of the Zuid-Limburg and Kempen fields explains the small number of mines and the consequent large output per pit in these fields, evident in Table 3.4. Differences in the economies of scale, as determined by output per shift in respect of underground workers, also reflect the different eras of development. However, in order to account for the striking decline in output and drastic reduction in the number of pits experienced by some of the fields between 1957, when production was at its post-war peak, and 1970, and the remarkably rapid contraction of Dutch output since 1965, factors other than scale economies must be considered.

Physical factors

The waterlogged nature of the sands and clays through which the Zuid-Limburg and Kempen pits had to be sunk has been referred to above.

TABLE 3.4

Some characteristics of the Benelux coalfields in 1957 and 1970

	Production '000 tons		% change	Number of pits		Output per pit '000 tons	Productivity kg per shift
	1957	1970		1957	1970	1970	1970
Borinage-Centre	7 475	822	− 809	39	3	274	1 831
Charleroi	6 958	2 144	− 224	58	9	238	1 831
Liège	4 332	1 299	− 223	36	7	185	1 767
Wallonie	18 765	4 265	− 400	133	19	224	1 799
Kempen	10 331	7 095	− 46	7	5	1 419	2 710
Z-Limburg	11 376	4 334	− 162	12	5	867	3 108

The cost of driving galleries through unstable material is also higher than in Wallonie, but the latter fields are plagued by copious water in the workings, a problem virtually absent in Zuid-Limburg. In terms of thickness of the seams and depth of pit, Zuid-Limburg has a slight advantage, but in respect of the quantity of sterile material found in the seams, Wallonie is at a great disadvantage. The Kempen, Zuid-Limburg and Walloon seams average an output of 8·0, 5·0 and 1·5 tons of coal per cubic metre of material extracted respectively, with the consequence that investment in washing and screening equipment is greatest in the oldest fields. Walloon seams dip more sharply than those in the northern fields, where only 5% of the output comes from seams with a slope of more than 20%; the figure for Wallonie is 51%. Walloon pits, above all those in the Borinage-Centre, are bedevilled by the presence of methane, and its dispersal adds to the cost of production. Together with the organisa-

tion of the pits, these physical considerations are the basis of the productivity data shown in Table 3.4. Zuid-Limburg has the best record and
production costs are thus the lowest of the Benelux fields. It is not surprising that within a shrinking market for coal, Walloon production has been
cut back since 1957, but that contraction in Zuid-Limburg did not begin
until 1965. In fact when natural gas was found in Groningen, the Staatsmijnen were sinking an entirely new pit, the Princess Beatrix near
Roermond to the north of the original concession area, and work on this
was not halted until 1961.

The demand for different types of coal

The European Coal and Steel Community (ECSC) recognises six basic
types of coal, ranging from anthracite, general purpose coal, coking coal
to gas coal. Because there is different demand for each category, the price
obtainable for each type is related to this demand. Most Benelux coalfields are well endowed with certain grades of coal, and in this way the
demand for coal has a geographical expression. Only Zuid-Limburg spans
the range from anthracite to gas coal, and the Dutch have been able to
substitute between coals according to demand.

Despite the competition provided by oil and natural gas in the domestic
market, there is still a considerable demand for anthracite, such that
anthracite prices are more than twice those commanded by coking coals.
In this way anthracite mines can remain open even though they are high
cost producers of coal, and this, coupled with social factors, is the reason
why it is possible to justify the existence of most Walloon pits. In 1969
some 83% of Walloon coal was anthracite and the Liège field produced
nothing else, thus explaining the apparent paradox of low productivity
and relatively modest contraction between 1957 and 1970. The same
reasoning can be applied to the Charleroi field, where anthracite accounted
for 85% of output in 1969. The very absence of anthracite from the
Borinage-Centre field, on the other hand, is one of the principal reasons for
its 80% contraction between 1957 and 1970. The demand for anthracite
has enabled output in Zuid-Limburg to be maintained at about one-third
of its 1957 level, and production of this type of coal increased during the
1960s. However, anthracite will be replaced by natural gas in the Netherlands in the early 1970s.

Three fields, the Borinage-Centre, Kempen and Zuid-Limburg, possess
reserves of coking coal, the demand for which is gradually increasing as
its consumption by blast furnaces grows. Unfortunately the price of
Borinage-Centre coking coal has become so high in relation to Kempen and
Zuid-Limburg prices that production has ceased. Coking coal accounts for
three-quarters of the output of the Kempen field, and coupled with the

ECSC policy of subsidising deliveries of coking coal to iron and steelworks to keep the cost of pig iron competitive, this has enabled production to be maintained. The future for Kempen coking coal is not assured, however, for imports from the USA can be delivered to Antwerp below Kempen prices, and were it not for the imposition of quotas and subsidies, Kempen coking coal would have no market at all. In contrast the Dutch have chosen to make use of cheap imported fuel in their blast furnaces at Ijmuiden; and although Zuid-Limburg has good quality coking coal, its production has been run down.

The demand for gas coal in Benelux has never been great because of the practice of utilising blast furnace gas and the gas made as a by-product of the coking process for domestic and other purposes. Thus in 1970 80% of Belgian gas originated from steelworks and from coking plants situated either on the coalfields, as at Tertre in the Borinage, or on canal-bank sites in Flanders. The distribution of coking plants in Benelux is shown in Fig. 3.7. It is worth observing that there were formerly two large coking plants in Zuid-Limburg, but they have been shut down as part of the contraction programme, and that despite the presence of blast furnaces in Luxembourg, coke is imported from West Germany and is not made *in situ*. The advent of oil refinery gas and natural gas has completely removed the limited market for gas coal and this has adversely affected the Borinage-Centre field in particular. The completion of the Belgian natural gas grid fed from the Groningen gas field should see the end of the demand for Kempen gas coal.

The market for power station coal depends principally upon the price of the coal available, since all coals can be used. At one time coal was the only fuel burnt, and power stations were established either on the coalfields or at sites such as Antwerp, Dordrecht and Rotterdam capable of receiving coal by barge. As coal prices rose in relation to oil prices, many power stations were converted to multiple firing, that is, they were capable of burning oil or coal, and more recently natural gas. The Belgians prefer to use their own high cost coal, which the government guarantees a market at power stations, in conjunction with oil and natural gas, but the Dutch see no future in coal for electricity generation and plan to phase out the use of this type of fuel. In 1970 one-third of Dutch power stations had no arrangements for burning coal at all, in contrast with those in Belgium, all of which could do so. Even so, there was a 43% fall in the tonnage of coal consumed in Belgian power stations between 1965 and 1970. Table 3.5 indicates the relative importance of the various fuels used in the production of electricity in Benelux in 1970. The distribution of the power stations with an installed capacity of more than 100 MW and three of the more common combinations of fuels burnt are shown in Fig. 3.8.

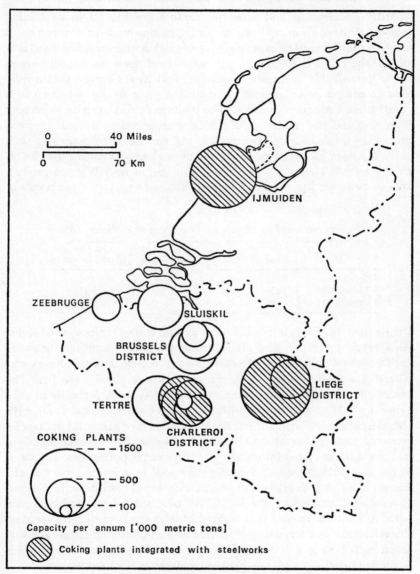

Fig. 3.7 Coking plants in Benelux in 1970

Government and European Coal and Steel Community policy

Although physical and economic factors are helpful in explaining regional differences in coal production, decisions made at governmental and Community level have proved to be of vital significance. The inauguration of the ECSC in February 1953 highlighted the economic differences between coalfields in member countries, and it was agreed that a five-year transition period should be instituted prior to the operation of a competitive Community market. The Walloon fields were seen to be very high cost and the mines, all of which were privately owned, received grants from the Belgian government and the ECSC to carry out such rationalisation as would make them able to compete with other ECSC fields by 1958. This policy had little effect and in 1957 Walloon production costs were 1 047 Belgian francs per ton compared with 792 francs in

TABLE 3.5

Fuels consumed in Benelux thermal power stations, 1970

	Coal	Oil	Natural gas	Coke oven/ blast furnace gas
Belgium	27%	50%	13%	10%
Netherlands	19%	34%	44%	3%
Luxembourg	1%	18%	—	81%

the Kempen field, 653 francs in Zuid-Limburg and 603 francs in the Ruhr. As a result the ECSC and the government had to continue financial assistance and for a time in the early 1960s the Belgian coal industry was partially isolated from the ECSC market to give it added protection. The prices quoted had little reference to production costs, for without subsidies it would have been very difficult to have sold any coal at all, with the possible exception of anthracite. Production levels thus did not rest on economic factors but rather on the social consequences of closing uneconomic pits in the absence of alternative employment opportunities. The speed of the contraction has subsequently depended in very large part on the success of regional development programmes set in motion by the Belgian government, assisted by the ECSC. By 1969 subsidies were being paid equal to $16.20 on every ton of coal mined, and $10.80 of this was spent on the retraining and rehousing of miners and on industrial redevelopment schemes. It is clear therefore that without massive aid the Walloon fields would have declined very much more rapidly than has been the case.

The level of production in coalfields outside Wallonie has also been influenced by governmental and ECSC action. The imposition of quotas on imports from non-member countries, the most important of which is the USA, has allowed coking coal output to be kept up, particularly in the Kempen. The decision made in 1967 to help the iron and steel industry by aligning ECSC coking coal prices with the landed price of United States coal, and to pay a subsidy to cover the difference, worked in the same direction. Coking coal also qualifies for a freight subsidy which in 1970 was $0.70 per ton, although this will be reduced to $0.40 by 1972. The Belgian government has introduced taxes which discriminate in favour of industrial coal and against oil, giving a small advantage to certain fields such as the Borinage-Centre. Membership of the ECSC itself has not only hastened the decline of the Walloon fields, but the availability of coking coal from the Ruhr was an important factor in the Dutch decision, in line with Community energy policy, to phase out coal production in Zuid-Limburg by 1974. This decision was particularly forward looking, for rather than take comfort from the fact that Zuid-Limburg prices were 12% lower than those in the Ruhr in 1965, and as such the lowest in the Community, the government took the view that this was not the fundamental issue and that the test should be whether coal could compete with other sources of energy. The task of closing down the Zuid-Limburg pits was made easier because of state control of a large part of production capacity, in contrast to Wallonie where the pits are not publicly owned, and closure more difficult to effect. In fact the Dutch programme of closures is running ahead of schedule and the last mine, Emma, is due to be closed in 1974.

3.5 OTHER ENERGY-PRODUCING INDUSTRIES
Oil production

Although oil plays such an important part in the economies of the Benelux countries, indigenous production is very small, and is limited to the Netherlands. The first discovery was made at Schoonebeek in Drenthe in 1943, and this field is still the largest in the country with an output of 850 000 tons a year. In 1950 Schoonebeek could provide one-fifth of Dutch oil requirements, but consumption has since outstripped production to such an extent that it can now meet only one-twentieth of the country's needs. The second most important field is Ijsselmonde-Ridderkerke, east of Rotterdam, opened in 1956 and currently providing 634 000 tons of oil a year. Other oil wells are located in the province of Zuid-Holland at Wassenaar, De Lier and Zoetermeer, but they are not large producers and the Dutch output of oil amounts only to 2 million tons per annum. The second North Sea oil find was effected 80 km off the Dutch coast in 1970, but it is too soon to estimate the role it will play in the market for energy.

Natural gas

If the Netherlands possesses a modest endowment of oil, it has in the province of Groningen one of the world's largest natural gas fields. It was not the first natural gas to be found in the country, for successful if small strikes had been made at Ijsselmonde-Ridderkerke in 1956 and at De Lier in 1958 before the major find at Slochteren the following year. Production figures reflect the time elapsing between the discovery of the Slochteren reserves and the operation of a comprehensive gas grid, for it was not until the mid-1960s that substantial quantities of gas appeared on the Dutch market. Table 3.6 shows the speed with which production has been expanded and indicates not only the way in which it is being increasingly used in industry, but also in thermal power stations. It is anticipated that between 60% and 65% of Dutch electric power will be derived from natural gas by 1975. Natural gas is extremely well suited to space-heating and has captured the domestic market from anthracite and coal gas. It is

TABLE 3.6

Production and consumption of natural gas in the Netherlands, 1963-1970 Tcal*

	1963	1968	1970
Production	5 814	119 428	266 844
Consumption			
Power stations	389	10 592	41 773
Domestic	667	27 132	n.a.
Exports	38	36 554	95 191
Industry	1 178	29 687	57 251

* 1 tera calorie is approximately equal to 160 tons of coal.

also very much cheaper than gas from coking plants so that the industrial market for coke oven gas has been lost. Natural gas is attractive to industry, for apart from its cheapness no storage facilities are required, its purity adds to the life of the furnaces burning it and it has a higher calorific value than oil. The consequence has been that it is widely used in the Dutch heat-raising industries such as iron and steel, ceramics, glass and the metallurgical industries. It is also an important raw material for the chemical industry, being used as a base for fertilisers, plastics, ashesives and organic chemicals.

The timing of the discovery of Dutch natural gas was particularly fortunate, for the technology of gas transmission by pipe had been sufficiently developed by the early 1960s to allow Groningen gas to be piped throughout the Netherlands and, from 1966, exported to Belgium, West Germany and France in addition. The pipeline network is shown in Fig. 3.9. The presence of important markets within 200 km was also fortunate, for natural gas is costly to transmit over long distances, but the proximity of the Ruhr and Belgium has enabled production to reach a high level with resulting economies of scale. The high-pressure transmission grid is operated by Gasunie, in which the Staatsmijnen have a 40% interest. The other shareholdings are Shell (25%), Esso (25%) and the Dutch government (10%). Gasunie is responsible for all gas distribution in the Netherlands, including the grid formerly operated by the Staatsmijnen. The Nederlandse Aardolie Maatschappij (NAM), a consortium of Shell and Esso, is responsible for the exploitation of Slochteren and most of the smaller finds in Friesland, Drenthe and Noord-Holland, but since 1969 a number of other companies have begun operations. One consortium, Petroland, exports gas from its Leeuwarden field in Friesland to France. It is anticipated that by 1975 natural gas will account for half of Dutch energy consumption, giving it a more important part in the economy than anywhere else in the world.

Electricity

Electric power in Benelux is almost entirely generated from the three sources of energy which have been considered, that is, coal, oil and natural gas, and the factors involved in their share of the power station market have been implicitly discussed. Given a free market, thermal power stations are very sensitive indicators of fuel prices, for they are able to switch fuels without major modifications. In all three Benelux countries there are many small power stations linked by low capacity grid systems. Particularly in Belgium, the production of electric power has remained in private hands, and most of the companies are fairly small rendering the construction of really large plants unjustifiable. The well-developed systems of river and canal transport in Belgium and the Netherlands have kept the cost of coal and oil supplies down, to some extent offsetting the diseconomies of small generating stations. However, of recent some large plants have been built in the Netherlands, where public ownership is better developed, and this trend is likely to continue. The majority of power stations are oriented to their markets, that is, the power they produce is consumed in the locality rather than being transmitted to distant markets. As a result, large stations are located in the areas of the greatest concentration of population. With one exception, all the Belgian stations with a capacity of more than 200 MW are situated in major towns. The exception, Ruien in West-Vlaanderen, represents the beginning of a new locational trend for large generating stations, a trend better developed in the Netherlands than Belgium. As power stations increase in size, they are able to produce more electricity than can be consumed locally, and it is therefore necessary for them to be located in respect of groups of towns. The large plants at Geertruidenburg (954 MW) in Noord-Brabant, Dordrecht (536 MW) and at Velsen, where there are two stations with a

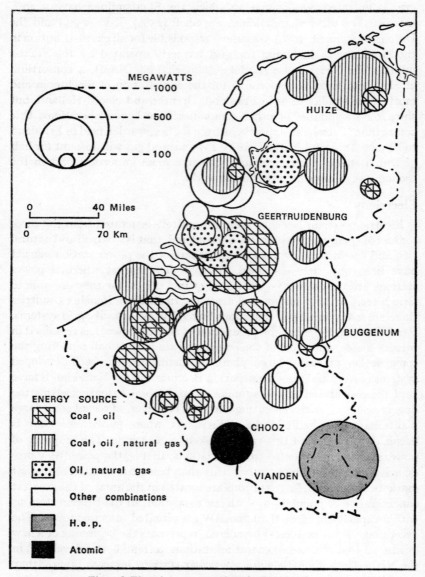

Fig. 3.8 Electric power stations in Benelux in 1970

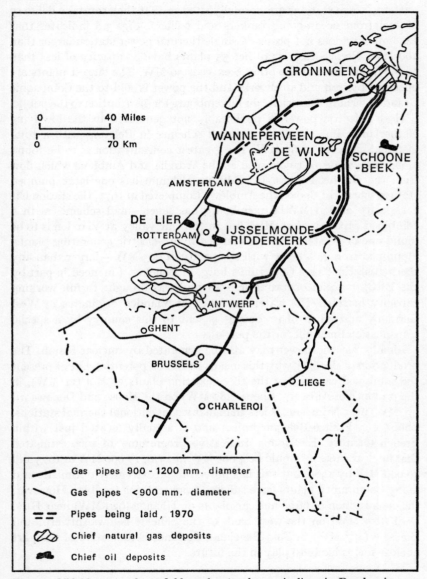

Fig. 3.9 Oilfields, natural gas fields and natural gas pipelines in Benelux in 1970

combined capacity of 860 MW, are examples of the new distribution pattern. These stations are normally sited so that they can take delivery of fuel from ocean-going tankers and colliers. Fig. 3.8 indicates that Luxembourg does not possess a single thermal power station larger than 100 MW. No less than 47 of her 55 plants have a capacity of less than 10 MW, and none of the other 8 exceeds 50 MW. The largest plants are operated by iron and steelworks and the power is sold to the Compagnie Grande-Ducale d'Electricité du Luxembourg for distribution to the public.

Hydro-electric power is predictably not generated in the low-lying Netherlands, but there are 18 small schemes in Belgium with a total installed capacity of 65 MW. The greatest concentration is to be found along the valleys of rivers such as the Warche and Amblève which flow from the Hautes Fagnes. In addition, Belgium has one large pumped storage scheme at Coo on the Amblève. Completed in 1971, the station has a capacity of 830 MW. Luxembourg has seven small schemes with a combined capacity of 26 MW, but in the Our valley at Vianden is to be found one of Western Europe's largest hydro-electric generating plants, a pumped storage scheme with a capacity of 903 MW—larger than any thermal station, save Geertruidenburg, in Benelux. Financed in part by the EEC, it began operating in 1961 and was brought to full working capacity in 1964. The water employed at Vianden originates in West Germany and much of its output is sent to this country by a special transmission line built for the purpose.

Finally, electric power may also be generated by nuclear fission. The production of electricity by this means has much potential, but at present the combined capacity of the three existing plants at Mol (11 MW), in the province of Antwerp, Chooz (282 MW) on the Meuse and Dodewaard (55 MW) near Nijmegen, is less than many conventional thermal stations. Chooz is a Franco-Belgian project and is actually located just within French territory. Euratom's 'Indicative Programme' of 1966 estimated that nuclear capacity would be 4 000 MW in 1970, 17 000 MW in 1975 and 40 000 MW by 1980, but this has proved to be extremely optimistic and many Community plants have suffered from teething troubles. However, the construction of large nuclear plants at Tihange (920 MW) near Huy, Doel (820 MW) on the west bank of the Scheldt below Antwerp, and Borssele (477 MW) in Zuid-Beveland, Zeeland, is indicative of the part nuclear fuel is likely to play in the future.

Further Reading

A. M. Lambert, 'Farm Consolidation and Improvement in the Netherlands: an Example from the Land van Maas en Waal', *Economic Geography*, 37, 1961, pp. 115-123.

—— *The Making of the Dutch Landscape. An Historical Geography of the Netherlands* (Seminar Press, London), 1971.

Ministry of Agriculture and Fisheries, *Agriculture in the Netherlands*, The Hague, 1968.

Peter Laut, *Agricultural Geography*, Vol. 2 (Thomas Nelson (Australia)), 1968, pp. 220-260 gives a very full account of agriculture in the Netherlands.

A dated but useful account may be found in S. W. E. Vince, 'The Agricultural Regions of Belgium' in L. D. Stamp and S. W. Wooldridge (Eds), *London Essays in Geography*, London, 1951, pp. 255-287.

F. J. Monkhouse, *The Belgian Kempenland* (Liverpool University Press), 1949.

—— 'The South Limburg Coalfield', *Economic Geography*, 31, 1955, pp. 126-137.

R. C. Riley, 'Recent Developments in the Belgian Borinage. An Area of Declining Coal Production in the ECSC', *Geography*, 1965, pp. 261-273.

—— 'Changes in the Supply of Coking Coal in Belgium since 1945', *Economic Geography*, 43, 1967, pp. 261-270.

G. R. P. Lawrence, 'The Changing Face of South Limburg', *Geography*, 1971, pp. 35-39.

European Communities' Statistical Office, *Energy Statistics Yearbook*, 1960-1970, Luxembourg, 1971. This is an outstandingly useful source of data.

Chapter 4

THE SECONDARY AND TERTIARY
INDUSTRIES OF BENELUX

Reference was made to the nature of industrial activity in Chapter 2, but comment was restricted to the national level. It is the object of this part of the book to investigate the reasons for the distribution of industry at the regional and local scales. The historical narrative of the growth of industry was taken down to the early part of the 19th century in Chapter 1. Subsequent events are taken up in this chapter, for many of today's manufacturing regions were set in motion during the last century, and many of their problems can be related to the date of their establishment and to the nature of their industries. The chapter therefore traces the evolution of the principal manufacturing regions in Benelux before considering some of the more important industries. Also included is a brief glance at the tertiary or service sector.

4.1 MANUFACTURING INDUSTRY IN BENELUX
IN THE NINETEENTH CENTURY

The evolution of manufacturing industry in Benelux during the last century followed different courses in each of the three countries, not so much because of policies pursued by governments but rather the result of differences in resource endowment. The Netherlands was short of the raw materials vital to large-scale industrial development in the 19th century, for it was not technically possible to exploit the coal reserves of Zuid-Limburg until this century. Belgium, on the other hand, possessed a range of materials such as coal, iron, copper and zinc which were conducive to industrialisation, and the same is true of the *minette* deposits of southern Luxembourg. The classic era of steam-industrialism is thus best exemplified in Belgium, for in Luxembourg the process gave birth to a single activity, iron and steel production, while the phenomenon was virtually absent from the Netherlands. Since industrialisation followed a separate path in the three countries, it is convenient to consider each in turn.

Belgium

For the first three-quarters of the century Belgium was Britain's principal competitor as an industrial power, and as in Britain the first

110

important technical advances were made in the textile industry, already a thriving domestic activity in Flanders, Brabant and in the Verviers region. The first spinning jenny for the production of cotton yarn was installed in Ghent in 1798, the year in which the Lancastrian William Cockerill arrived in Verviers to build wool-spinning machinery. Power looms were introduced in both Ghent and Verviers shortly after this in 1805. Cockerill and his son John, proved to be innovators of unusual ability and they perfected combing and carding engines for use in the production of woollen and worsted cloth. It is not surprising that the Verviers district quickly came to be responsible for half the Belgian output of wool textiles, but the greatest proliferation of steam-driven textile mills occurred in Flanders. Here, in particular along the Leie valley between Kortrijk and Ghent, the linen industry had long flourished. Because manufacture of the cloth and the cultivation of the raw material, flax, were carried on in the same locality, providing industrial employment for a rural population, linen manufacture was well suited to this area which was beginning to suffer from population pressure. Important though it was, linen manufacture was a domestic industry, and it was the cotton industry which was the first to mechanise, overtaking linen in respect of the number employed in 1846. Cotton was a factory industry employing mass-production techniques in large mills concentrated in the towns where the labour supply and transport facilities were good. The greatest concentration of mills was at Ghent, and by mid-century the industry had diffused thence up the Scheldt to Oudenaarde and Ronse, and down the Scheldt and up the Dender to Aalst and Ath. The linen industry reacted to competition from British mills and the loss of labour to local cotton mills by becoming a factory industry itself, although locationally the only change was a shift to the towns of the Leie valley and vicinity.

The industrialisation of the provinces of West- and Oost-Vlaanderen was almost entirely achieved by the textile industry, but unlike the experience of Great Britain, it was not effected on a coalfield. Four reasons may be advanced for this. Firstly, Flanders was not only an area of traditional skill in textile production but it was also a region of plentiful labour supply, caused by a rapidly growing population and by redundancies consequent upon improving agricultural techniques. Secondly, the comprehensive inland waterway network ensured that the steam-mills were able to take delivery of coal, initially from South Wales and Northumberland and Durham, and later the Walloon coalfield, at very low cost. Thirdly, a great many of the Belgian mills were built in the second quarter of the century, much later than in Britain, by which time the design of steam-engines had been greatly advanced. The early Watt engines were voracious consumers of coal, but by the use of compound engines, developed in the 1820s, the consumption of fuel was drastically reduced. Fourthly, a rather less important consideration was the advantage to be gained from a location close to the ports of Ghent and Antwerp, for all cotton, a large proportion of the wool and, later in the century, flax as well, had to be imported. The pattern of distribution established at the time of the first textile factories has endured for over a century and serves to underline the need to explore the initial location factors in order to understand the current situation.

The mills of the textile industry may have been the first to develop, but they could not match the number of multifarious factories that later sprang up on the Walloon coalfield. Local iron, lead and zinc, charcoal from the forests and water power provided by the abundant streams had given rise to small-scale metal-working between Liège, Namur and Charleroi and in the pre-Ardennes since the Middle Ages. The use of coal for smelting, refining and for the provision of power changed the emphasis to large-scale operations and made a coalfield location virtually *de rigeur*. The early introduction of steam-pumps for mine drainage allowed the production of coal to rise rapidly and by 1800 the Belgian coal industry was the most technically advanced in continental Europe. The availability of coal at Liège, for centuries a high quality metallurgical centre, rendered it likely that experiments with coal should take place there. The presence of John Cockerill made it inevitable. He had moved out of textile machinery and at Liège in 1817 he built the first continental puddling furnace, following this in 1823 with the first successful coke-fired blast furnace outside Great Britain. At the same time he produced mechanically operated blast furnace bellows, and it was predictable that in 1835 it was his firm that built the first Belgian locomotive. A further outlet for the iron he produced at Liège was the shipyard he opened at Hoboken, Antwerp, in 1824. The use of coke in smelting spread westwards to Charleroi, and at the same time the small-scale industry in the pre-Ardennes collapsed, a process virtually complete by 1840. A further 120 years elapsed before a major iron and steel plant was built outside the two great centres of Liège and Charleroi.

Coal and iron ore were not the only raw materials to be found in the Walloon industrial belt. A deposit of zinc near Liège, the mining concession for which was granted in 1806, gave rise to a zinc smelting industry. The deposits were sufficient to meet local demand until 1875, and although the industry was obliged to rely increasingly upon imports, it continued to prosper in the old-established district. For much of the 19th century Belgium was the world's leading producer of raw zinc. The juxtaposition of glass sands and coal at several sites on the coalfield, above all at Charleroi, was conducive to the development of a large glass industry. The activity was assisted by the settlement of Venetian glass blowers near Charleroi in the 14th century, and later by the decision of the works at Val-St. Lambert near Liège, to specialise in high quality crystal ware. Until the 1880s Belgium held a virtual monopoly on the world market for many glass products. Not all the coal mined was used for fuel and power, some was used as a raw material by the chemical industry for the production of gas from which a wide range of chemicals was derived. Other chemical plants used coal as a fuel and for this reason Ernest Solvay established his plant for the manufacture of soda at Couillet, near Charleroi, in 1865.

The activities described owed their location to the distribution of natural resources, but of great importance were those industries which clustered on the coalfield to process the products of the basic industries. The best example was metal working and engineering, using the output of the iron and steel works and rolling mills to fashion a myriad of items from steam engines, boilers and rolling stock to tools, guns and nails. Great impetus was received from the country's early lead in the continental industrial revolution and from innovators such as Walschaert (valve gear), Belpaire (boilers) and Flamme (superheating), to name some associated with locomotive technology. The presence of materials, fuel and power, labour and a well-established transport system gave the Walloon coalfield unparalleled advantages for manufacturing, and although subsequent developments have weakened its attraction, Charleroi and Liège remain the largest steel-using districts in Benelux.

Luxembourg

In many respects the growth of industry in Luxembourg was similar to that in Belgium. The major activity, iron and steel production, grew up because of the availability of a basic raw material, iron ore, and in order to minimise the cost of transporting the ore, blast furnaces were sited on the orefield. In Belgium there was coalfield industrialisation, in Luxembourg the phenomenon occurred on the ironfield. As in the Ardennes, small charcoal-burning furnaces using local iron ore bodies had long existed, and it was not until 1845 that a furnace was set up at Eich to smelt the lean ores (with an average iron content of 30%) of the Lorraine ironfield, the northern tip of which extended into the Duchy. However, this ore, known as *minette*, was highly phosphoric, and some of the older works continued using alluvial iron ores, smelting them with coke brought from Liège after 1862 when the railway line was finished. Rapid expansion did not really occur until the introduction of the Thomas-Gilchrist process, which enabled good steel to be produced from phosphoric ores. The first works to employ the process was established at Dudelange in 1884, and from then

H

on blast furnaces were quickly built at locations suitable for the transport of ore and pig iron, such as Rodange, Differdange, Belval, Esch, Rumelange and Dudelange. Some 28 were in blast by 1900.

The question arises as to why it was preferable to move coal or coke to the orefield rather than iron ore to the Belgian coalfield. The answer is simply that for every ton of pig iron made, only 2 tons of coal were required, compared with 3 tons of *minette*. It is true that some *minette* was sent to the Walloon and Ruhr coalfields, but larger tonnages were smelted *in situ* and the pig iron sent to be refined in the coalfield regions. Pig iron has a much higher value than *minette* by weight, and it was more easily able to stand the costs of transport. This is the reason why the production of pig iron was much more important than that of steel in Luxembourg until the 1920s. Similar reasoning led to the introduction of blast furnaces at Athus, Halanzy and Musson on the *minette* escarpment in Belgian Luxembourg.

The Netherlands

The development of industry in the Netherlands followed quite a different pattern. The country possessed few mineral ores with the consequence that iron, coal and steam-engines had to be imported. Import duties on coal, not removed until 1863, were an additional disincentive to industrialisation. There was little large-scale industry at all until after mid-century, and those manufactured goods which were required were purchased from Britain and Belgium. Thus the great reclamation works of the century, for example the drainage of Haarlemmermeer, were executed with foreign, usually British, steam-pumps, as the Cruquius engine house still testifies. It has been estimated that in approximately 1850 steam-engines in Belgium were developing six times more power than the total produced in the Netherlands. The many inland waterways did not encourage the construction of railways, and this reduced the need for ironworks to provide track and rolling stock. The Dutch industrial revolution did not in fact get under way until the 1860s, and even then it differed from that in both Belgium and Luxembourg because it was not based on the processing of mineral resources. Prior to these events industrial activity in the Netherlands was primarily linked to the trading activities of flourishing ports such as Amsterdam and Dordrecht.

There was one exception to this emphasis on international trade, and that was the textile industry, which, although it was a domestic activity, was an important form of employment in the Twente district of Overijssel and in Noord-Brabant. Agriculture in these heathland areas was unable to support the growing population, causing increasing numbers to have recourse to an industry which could be pursued in rural areas. The abundant supply of labour kept wages low and textile production gradually vacated the towns of the Western Netherlands. Noord-Brabant in particular received considerable stimulus from the influx of Belgian textile manufacturers anxious to retain the valuable Dutch colonial markets lost to Belgium after the separation of the two countries in 1830. Willem I established the Nederlandsche Handel Maatschappij in 1824 to encourage trade with the Dutch East Indies, and this increased the demand for cotton goods, largely made in Twente. The first steam-driven cotton spinning mill was opened in Twente in 1829 and the application of steam to weaving followed in 1852. Coal was brought in at low cost by barge from the Ruhr. Expansion took the same pattern in Noord-Brabant, the principal difference lying in the province's specialisation in wool textiles. The first steam-mill was established at Tilburg in 1827, but this example was followed only slowly, and by 1864 two-thirds of the mills had still to be converted to steam power. The coming of the railways in the 1860s greatly assisted further growth, with the consequence that textile production became firmly established on a factory basis both in Noord-Brabant and Twente, a regional specialisation that persists today.

Despite the industrialisation of the textile industry in peripheral areas, it was in the ports of the west that the most important changes took place. Amsterdam was a major entrepôt for colonial produce and a number of industries based on the processing of these commodities had sprung up. These industries, at one time called *trafieken*, included biscuit-making, rubber production, cigar manufacture and distilling, but in the 19th century they became large-scale activities. The most remarkable case was the expansion of distilling, not in Amsterdam but in Schiedam, where there were almost 400 works in 1881, and where other activity was virtually absent. Further *trafieken* were added to the list as a result of innovation, an excellent example being cocoa manufacture which resulted from Van Houten's experiments in 1825. In 1834 the first power-driven paper-making machine was set up at Zaandijk near Amsterdam, based on imported materials. Towards the end of the century, in 1883, tropical vegetable oils began to be used in the manufacture of margarine, and in 1891 a processing plant was built in Rotterdam.

The development of industry in the ports was related to the opening up of the Dutch East Indies, to liberal trading policies and to the growth of the transit trade. The latter was largely a result of the position of the Netherlands in relation to the Ruhr, whose major expansion was effected during the last third of the century. So important was the German traffic that the Dutch transport system was virtually designed to link the ports with the Rhine hinterland rather than to bring the various regions of the country into a cohesive unit. The New Waterway and North Sea ship canals, built to improve accessibility to Rotterdam and Amsterdam respectively, date from the late 1860s, but it was Rotterdam, with a better position in respect of the Rhine distributaries, that benefited more from German industrialisation. An essential service offered by the ports is ship repairing, and this activity increased proportionately with the number of vessels using the Dutch ports. It was a short step to marine engineering and shipbuilding itself, the metal for which could be obtained cheaply by means of water transport from the Ruhr. In this way the engineering industry evolved—associated with trade and not, as in Belgium, with coalmining and iron and steel production. Only in a few instances did engineering develop outside Noord- and Zuid-Holland; both at Hengelo in Twente and at Eindhoven there was an important human element in the form of dynamic business enterprises (Stork and Philips respectively) making good use of local labour resources.

For all these developments, the Netherlands was still an agricultural country at the end of the century, when 31% of the working population was employed in farming compared with 23% in manufacturing. The agricultural sector was very efficient, for much of its produce was sold abroad, and it was this progressive attitude that led to the introduction of agricultural product processing industries. After 1867 rye began to be grown for strawboard manufacture in Groningen, and in the same area potatoes were used as the basis of potato-flour. The manufacture of margarine was begun at Oss in Noord-Brabant in 1871, and in the last decade of the century large butter-making plants began to make an appearance, together with condensed and powdered milk factories, in many rural areas. These factories gave a new dimension to the distribution of industry in the Netherlands, for they represented the beginnings of the industrialisation of hitherto wholly agricultural areas. Unfortunately the Western Netherlands had established a commanding lead over the peripheral areas, and the task of attracting additional industry thence since 1945 has proved to be a major problem.

4.2   THE DISTRIBUTION OF MANUFACTURING INDUSTRY IN THE TWENTIETH CENTURY

The fundamental pattern of the distribution of industry in Benelux had been established by the end of the 19th century, and most of the industrial regions illustrated in Fig. 4.1 had their origin in these years. Three categories of manufacturing regions may be recognised. Firstly, regions of heavy industry were located on the Walloon coalfield and on the *minette* outcrop in Belgium and Luxembourg. Secondly, the ports of the Western Netherlands were associated with the processing of colonial imports, ship repair, shipbuilding and many branches of engineering.

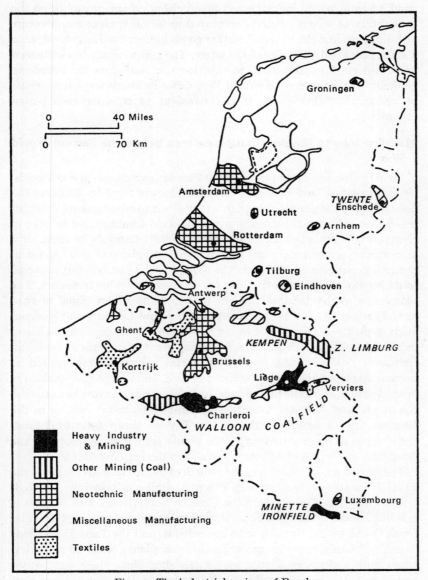

Fig. 4.1 The industrial regions of Benelux

Antwerp also belongs to this category. Thirdly, there were a number of rural areas in which industry was based either on agriculture or on the availability of labour formerly employed in farming; cigar manufacture at Eindhoven and the shoe and leather goods industry of Langstraat, near Tilburg, are good examples of the latter. The 20th century has witnessed some important modifications to this situation, but since the influences at work before the Second World War differ in many ways from those obtaining after this event, it is convenient to consider each period separately.

Modifications to the distribution pattern before the Second World War

Shortly after the turn of the century Benelux gained two new coalfields, the Kempen and Zuid-Limburg. The chronology of their development has been traced in the previous chapter, and suffice it to reiterate here that coal was first brought to the surface in 1906 in Zuid-Limburg and in 1917 in Kempen. The era when a coalfield was a highly desirable location for a manufacturing plant was over, however, for not only were there powerful external economies to be had in the old industrial districts but also coal could be moved out of both fields by inexpensive water transport. The completion of the Juliana Canal in 1936 and the Albert Canal in 1940 served further to reduce the attraction of the Zuid-Limburg and Kempen fields respectively. This is not to say that there was a complete absence of industrial activity in these areas, for coking plants were built at Beek and Geleen in Zuid-Limburg, non-ferrous metal refineries were located at seven sites on or adjacent to the Kempen field, and a large glassworks was opened at Mol, adjacent to both coal and glass sands. It must be noted, on the other hand, that specialisation in non-ferrous metal refining in the Kempen was a result of the availability of cheap industrial land, the absence of large settlements (the plants emit toxic fumes) and the proximity of the port of Antwerp, as much as the presence of coal.

The second modification was the growth of industrial activity along the navigable waterways in northern Belgium, similar in principle, although not in scale, to earlier events in the Western Netherlands. The waterways involved included the lower Scheldt, especially above Antwerp, the Willebroek Canal linking Brussels with the Scheldt, and the Terneuzen-Ghent Canal. Shipyards, engineering works, chemical plants, small oil refineries, paper mills and coking plants were established along these waterways, and in many cases they used imported materials. It was in this era that the coking plants carbonising German coal at Sluiskil in Zeeland, Zeebrugge and in the Brussels district (Fig. 3.7) were erected.

The third modification was one that was incipient in the 19th century, but which gathered strength in the 20th, that is the development of Brussels as a major manufacturing region. In addition to the industries, described above, which grew up on the Willebroek canal as it entered the city, Brussels generated a number of activities by virtue of its position as capital of Belgium. The demand for goods of high quality was greater than elsewhere in the country, and to meet this a wide range of industries producing *articles de luxe* arose. Examples include non-ferrous metalworking, coach building, printing, fine cotton, wool, lace and glove manufacture and the production of musical instruments, furniture and leather goods. These were the urban craft industries typical of so many capital cities. The presence of raw materials was irrelevant, for the manufacturing process greatly added to the value of the materials used, and transport costs were not important. Much of the workforce was skilled, but unskilled labour was readily recruited in such a large city. By way of contrast a metalworking and engineering district grew up in the valley of the Senne at the southern edge of the town, further widening the range of manufacturing.

The changes effected in the first four decades of the century were accompanied by the beginnings of decline in the Walloon coalfield, and by an increasing gap between the rates of growth in the Dutch peripheral provinces and the Western Netherlands. The continued expansion of Zuid- and Noord-Holland, where heavy industry was at last established with the construction of blast furnaces at Ijmuiden in 1918, and the developments in the Antwerp-Brussels axial zone, suggested the existence of two growth areas to the north and to the south of the Rhine-Maas-Scheldt delta by 1939.

The distribution of manufacturing after the Second World War

Events since the Second World War have involved not so much the growth of entirely new industrial areas as the expansion or decline of existing manufacturing districts. The older regions have failed to expand as rapidly as the Western Netherlands and the Antwerp-Brussels region largely because those industries which are expanding at the fastest rate are in the main located in the two latter rather than the former areas. The textile industries have been badly affected by foreign competition and the introduction of man-made fibres, the ceramics industry of the Walloon coalfield has virtually collapsed in the face of competition from plastics and the demand for the products of the older engineering firms has fallen. The contraction of coalmining has had an adverse effect on the demand for mining equipment, largely made in the older industrial districts. Meanwhile the iron and steel industry on the coalfields and ironfields has been forced to rationalise. The most profitable industries are the neotechnic

industries such as electronic engineering, vehicle production, pharmaceuticals, plastics and the manufacture of consumer durables, in which
advanced technology plays an important part. Of importance to the location of these industries is the considerable value which is added to the
materials used during the manufacturing process, (they are sometimes
referred to as the 'high value-adding industries') and the fact that transport costs account for a small part of total costs. This freedom from ties
to sources of materials, coupled with the advent of electric power and
natural gas, endows neotechnic industry with great mobility, allowing a
location to be effected in respect of considerations such as labour supplies
and access to national and international motorway systems because of the
convenience this ensures. These conditions are best met in the two growth
areas.

The declining areas, on the other hand, are often rejected by expanding
firms precisely because they are in decline, and sometimes visually un-
pleasing, and decline is thus accelerated. It is not only the outworn social
and economic infrastructure that repels manufacturers, it is also the
belief that labour relations will be better in the newer areas. This has
certainly benefited parts of Belgian Flanders, for in the 1950s and 1960s
the Antwerp-Brussels axis was not only a growth region but an area of
cheap labour as well. Having participated only to a limited extent in the
industrial revolution of the previous century, the Flemish were enthusias-
tic participants in the process when their turn came, and this was reflected
in the cost of labour. Some firms, however, have chosen to expand outside
the growth areas to take advantage of cheap labour. An example is the
electronics firm of Philips, which has established large branch plants at
Drachten in Friesland, Stadskanaal in Groningen, Zwolle and Hengelo in
Overijssel, Nijmegen in Gelderland, Roosendaal, Tilburg and Oss in
Noord-Brabant, and at Roermond and Sittard in Limburg. Only three
major branch plants exist in the west, at Weesp, Hilversum and Huizen
in Noord-Holland.

There is one neotechnic industry which does not possess great mobility,
oil refining. This industry, which has experienced phenomenal expansion
over the last two decades, is almost as immobile as the iron and steel
industry in the 19th century. Apart from the small Dutch production, all
Benelux crude oil must be imported and the cheapest location at which to
refine it is the importing port. The industry is thus found at Rotterdam,
Antwerp, Ghent and Amsterdam, all of which are integral parts of the
growth regions of Benelux. Moreover, because the cost of shipping a ton
of crude oil declines as the size of tanker increases, the capacity of these
vessels increased dramatically in the 1960s. Of the four ports mentioned,
only Rotterdam has been able to extend its facilities to accommodate the

largest tankers, becoming in the process the major West European oil refining complex, re-exporting a large proportion of her crude oil imports as refined products, in short a modern *trafiek*. Such has been the growth of oil refining and its associated petrochemical production, that the extension of Rotterdam westwards to Europoort and Antwerp northwards to Zandvliet is a direct demand for sites for these activities. Although the industry is not expanding at the same speed, it is no accident that the two newest iron and steelworks to be built in Benelux, at Ijmuiden and Zelzate, north of Ghent, are both at sites close to the sea. It seems that coastal sites for industry processing cheap and bulky imports are increasingly desirable, and this emphasises the potential of the two growth areas.

So far the discussion has considered only the technical and economic background to the present-day distribution of manufacturing in Benelux, assuming that market forces are allowed free play. This is a false assumption, for one of the most powerful influences upon the distribution of industry in the post-war period has been intervention by provincial and national governments and by the EEC itself. Without such action the gap between the growth areas and the rest of Benelux would be very much greater, for the aim of regional policy has been to reduce unemployment and to assist the industrial development of the areas of indifferent economic health, and to control the progress of the favoured areas. Criteria other than unemployment, for example, *per capita* income, net emigration and the incidence of long-distance commuting, are also used by governments to determine whether financial aid should be granted. It is not unfair to suggest that regional policy is the most important location factor in the case of plants setting up in the assisted areas, since in the absence of such assistance most of them would have selected alternative sites. The benefits of regional policy are also largely responsible for the continuation of many industries in the old industrial areas which, in the absence of intervention, would become decreasingly attractive as plants shut, population migrated and the economic infrastructure ran down. The importance of government policy with respect to both the location of industry and regional development as a whole justifies particular attention being paid to the subject.

Regional policy in Benelux

(i) *The Netherlands* Following the long history of governmental action in such spheres as land reclamation and water control, the principle that areas of sluggish economic growth should be assisted on the grounds that unemployment represents a wasting national asset, was readily accepted. The first region to receive assistance was south-east Drenthe in 1951, where there was high structural unemployment among the peat workers consequent upon the final collapse of the demand for peat. The same concern for unemployment in peripheral regions caused the government to designate eight districts as development areas in 1952. At the same time some 44 towns were declared development centres. The financial incentives designed to attract new industry included grants of up to 25% of the cost of new buildings and loans at low rates of interest. Extensions to existing factories also qualified for aid. Attention was also paid to the improvement of roads, waterways, water supplies and to technical education facilities. Migration grants were made available to people living in outlying parts of the development areas to help build up the population of the development centres. To assist this process modern housing estates were constructed in these centres. Since 1958 greater stress has been placed upon industrial decentralisation from the congested regions in the west, concomitant with the restructuring of the old industries and the encouragement of new developments in the peripheral districts. Thus firms setting up in the Rotterdam-Europoort area were required to show that access to deep water was essential before they were allowed to establish themselves in the area. If this was not the case, firms were encouraged to go to the problem areas, designated in 1958. These areas were larger than the original development areas and consisted of Friesland, Groningen, Drenthe, parts of Overijssel, Zeeland and large areas of Noord-Brabant and Limburg. The problem areas extended over one-quarter of the Dutch land surface.

By 1964 sufficient industry had moved into most of the development centres for their number to be reduced to 20, and firms have since been guided to these sites as part of a policy of 'nucleated deconcentration'. The 1969 regional policy legislation has followed the same principles, but a novel feature is the recognition of *herstruktureringsgebieden*, or restructuring areas, where the old economic base has declined to such an extent that complete re-organisation is necessary. Among the particularly favourable financial incentives available in these regions is the 50% subsidy on the cost of buying industrial sites. As Fig. 4.2 shows, there are two such areas, the textile district of Tilburg and Zuid-Limburg where special measures have been occasioned by the very rapid phasing out of coal production. In the latter region three towns, Roermond, Born and Maastricht, and the entire Eastern Mining Region have been declared development centres. The problem areas are now known as *stimuleringsgebieden*, or stimulation areas, where industry is regarded as being at the beginning of sustained growth. Although Groningen is not a re-structuring area it has benefited from the decision by the government to offer preferential natural gas prices to plants considered to be of great importance

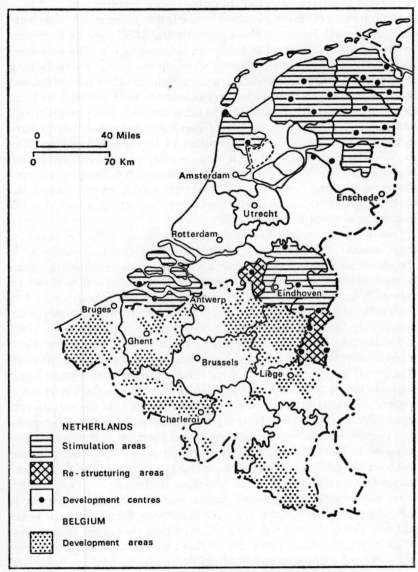

Fig. 4.2 The assisted areas of Belgium and the Netherlands

for the industrial development of the country. The aluminium smelter and the methyl alcohol plant at Delfzijl spring from this policy.

In addition to the measures taken by the Dutch government to promote economic growth is the assistance given by the ECSC towards the reconversion of coalfield areas. The European Community is no less concerned with the future prospects of regions formerly dominated by coalmining than are national governments, and since 1965 loans at low rates of interest of up to 30% of the cost of the investment have been available in Zuid-Limburg and in the Walloon field. The loans are made in conjunction with national policy on the suitability of particular industries, and governments are responsible for the execution of the agreed measures. The ECSC also makes grants, which it terms re-adaptation payments, for the retraining of miners, thereby removing the onus of retraining labour from the incoming firms. Since they are in receipt of aid from two sources, the coalfields are clearly much more attractive to industry than would be the case in the absence of regional policy.

Dutch regional policy has succeeded in influencing the location of a large number of plants, particularly those that could operate outside Randstad, and the industrial structure of the development centres must be regarded almost entirely as a function of government action. However, the north has proved unattractive for industries strongly dependent on links with other industries, and there is thus a scarcity of plants producing semi-finished and consumer goods. Foreign firms in particular have chosen to forsake the financial incentives that go with a location in the peripheral areas in order to benefit from the agglomeration economies of the west. A study of foreign firms establishing themselves between 1950 and 1963 showed that 54% of employment in such firms was in the western provinces, compared with 9% in the northern and 14% in the eastern provinces. An important part of this expansion was determined by the requirement of the oil refining, petrochemical and chemical industries for sites adjacent to tidewater, but this consideration did not apply to such firms as Coca Cola, IBM, Honeywell and General Tire who set up in Amsterdam, and to Cincinnati (machine tools) who chose Rotterdam.

(ii) *Belgium* The Belgian dislike of authority is reflected in the way in which regional policy has evolved. The first efforts did not originate at the national but at the regional level, and even then the Conseil Economique Wallon (1945) and the Economische Raad voor Vlaanderen (1954) were the result of private as much as public initiative. Lacking funds and government backing, these bodies often did little more than lobby the government and air Flemish and Walloon grievances, although there was notable success at Mechelen and Bruges where industrial estates were set up. Government action was slow to materialise firstly because of the traditional mobility enjoyed by the labour force owing to the very low prices of workmen's rail season tickets, allowing both rural-urban and inter-regional commuting, and secondly for fear of favouring one linguistic region at the expense of the other. The coalmining crisis at the end of the 1950s brought matters to a head, and in 1959 a number of regions, the largest of which were in Hainaut, Luxembourg, Kempenland and West-Vlaanderen, were declared development areas. Loans at low rates of interest and grants of 20% of the cost of buildings and 7·5% of the cost of equipment were made available. At the same time a new type of *inter-communale* was established. The first *intercommunales* dated from 1922 when they were begun as a response to the need for small *communes* to amalgamate to provide more efficient public utility services. The new *intercommunales*, known as *sociétés d'équipement économique régionale*, were set up to execute the legislation. They are 24 in number at present.

The level of assistance allowed for in the 1959 legislation was lower than that in the Netherlands, but by 1966 increasing unemployment in, and emigration from the coalmining districts in particular caused the government to increase both the amount of assistance and the size of the development areas. Grants for buildings were raised to 30% of the total cost, and those towards machinery to 10% of the total cost. Depreciation allowances were also raised. Fig. 4.2 indicates the extent of the assisted areas designated by the 1959 and 1966 legislation, which benefited one-third of the country. It is evident that assisted areas exist close to the Antwerp-Brussels axis, and this has been a powerful influence on firms locating in eastern Oost-Vlaanderen and in Kempenland, much to the disgust of the Walloons. It is not surprising, therefore, that the advantages of access to the port of Antwerp, a comprehensive motorway network, a cooperative labour force and financial aid have made the development areas in the provinces of Oost-Vlaanderen, Antwerp and Limburg extremely attractive to foreign investment. Between 1959 and 1969, 80% of the investment made by foreign companies in Belgium was effected in these three pro-vinces, Oost-Vlaanderen leading with 36%. The greatest expansion has been in petrochemicals, organic chemicals, engineering and vehicle assembly, and American firms such as Union Carbide and Amoco at Antwerp and Ford at Genk in Limburg, have been responsible for 55% of the total investment. Such investment that has been allocated to Wallonie has been designed to improve the efficiency of existing plants, especially iron and steelworks, and not many substantial new firms have entered the region.

The success that Belgian regional policy has had in attracting new industry has prompted the government to increase still further the financial assistance to the development areas. However, this legislation,

enacted in 1970, has run into severe difficulties, for the EEC Commission
does not accept that Belgium is justified in offering such a wide range of
financial incentives to industry in an area which, in the context of the
EEC, is certainly not a 'priority region'. Nor is the Commission happy
about some of the methods employed by the Belgian *intercommunales* to
attract industry, considering that discriminatory tactics are being used
against other member countries. The Commission takes the view that
regional aids to the central areas of the Community, including Belgium,
should not exceed 20% of the value of the investment, and that some of the
Flemish development areas should lose their status. The Belgian case is
that if it is to help Wallonie, it must support Flanders to the same extent
to preserve the finely balanced equilibrium between north and south. A
solution to this seemingly intractable problem had still not been found by
the summer of 1972. In this instance, assuming that the EEC Commission
has its way, the supranational authority will exert a negative influence on
the location of industry in the areas which lose development area status.

(iii) *Luxembourg* The small size of the Grand Duchy makes it difficult
for the country to have a regional problem, although the great bulk of
economic activity does take place in the south. The principal difficulty
facing the country is the adaptation of the labour force from mining and
iron and steel production towards manufacturing industry in general. To
effect this a comprehensive policy aimed at attracting foreign investment,
similar in scope to Belgian regional policy, was inaugurated in 1962. At
the present time financial incentives include grants of 15% of the cost of
total investment, exemption from 25% of corporation taxes for 8 years,
subsidies on the interest on money borrowed for investment, grants for
research and training schemes, tax rebates and depreciation allowances.
The EEC Commission has not objected to this formidable array of aids,
and the diversification that the country's manufacturing sector has under-
gone in the last decade owes a great deal to government action. The characteristics of industries wishing to develop in the country are taken into
consideration, for example firms liable to cause pollution or require a
large labour force are discouraged, while firms based on advanced technologies are welcome. Thus in yet another way a government may
influence the distribution of manufacturing.

4.3 CASE STUDIES OF BENELUX INDUSTRIES

Having considered the principal factors influencing the location of
industry, it is useful to examine some of the more important industries to
observe their present-day patterns of distribution. The industries selected
possess differing locational characteristics. Thus the iron and steel
industry is powerfully influenced by the supply of materials, the manu-

facture of vehicles is a neotechnic activity and is particularly mobile, oil refining is largely tied to break of bulk points and the textile industry is located in areas of cheap labour.

The iron and steel industry

The production of iron and steel is an important activity in Benelux, more especially in Luxembourg and Belgium, and these countries rank first and second respectively in the world in respect of output *per capita*. In 1971 Luxembourg produced 15·3 tons and Belgium 1·3 tons per inhabitant, data which clearly suggest the massive significance of the industry in the former country. However, as Table 4.1 indicates, steel output in the Netherlands is increasing at a faster rate than in either of the other two countries, and by 1971 output was virtually equal to that in Luxembourg. Indeed if plans drawn up by Hoogovens, the major Dutch

TABLE 4.1

Benelux pig iron, steel and iron ore production, 1965-1971
in '000 tons

| | 1965 | | | 1969 | | | 1971 | | |
	Pig	Steel	Ore	Pig	Steel	Ore	Pig	Steel	Ore
Belgium	8 436	9 162	91	11 313	12 832	93	10 527	12 442	90
Netherlands	2 364	3 145	—	3 461	4 712	—	3 759	5 081	—
Luxembourg	4 145	4 585	6 615	4 865	5 521	6 311	4 588	5 241	4 540

plant, come to fruition, output will be substantially in excess of that in Luxembourg by the mid-1970s. The different rates of expansion are to some extent a function of the dominant types of location in each country, and it is useful to examine the four categories of site in turn.

(i) *Coalfield sites* It is evident from Fig. 4.3 that in terms of the number and variety of plants the Walloon coalfield is the leading iron and steel district in Benelux. It is responsible for 40% of Benelux steel output, and for three-quarters of the Belgian total, with 9 of the 12 Belgian integrated works, that is those combining pig-iron production and steel-making. The integrated plant at Clabecq, to the north of Charleroi on the Charleroi-Brussels Canal, owes its location at least in part to its ability to take delivery of coal at low cost from the mines to the south. Because of the long industrial history the coalfield possesses, it is to be expected that there should also be a multiplicity of works, many of them only medium-sized, taking their materials from the larger integrated works around which they are clustered. Thus only 6 of the 23 Belgian steelworks and rolling mills are sited beyond the confines of the coal measures. The concentration of the industry around Liège and Charleroi continues, and these districts

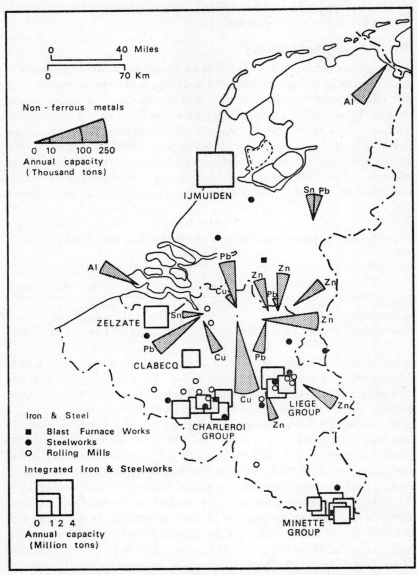

Fig. 4.3 The iron and steel and non-ferrous metal industries of Benelux

claim 8 of the 9 integrated plants on the coalfield. The other is at La Louvière to the west of Charleroi.

The major advantages possessed by the coalfield plants do not now lie in the availability of local coal supplies, for as we have seen in Chapter 3, production costs are so high that coking coal is no longer mined, and fuel must be brought from the Kempen, the Ruhr and the USA. Further, iron ore must be imported from Sweden and French Lorraine, with the consequence that transport costs, which account for about one-third of total costs, are onerous. The reason for the continuation of the industry on the coalfield lies in the strength of the external economies resulting from the presence of so many steel-making activities and supporting services in the area, together with the sheer cost of building a new plant elsewhere. Even so the iron and steel firms have had to institute changes to offset their poor location, especially since more Belgian steel is exported than is consumed within the country, making competitive prices essential. One strategy is to produce standard steels, and another is to try to reap the advantages of large-scale production by having big plants, but the latter advantage has been lost to coastal works like that at Ijmuiden, which is more than three times the size of the largest coalfield plant. The solution has been a series of mergers allowing separate plants to function as a unit, with appropriate economies. Thus the Cockerill company merged with the Ougrée group in 1966, and the subsequent merger in 1969 of Cockerill-Ougrée with the other major Liège group, Espérance-Longdoz, has caused the Liège region effectively to pass into the control of one firm. In addition to the three integrated works, Cockerill owns, or has an important financial interest in four of the six steelworks and rolling mills in Liège, and is able to effect specialisation as between plants. The company also has integrated works at Charleroi (Marchienne), at Athus in Belgian Luxembourg and at Genk, which is a stainless-steel-making works. Similar in principle if not in scale is the control of the Charleroi district by the two firms Hainaut-Sambre and Thy-Marcinelle et Monceau.

(ii) *Ironfield sites* The *minette* ironfield differs from the coalfield in that outside iron and steel production, industrial activity is poorly developed. The reason is that although the very lean *minette*, whose average iron content is now only 22%, argued in favour of ironfield blast furnaces, the absence of coal militated against other forms of industry. Consequently, with the exception of the small Dommeldange steelworks to the north of the field, a survival from the era of charcoal fuel, the ironfield industry comprises six integrated works and a blast furnace works at Terres Rouges. Unfortunately the advantages of a location close to supplies of iron ore is diminishing, for Luxembourg output is declining (Table 4.1) as it becomes increasingly costly to mine, and in 1970 some 71% of the iron ore consumed

I

was imported, largely from French Lorraine to the south. However Lorraine iron ore costs are rising more rapidly than the landed prices of Brazilian and Venezuelan ores at Antwerp or Ijmuiden. Moreover, although the rationalisation of freight rates by the ECSC has helped to keep down the transport costs on imported Ruhr coke, the ironfield plants are at a disadvantage in respect of coastal works. Hence the locational problems of the *minette* plants are the cause of the slow growth of Luxembourg steel output evident in Table 4.1.

The solutions to the locational difficulties are similar to those adopted on the Walloon coalfield. There are only two companies in Luxembourg, and one of them, Aciéries Réunies de Burbach-Eich-Dudelange (ARBED) owns four of the five integrated works, the blast furnace works and the steelworks at Dommeldange. There are thus opportunities for integration between plants; for instance all the pig produced at Terres Rouges is sent to the two plants at Esch to be refined. ARBED is only marginally smaller than Cockerill, the largest Benelux group, producing 4·69 million tons of steel in 1971, compared with 4·83 million tons by Cockerill. A further strategy undertaken by ARBED is the purchase of iron mines in Lorraine and coal mines in the Ruhr, but there can be no doubt that the future advantage lies with the coastal plants. A portent is the production by Hoogovens at Ijmuiden of 4·63 million tons of steel in 1971.

(iii) *Coastal sites* At present only two works belong to this category, Koninklijke Nederlandsche Hoogovens at Ijmuiden, at the entrance to the North Sea Canal, and Sidérurgie Maritime (SIDMAR) on the Terneuzen-Ghent Canal just within Belgium at Zelzate. The establishment of Hoogovens in 1918 was a reaction by the government to the country's dependence on foreign supplies of steel during the 1914-1918 War, and the plant, which began smelting in 1924, was designed at the outset to utilise imported raw materials. Steel-making capacity was not added until 1939, although prior to this a fertiliser and a cement works were built as an integral part of the plant. The rise in price of European coal and iron ore, coupled with the favourable price of imported materials, have given Hoogovens a distinct advantage over inland works, and its expansion has been rapid. The seventh blast furnace was blown in early in 1972 and it is expected that an output of 6 million tons will be reached during 1973. The firm has not been content with the expansion, and the economies that can be achieved at Ijmuiden however, and in 1972 a merger with Hoesch of Dortmund was finalised. The new company has taken the name ESTEL and has an annual capacity of 12·5 million tons, akin to many American and Japanese firms. ESTEL is the third largest West European steel firm, behind the British Steel Corporation and August Thyssen Hutte.

The SIDMAR plant dates from 1966. It was built by a consortium of companies including ARBED, Cockerill, the French Schneider and Knutange groups and the Italian firm of Falck, all of whom were anxious to participate in the profits accruing from steel-making on the coast. Initially a site at Antwerp was favoured, but the group was persuaded to set up in Oost-Vlaanderen, where at that time there was a high level of unemployment. The works stands on a plot of land bought with some forethought by ARBED some years earlier. The ship canal can accommodate vessels of up to 50 000 tons, consequently all but the very largest bulk carriers can discharge at the plant's quay. Production amounted to 2·04 million tons in 1971, and there are plans for expansion to 2·5 million tons by 1975.

During the 1960s Hoogovens and Hoesch seriously considered building a plant at Maasvlakte on land reclaimed from the North Sea at the western end of the New Waterway, but there were several difficulties, not the least of which were objections to pollution, and the plan was shelved in 1971.

(iv) *Market sites* There are a number of works which do not fall into the categories discussed, and the majority of these are small- to medium-sized steelworks and rolling mills established to meet local or regional demand. The steelworks are frequently concerned with the manufacture of special steels using electric arc furnaces, and this is the case with the plant at Ghent, the Demka works at Utrecht founded in 1861, and the ‹covered› Alblasserdam which produces steel

‹covered› industry

‹covered›g industry was established, as we have ‹covered›e reason for its growth was the discovery ‹covered›eposits of copper, zinc, silver, cadmium, ‹covered›were brought to Belgium to be smelted ‹covered›rt, later re-exported in the style of the ‹covered›ing of metals was organised by Union ‹covered›en over by the Congolese government in ‹covered›rried out by firms such as Métallurgie ‹covered›Vieille-Montagne. The Société Générale ‹covered›n, and was responsible for the eventual ‹covered›verpelt-Lommel in 1970. ‹covered›ave for the zinc deposits at Liège, the ‹covered›d the port of Antwerp with an eastward ‹covered›ig. 4.3 shows. Here pollution appeared

to do little harm, coal was available and materials could be moved to and from Antwerp by barge. The result is an impressive concentration of the activity, broken only by the continuation of zinc smelting in the Liège area at Flône and Prayon. There seems little sign that other regions have become more favoured and new plants have been, or are being constructed in the established area at Oolen, Overpelt and Budel (within Dutch territory). These new plants have been occasioned by increased demand and by the introduction of more advanced technology. Thus the new electrolytic zinc plant at Overpelt will replace zinc smelters at Overpelt and Lommel which date from 1893 and 1904 respectively. In the same way the old plant at Budel is to be closed and replaced by an electrolytic works. Incentive to remain in the existing areas is increased by the assistance granted under regional policy legislation. A further factor conducive to inertia is the production of several metals at the same site or even from the same ore, so that should market conditions for one metal deteriorate, the plant is able to continue operations. This has happened at Arnhem where the plant was designed to use high-grade tin concentrates which are no longer available. Tin smelting has been discontinued, but the production of lead remains unimpaired. The chemical abbreviations used in Fig. 4.3 indicate the most important metals produced at each plant. That Métallurgie Hoboken-Overpelt produce at least twenty different metals from its seven plants is an indication of the range of the industry. Of the more important non-ferrous metals, only aluminium is lacking in Belgium, although Alusuisse plans to build a smelter at Amay to the west of Liège.

Aluminium smelting is comparatively new to Benelux, the first plant starting at Delfzijl only in 1966, and the second at Vlissingen in Zeeland in 1971. The attraction of both these sites is the presence of deepwater harbour facilities allowing imported alumina to be unloaded adjacent to the smelters, the availability of natural gas for the generation of electric power and development area grants. Both plants have been established by international aluminium corporations, the first by Alusuisse in association with Hoogovens, and the second by the French concern Pechiney. There is the same emphasis on the export of refined aluminium as there is in the case of the older metals produced in Belgium. Should the Amay smelter go ahead, its inland site will certainly conflict with the practice followed in the Netherlands.

The motor vehicle industry

The manufacture of motor vehicles is essentially a 20th-century activity, relying upon sophisticated machinery to assemble a large number of components which have a high value in relation to their weight. The industry is therefore not tied to its supply of materials and is free to establish itself at any point within manufacturing areas. As Fig. 4.4 illustrates, within Benelux the activity has been particularly selective and with few exceptions has chosen to locate itself in the most rapidly expanding manufactur-

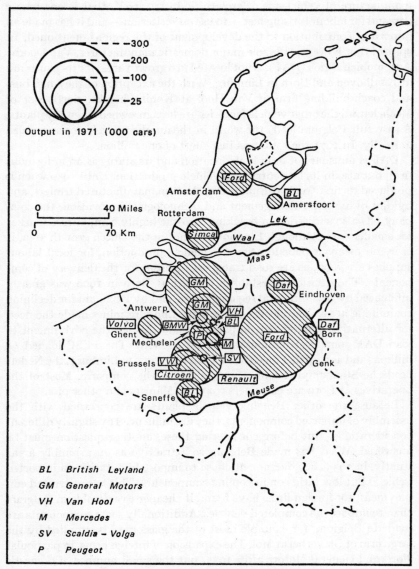

Fig. 4.4 The Benelux motor vehicle industry

ing areas of the Antwerp-Brussels axis and the western Netherlands. The manufacture of vehicles is a 'growth' industry itself, that is one whose demand for labour is rising fast—to use one criterion—and it has made an important contribution to the development of the regions mentioned. In spite of this, however, the sole major domestic manufacturer, Van Doorne Automobielfabriek (DAF), is not located in a growth area, for its plants are at Eindhoven and Born in Limburg. With the exception of the small bus- and coach-building firm of Van Hool at Koningshooikt, north-east of Mechelen, all the other vehicle factories are foreign-owned assembly plants. As a result Belgium leads the world in the number of vehicles assembled annually. In 1971 the total was just short of one million.

DAF is unusual not only in its location and its status as an indigenous firm, but also in its late entry into vehicle production. Until 1950 when it produced its first truck at Eindhoven, the firm manufactured trailers, and by dint of dynamic management and technological innovation, the company has also succeeded in breaking into the highly competitive market for smaller cars. Although Eindhoven is not in the Dutch growth area, it is by no means a poor location for vehicle production, for local labour supplies are good, as are road transport facilities for the delivery of components. The decision to establish a plant at Born in 1966 was greatly influenced by governmental regional policy and by ECSC aid for declining coalmining areas. The closure of the Zuid-Limburg mines made the need for alternative employment imperative, and this led the government to loan DAF some $30 millions to set up at Born. The ECSC loaned £4 millions and as a further incentive for DAF to come to Limburg, the Nederlandsche Staatsmijnen took a 25% share in the company. Most of the operatives at Born are ex-miners from the Maurits and other pits.

Because the other Benelux vehicle plants are concerned with the assembly of imported components, they are influenced by slightly different considerations. But before considering these, another question must be answered. What has made Belgium so attractive as an assembly area? Firstly, in 1935 the government chose to impose high tariffs on imported vehicles but low tariffs on in-coming components. This has generated employment, for foreign firms have found it cheaper to assemble in Belgium than to import the completed vehicles. Additionally some components are made in Belgium, for example most of the glass used is supplied by the large firm of Glaverbel at Mol. The expansion of foreign firms, in particular Ford and General Motors after 1935, put the small number of domestic firms out of business. Secondly, legislation enacted in 1952 virtually ensured assembly rather than the import of finished vehicles by placing a maximum of 250 on the number of assembled vehicles of each make that could be imported annually. Thirdly, the advent of the EEC has placed

Belgium in a strategic position to supply member countries with vehicles built from imported components. Britain's entry into the Common Market will remove the existing tariffs and should make Belgium even more attractive to British firms.

In respect of location within Belgium and the Netherlands, four factors are at work. Although components have a high value in relation to their weight, economies are to be obtained by a quay-side location, enabling crates and containers to be unloaded directly into a storage area. This seems to have been an overriding consideration with the American firms, since all their early plants were established in Antwerp and Amsterdam docks. Ford were persuaded to expand in a development area at Genk in 1962 (their Antwerp factory has been converted to the production of tractors), but the most recent (1967) General Motors plant was once again in the docks at Antwerp. The second influence has been the availability of cheap labour in Flanders. Non-industrial labour was paid lower wages than that in the manufacturing areas, and certainly in the early years, it was extremely reliable and diligent. This is an important reason for the colonisation of Mechelen by vehicle firms before the 1959 regional policy legislation provided incentive to develop outside the Antwerp-Brussels region. Peugeot, Mercedes and Triumph (now British Leyland) all built works at Mechelen between 1953 and 1956. The BMW plant at Kontich, south of Antwerp, dates from 1959. Regional policy has been a third and more recent influence, for of the 6 plants constructed since 1960, 3 have chosen assisted areas. Ford at Genk and Volvo at Ghent initially also benefited from low labour costs (the unions have now obtained equal pay irrespective of the location of the factory), but British Leyland have broken new ground in selecting Seneffe on the fringe of the Walloon coal-field for its most recent works. Finally, the French firms of Renault and Citroen chose Brussels in the 1920s because of the skilled labour supply that existed there at that time, and because both firms produced cars in Paris and it was natural that they should select the capital city of the country in which they chose to assemble. However, apart from the VW plant at Forest, opened in 1954, and the small Scaldia-Volga works at Diegem, no other factories have followed this lead, probably because of the high cost of labour.

The chemical industry

During the last decade and a half the Benelux chemical industry has been growing almost twice as fast as the combined rate for all industry, but expansion has not been spread evenly over the different sectors of the activity. The production of heavy inorganic chemicals, such as nitrogenous fertilisers, and the carbochemical industry have lagged, but oil refining, the petrochemical, plastics, and man-made fibre industries have experienced boom conditions. Initially the foreign firms who for the most part engineered the expansion preferred the Netherlands, and between 1959 and 1970 the annual output of the Dutch chemical industry rose from £310 millions to £1 100 millions. Until the mid-1960s Belgium remained the province of the older, traditional firms based on the Walloon coalfield, but of recent there has been a great upsurge in investment by foreign companies. Needless to say the leading beneficiaries of these developments have been the regions of the large ports; the province of Antwerp received half, and the province of Zuid-Holland one-third of the total investment in the chemical industry in Belgium and the Netherlands respectively in 1971. Investment in this year in the Netherlands was £610 millions compared with £453 millions in Belgium, suggesting that the earlier trend has not yet been reversed.

(i) *Oil refining* The refining of crude oil is the basic process in the modern organic chemical industry. Growth here stems from increased demand both for chemicals for subsequent processing, and for energy, in particular petrol and fuel oils. The economies to be obtained from a location at the deepwater ports where large tankers can be berthed have been noted, and until the early 1960s there were no inland refineries in Western Europe. The major refining centre is the largest port, Rotterdam-Europoort, with five plants with a total capacity of 64 million tons per annum, although when the BP refinery at Europoort is expanded to 25 million tons in 1974, this figure will reach 83 million tons. The difficult navigational approaches to Antwerp coupled with its restricted hinterland have caused the port to be a much less important refining centre. The five refineries here have an annual capacity of 30 million tons, with half of this contributed by one plant belonging to the Société Industrielle Belge des Pétroles. The opening of the Rotterdam-Antwerp oil pipeline in 1971 removes the problem caused by the inability of Antwerp to handle large tankers, which will now be able to discharge crude oil for Antwerp at Rotterdam. The result may well be further expansion of oil refining in the port. As Fig. 4.5 illustrates, there are also refineries at Amsterdam and Ghent. In both cases they are fed, in part, by crude oil pipelines from Rotterdam and Zeebrugge respectively, both ports with superior handling facilities.

Several new refineries are planned or are in the course of construction, and some, like those at Sloe and Borssele near Vlissingen, Rotterdam and Amsterdam, reinforce the existing practice of siting refineries adjacent to deep water. However the development of demand at inland sites has begun to reach the level at which the entire output from a refinery can be consumed in the vicinity. The Rotterdam-Ruhr pipeline built in 1960

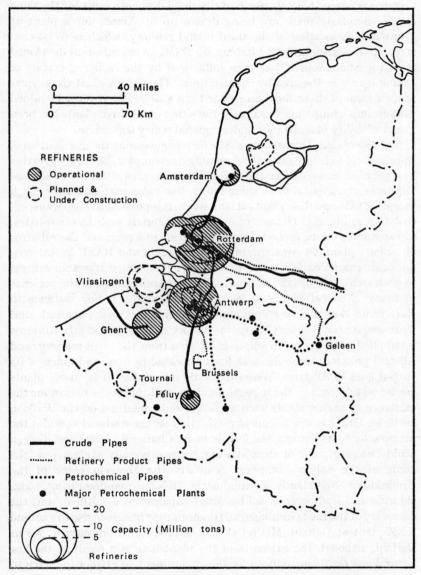

Fig. 4.5 Oil refining and petrochemical production in Benelux

was a response to the occurrence of this situation in the Ruhr, and the Chevron refinery at Féluy, north of Charleroi, has been built for the same reason. Similarly plans are being drawn up by Amoco for a plant at Tournai. The location of the third inland refinery, which is to be constructed at Geleen in Zuid-Limburg by DSM, an organisation developed from the Staatsmijnen, has been influenced by the earlier operation of coking plants in the area by Staatsmijnen. The Geleen plant thus represents a form of diversification rather than a new site. It must be added that an important consideration in the siting of all three plants has been the availability of assistance under regional policy legislation.

(ii) *Other chemical manufacture* The factors governing the distribution of the chemical industry outside oil refining are complex, but it is nevertheless possible to recognise three sectors, each with different locational requirements. Firstly, firms using bulky, low-value materials have much incentive to locate their plants at sites where it is possible to keep transport cost to a minimum. The use of imported materials such as phosphates, nitrates and sulphur is conducive to a location in a port, and the Albatros phosphate plants in Amsterdam and Rotterdam and BASF in Antwerp docks are examples. It is not only transport costs which draws these firms to dock areas, but also the external economies springing from the presence of many chemical plants as suppliers and markets. For instance in Rotterdam Zoutchemie manufactures chlorine for Shell Chemicals and hydrogen for the Brinkers Margarine factory from imported salt; Albatros is supplied with hydrogen sulphide by pipe from the Shell refinery, and Albacid produces sulphuric acid from imported pyrites, and much of its output goes to Albatros. Where domestic raw materials are used, plants are found adjacent to the mineral deposits, and this is the reason for the existence of coking plants such as Tertre and Anderlues on the Walloon coalfield. Other heavy chemical production on the coalfield includes the manufacture of nitrogenous fertilisers at Charleroi, Liège and Geleen (Zuid-Limburg), and of ammonia and soda, especially at Jemeppe, the home of the Solvay company. Similarly the Hengelo plant of the Koninklijke Nederlands Zoutindustrie (KNZ), manufacturing soda, chlorine and hydrochloric acid is sited adjacent to a saltfield, and the discovery of the East Groningen salt dome in 1957 has given rise to a second KNZ plant at Delfzijl. Methyl alcohol is produced from natural gas at Delfzijl, although the existence of the plant here is a result of the low natural gas tariffs introduced by the government to attract industry to this part of the country, rather than the presence of the gasfield.

The second sector is the manufacture of petrochemicals, an activity which is closely allied to oil refining, which is largely a coastal industry. The first petrochemical plant was built in 1949 by Shell close to its Pernis refinery, and there are now more than twenty plants in the ports of Rotterdam-Europoort and Antwerp. A vast range of products is manufactured and an extensive pipeline network links many of the plants bringing great external economies to the port areas. Indeed Rotterdam-Europoort above all may truly be regarded as what Jean Chardonnet has termed *un complexe à base de pétrole*. The petrochemical industry is not restricted to ports or to the vicinity of oil refineries, however, for where demand is sufficient petroleum products pipelines have been built from oil refineries (Fig. 4.5), endowing petrochemical plants with a degree of flexibility in their location. The DSM plant at Beek and Shell Chemicals at Moerdijk are supplied with products from the Shell refinery at Rotterdam, and 1971 saw the completion of an ethylene grid linking Dow Chemicals at Terneuzen with Rotterdam and Antwerp, Solvay at Jemeppe with Antwerp and the plants at Geel, Tessenderloo and Beek once again with Antwerp. The growth of pipelines thus presents old-established plants, such as that at Jemeppe, with the opportunity of diversifying their output, and as a result the petrochemical industry assumes a more dispersed pattern of distribution.

The final sector comprises that part of the chemical industry concerned with the manufacture of products whose value is high in relation to their weight. Plants in this sector are not tied to their material suppliers and are free to locate themselves in respect of other factors. For new plants the financial incentives offered in the development areas are an important consideration, and such firms as Beecham, Dow Chemicals and Hooker have chosen Heppignies near Charleroi, Seneffe and Genk respectively, largely in response to these inducements. There seems to be a tendency for pharmaceutical firms to favour the large towns and the growth areas, particularly in the Netherlands, but even in Belgium the large firms of Union Chimique Belge and Agfa-Gevaert are to be found in Brussels and Antwerp respectively. The production of man-made fibres exhibits some evidence of attraction to the textile districts with plants at Breda, Emmen, Nijmegen and Arnhem in the Netherlands, and at Zwijnaarde, south of Ghent, in Belgium. However, there is an equal number of plants, including that at Echternach in Luxembourg, distant from the textile regions. This dispersed pattern of distribution emphasises the increasingly footloose nature of many branches of the chemical industry in Benelux.

The textile industry

Unlike the other industries considered, the manufacture of textiles is a declining activity, and the distribution of the industry has changed little during the 20th century. The old-established textile areas of West- and Oost-Vlaanderen, Noord-Brabant, Twente and Verviers are in the main peripheral to the growth areas, so that labour at the wages that the textile industry is prepared to pay is still forthcoming. As a result no great locational shifts have occurred. Contraction has accelerated since the Second World War, particularly in cotton and linen textiles. This has been a result of dwindling overseas markets, which can be supplied at very low cost by producers in Japan and Hong Kong and other low-wage economies, competition from cheap imports from outside the EEC and from Italy within it, and falling demand for textiles goods within Benelux. The introduction of man-made fibres has also reduced the need for special-ist mills in the early stages of production.

The contraction of the industry has been accompanied by an increased concentration into the largest centres of production, although in the case of cottons, the Kortrijk district has overtaken Ghent as the leading area of production. This is in part a result of the severe rationalisation measures carried through in Ghent by Union Cotonnière (UCO), the leading Belgian cotton textile group, and in part a consequence of the very successful switch by the mills of the Kortrijk district into the manufacture of house-hold textiles such as carpets, curtains, upholstery cloths and tablecloths, making great use of man-made fibres. Household textiles account for more than half of the Belgian cotton textile industry's production, and to some extent the other important districts round Oudenaarde, Ronse and St. Niklaas have begun to follow suit. The concentration of cotton and linen production into a few districts in the Leie and Scheldt valleys has caused some centres, such as Bruges and Brussels, where the activity was once of moderate importance, to lie outside the textile region altogether. The declining fortunes of the cotton industry in the Netherlands has been accompanied by mill closures through bankruptcy, rationalisation and mergers which have created firms like the Koninklijke Nederlands Textiel Unie (KNTU) of Hengelo. There are now only a few important areas such as Enschede and Almelo in Twente, and Tilburg, Eindhoven and Helmond in Noord-Brabant. Enschede has a lead in the Netherlands similar to that of Kortrijk in Belgium, but the Dutch cotton industry is much less well developed than its Belgian counterpart.

By virtue of the demand for a large number of different cloths, rendering mass-production difficult to effect, the wool textile industry has not experienced quite the same contraction as the cotton and linen industries. The old patterns of distribution have continued with Tilburg and Verviers the areas where specialisation in wool textiles is greatest. There are a number of centres in the Leie and Scheldt valleys where the industry is as important as the manufacture of cottons, and in the Mouscron and Tournai districts the manufacture of woollens and worsteds is the principal activity. Some of the former wool textile mills in West- and Oost-

Vlaanderen have moved into the carpets trades and use a high proportion of man-made fibres in conjunction with woollen yarn, thus blurring the distinction between wool and cotton textiles. A further strategy is the production of knitting yarns for the hosiery trade, following the recent growth in demand for tights. The Danish-owned Danlon mills at Emmen in Drenthe, outside the traditional textile area, are the largest producers of these yarns. The future of the production of high quality worsted cloth seems assured, and it is unlikely that the worsted spinners of Veenendaal and the manufacturers of Tilburg and Verviers will cause changes to be made to the map of worsted production in the near future.

4.4 THE TERTIARY OR SERVICE INDUSTRIES OF BENELUX

In the Benelux countries as in most developed states, service industries employ a higher percentage of the national labour force and produce a larger part of the national produce than either agriculture or manufacturing industry. Increasingly prosperous consumers are demanding a more than proportional increase in services. In the last 25 years, for example, the expenditure of the average Dutch family on goods such as food, clothing and housing has declined from three-quarters to two-thirds of their total spending, while expenditure on services such as transport, health and insurance has risen from one-quarter to one-third of the total spent. Service industries have a special importance in Benelux, for in this sector raw material and power requirements are small, but the workforce is both large and highly skilled. Therefore the export of services is a profitable strategy for countries deficient in materials, rich in labour skills and advantageously located in respect of potential markets. The earnings of trade, transport and financial services were the mainspring of Benelux prosperity in the 17th and 18th centuries, and the export of similar services remains important in the modern economy.

There is a marked tendency for the location of the service industries to be related to the distribution of population, so that the largest settlements have the greatest numbers employed. Large towns are both markets and sources of labour supplies, and at the same time they provide the well-developed means and communication and transport essential for many service industries, with the consequence that they have a wider range of services than small towns. Many large towns benefit from the establishment of international institutions, which are seldom attracted to small settlements, thus helping to increase the strength of their tertiary sector. By virtue of its location within the EEC, its familiarity with the two principal international languages, French and English, its tradition of international contact and considerable government support, Brussels has become the home of the European Commission, the executive of the EEC. It is also the headquarters of NATO. Following this there has been an increase in the number of embassy staff, journalists, at least 100 of whom are accredited to the Commission, and some 300 interest groups, representing every imaginable sector of the Benelux economy, have sprung up. The forthcoming enlargement of the Community will add further increments to the tertiary sector of the city. Many firms have been encouraged by the selection of the city by the EEC also to locate themselves there, and this has led to the agglomeration of offices of international political and economic organisations over the last decade and a half. The position of Luxembourg City as the capital of the Duchy has caused a number of Community institutions to be located there, and the Dutch capital, The Hague, is the seat of the International Court of Justice. The tertiary sector of capital cities is also increased by the presence of government offices, leading in turn to the growth of offices of commercial firms who value close contact with the civil service. Specialisation in particular activities can occur in the tertiary sector as it does in manufacturing, and within cities specialist quarters have developed. Examples are the Damrak financial district of Amsterdam, the gemstone trading area around Pelikaanstraat in Antwerp and the tourist quarter in the Buitenhof-Spui area of The Hague. The importance of labour supplies can itself cause specialisation, for work-people are becoming increasingly discriminating in respect of their place of work and residence, giving attractive areas an advantage for the expansion of service industries. This certainly allowed The Hague to score over Rotterdam as a suitable location for offices.

Two examples of service activities which have important export functions will now be considered. Both exhibit an association with the distribution of population, but one, banking and finance, tends to cluster in one particular city in each of the three countries, and the other, tourism, is well developed in coastal and isolated regions in addition to the major cities.

Banking and finance

Banks and other financial institutions have traditionally played a more central rôle in the development of the Benelux economies than in Great Britain. Institutions such as the Dutch AMRO bank or the Belgian Société Générale have customarily concerned themselves with the direct financing of trade and industry. La Générale, as it is known, has a wide range of interests, and in the iron and steel industry alone it owns both Cockerill and ARBED, and through them has a controlling interest in SIDMAR. In all three Benelux countries the state has fostered a political and economic climate that has encouraged the development of a large and varied financial sector with interests in both domestic and international affairs. Both Dutch and Belgian banks have substantial holdings in Latin America and Africa, and the encouragement of the mobility of capital by the EEC has led to the banks of Benelux playing an active rôle in the financing of the Common Market countries.

Banking and finance is dominantly an urban activity and is especially well developed in the largest cities. Amsterdam contains about half the Dutch employment in banking, while The Hague, Rotterdam, Utrecht and Arnhem contain a further third. Additionally it is important to distinguish between the purely local functions of the smaller centres and the national and international functions of the financial capitals of Amsterdam, Brussels and Luxembourg City which contain almost the entire employment in the more specialised financial activities. Banks and financial institutions benefit greatly from proximity to each other, to government departments and, in the case of Brussels and Luxembourg City, to Community institutions. Such are the advantages of these financial agglomerations that an international bank opening a branch has little choice but to do so in the established centre. Each city has a well-defined financial quarter. Of the 37 000 workers in banking and finance in Amsterdam, some 33 000 are employed within the Damrak district. In Brussels the Avenue des Arts is rapidly becoming an international 'bankers' row', recent additions to its ranks including the Chase Manhattan Bank, the First National Bank of Chicago, American Express and the Chemical Bank.

Since the formation of the EEC there has been an upsurge in the volume of international financial transactions in the Community. This is a result of the growth of international trade, of international financial transactions involving both member and non-member countries, and of the development of international corporations, in particular those with headquarters in the USA. American industry is frequently served by American banks, and the rapid expansion of American investment in chemicals in Belgium is the principal reason for the establishment of the Chemical Bank in Brussels. Each of the three Benelux financial centres is bidding to become the financial capital of Western Europe, and they are assisted in this by their respective governments, for the growth of regional prosperity is greatly assisted by expansion in this sector. Amsterdam is the old established centre, her expertise going back to the golden era of the 17th century, and the strength of the guilder is reflected in the use of the Euroguilder as an international medium of exchange. Brussels is particularly fortunate in being the seat of many EEC institutions, making it the unofficial capital of the Community in addition to its status as the first city of Belgium. The largest Belgian bank, the Société Générale de Banque, is only 67th on the list of world banks, and it is the international banks which are providing the expansion in Brussels. There are now 52 foreign banks in the city, 18 of these being American, and foreign money now accounts for one-fifth of the total deposits in banks in Belgium. The Belgian banks have pioneered the formation of European banking consortia which coordinate international financial business, and the three leading consortia, BEC, EBIC and ABECOR, have their head offices in Brussels. By the end of 1971, more than 450 foreign manufacturing and other firms had established their European headquarters in Brussels, and this is likely to intensify the interest of the international banks in the city.

If Brussels has become a major banking centre, Luxembourg City has become a leading European financial centre. It is the seat of some of the EEC institutions such as the European Investment Bank, but its small size and poorly developed financial traditions clearly do not account for its position as the first European bond market. It has become an international clearing house for financial operations of all kinds as a result of legislation passed in 1929 exempting holding companies established in the Duchy from taxes on interest and dividends. There is also no capital gains tax nor exchange controls and the stock exchange regulations are liberal. It is not surprising that there are now about 2 000 holding companies in the city, and the growth in the number of banks, which play an integral part in the financial dealings, has been very rapid. In 1950 there were 14 banks in the city. By 1966 this had risen to 23, but only five years later, in 1971, there were 44, the number of employees doubling during this period. Bank employment is increasing at an annual rate of 13%, which compared with the rate for all industry of 1%, makes it a true growth industry.

The tourist industry in Benelux

Although tourism is not quite so closely correlated with the distribution of population as many service industries, it is most well developed in the larger towns, and therefore fits the locational model of the tertiary sector reasonably well. The industry is expanding very rapidly indeed as a result of the growth of affluence and car-ownership, which greatly improves the mobility of the individual. Consequently it is a valuable source of foreign exchange, representing 3·2% of the export earnings of the Benelux countries, and substantially helping to offset the foreign spending of Benelux nationals (Table 4.2). Additionally, spending by tourists directly assists such areas as the Ardennes, Oesling and the Drenthe Plateau, whose very isolation has inhibited other kinds of economic activity.

The benefits of the tourist industry must be weighed against its costs, and in particular the resources that it utilises. In the Netherlands for example, tourism employs about 110 000 people, rather more than the petrochemical industry, and the implementation of the tourist provisions in the second structure plan of 1966 would need a national investment of £712 millions. Above all in Benelux it is the utilisation of land for tourism that most often causes conflict with other potential users. In addition tourism has an inevitable physical and social impact upon the character of the tourist areas. The sprawling and haphazard camping and caravan development that runs the full length of the Belgian coast, and the rash of chalets and bungalows in the western valleys of the Ardennes are part of the cost of the industry. Further, the market for tourist services is both seasonal and capricious. The former condition makes for an uneconomic utilisation of the facilities available, and the latter places the economy at the mercy of changing tastes. At present the Belgian coast is more popular than the Dutch, Amsterdam more fashionable than Brussels, and the demand for camp sites and caravan parks is increasing relative to the

TABLE 4.2

Balance of tourist payments, 1972, *million* US $

	Receipts	Expenditure	Balance	Receipts as % total exports
Belgium Luxembourg }	262	493	−231	3·2
Netherlands	321	375	−54	3·2

demand for hotels and youth hostels. The nature and the location of future investment thus involves considerable risk.

An immediate contrast between the tourist industries of the Benelux countries can be seen in Table 4.3. In both Belgium and the Netherlands domestic demand is of much greater importance than foreign demand. In Luxembourg, however, the selling of tourist services to foreigners has a much greater significance to the economy, and receipts outweigh expenditure by Luxembourg nationals abroad, producing a considerable surplus on the tourist account. Foreigners account for 93% of the total nights spent in the Duchy by tourists. The domestic demand of the Benelux population (Table 4·3) is growing at an annual rate of 8%, with about 2·5% of *per capita* income being spent on this service. As a result some 60 million nights are spent by Benelux tourists in their own countries. In addition it has been estimated that 15% of car-passenger journeys, some 8% of bus journeys and 10% of train journeys have a tourist motive.

Foreign tourists may be fewer than those from Benelux itself, but each foreign visitor spends about twice as much as each domestic tourist, and the location of Benelux in respect of West Germany, France and the United

K

Kingdom is thus particularly fortunate. Indeed, the Dutch and Belgian coasts are the closest beaches for a majority of the West German population who form the world's largest tourist nation. The task of accommodating almost 5 million foreign visitors is complicated by the need to cater for an annual influx of between 70 and 100 million foreign day-excursionists, who make great demands on recreational facilities, in particular transport services. More than 30 million West Europeans live within a two hour drive of the Benelux boundary.

The Benelux countries have marshalled a formidable array of tourist resources to meet this demand. Large areas of special scenic value have been accorded measures of conservation, such as the Dutch National Parks at Kennermerduinen and Hoge Veluwe, and suitable landscapes have been created in the Delta and Ijsselmeerrandmeeren. It is unfortunate that often the regions of greatest landscape beauty are furthest from the main centres of domestic and foreign demand. Accommodation provided for

TABLE 4.3
Tourism in Benelux in 1969 in '000 visitors

	Domestic visitor-nights	Foreign visitor-nights	Foreign visitor-nights spent in hotels	Mean length of stay days	Foreign visitor-nights as % of total visitor-nights
Belgium	19 434	6 565	3 920	n.a.	25
Netherlands	39 600	n.a.	5 655	2·6	n.a.
Luxembourg	118	1 629	781	2·0	93

tourists exhibits a concentrated rather than a dispersed pattern of distribution. Hotel facilities are an urban phenomenon as is to be expected, but even the more dispersed forms of accommodation, such as camping sites, are concentrated into distinct areas, for example the Friesian Islands, North Zeeland and the river valleys of northern Luxembourg. Mention should be made of the current boom in second homes. At present an average of 1 in 60 of the Benelux population owns a second home, but this is expected to double by 1990. As a result, the erection of 200 000 second homes of various sorts is having a major impact upon the landscape and economy of favoured areas within four hours' driving time of the major population centres.

Three distinct tourist regions may be identified in Benelux: the major cities, the North Sea coast and a number of inland areas. An impression of this division may be obtained from Fig. 4.6 which shows the distribution of nights spent by tourists in Benelux during 1969.

(i) *The cities* In all three countries the largest number of tourists, and

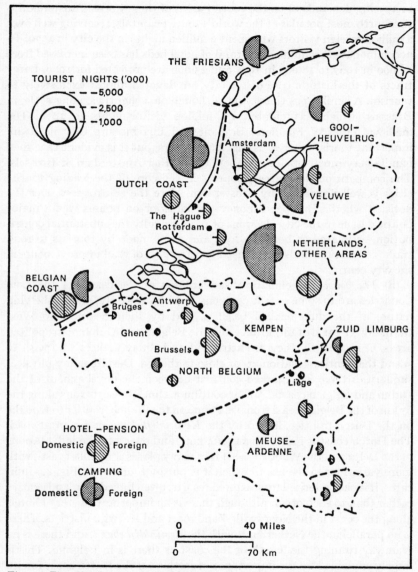

Fig. 4.6 The distribution of tourist-nights in Belgium, the Netherlands and in Luxembourg in 1969

the majority of all foreign tourists are found in the largest cities, making increasing demands upon the central areas of these towns. Amsterdam is the fourth most popular of the world's tourist capitals, receiving well over a million foreign visitors who spent 2 million nights in the city in 1970. To accommodate this number the total of hotel beds has been increased from 11 000 in 1967 to 18 000 in 1971 and 25 000 are projected for 1980. Large tracts of the historic core of the city are devoted almost exclusively to tourism. A similar position exists, although on a slightly smaller scale, in Brussels, which accumulated 1·5 million visitor-nights in 1970. The medieval cities of Flanders, Brabant and Luxembourg City itself are important tourist centres, as Fig. 4.6 suggests, but it is evident that they handle very much smaller numbers than either Amsterdam or Brussels. The competition for scarce resources in the core of the leading tourist cities is well illustrated by Amsterdam. Here the controversy over the decision whether to spend money on hotels or on houses was a major political issue in the city elections of 1970. Equally the substantial contribution, estimated at between 10% and 20%, made by tourists to road traffic congestion, adds to the need for, and cost of road improvements in the city centre.

(ii) *The coast* The climatic disadvantages of the coasts of the Low Countries are to some extent compensated by the sandy, gently shelving nature of the dune-backed beaches, and by their nearness to West Germany, Great Britain, France and the Belgian and Dutch metropolitan areas. Consequently they are attractive to holiday makers who wish to spend their entire vacation at, or close to the sea. Despite many physical similarities there is a marked contrast between the development of the Dutch and Belgian coasts. A near continuous line of resorts runs along the 67 km of the Belgian coast from De Panne on the French frontier to Knokke on the Dutch frontier, linked by the *Koninklijkebaan* or sea front road. The Dutch coast is much longer (864 km), and owing to the indentations of the Delta and the Wadden Zee it is in many places a 'double-coast', with more variations in the use to which it is put by tourists. As Fig. 4.7 indicates, it is characterised by scattered resorts, often linked to inland centres rather than to each other, although there is an important cluster of hotels along the coast in the Noordwijk, Zandvoort and Katwijk districts. There is no parallel in the Netherlands with the *Koninklijkebaan*, and there is no tramway running the length of the coast as there is in Belgium. This is largely explained by the importance of sections of the Dutch coast for sea defence, water collection and nature conservation, causing well over half of its length to be subject to restricted access. Table 4.4 and Fig. 4.7 show the much greater success the Belgian coast has had in attracting visitors, attributable in part to its concentration of facilities into a single resort

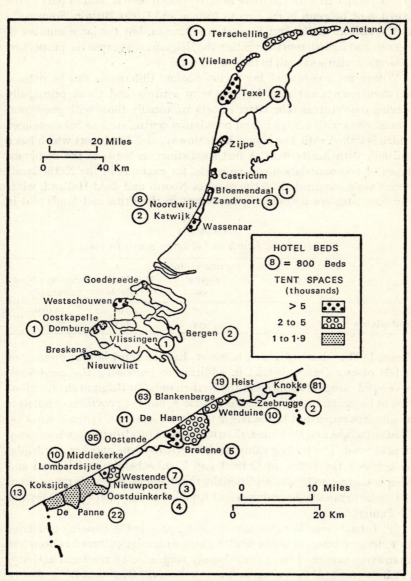

Fig. 4.7 The provision of hotel beds and tent spaces on the Benelux coast in 1969

region compared with the more isolated Dutch resorts, and in part to the position of Belgium in relation to France and Great Britain. Some 63% of the visitors to the Dutch coast are German, but the large number of French and British tourists visiting the Belgian coast cause the proportion of German visitors to fall to 18% of the total.

Within the coastal holiday region distinct differences can be noticed between resorts catering for long-term visitors and those principally serving day-visitors. The latter resorts are usually those with good communications with a large inland population centre, such as Scheveningen which is linked with The Hague by tramway, and Zandvoort which has a rail link with Amsterdam. A further distinction between the dominant types of accommodation can be made, for example in the Netherlands hotels are concentrated on the coast of Noord- and Zuid-Holland, while camping sites are particularly important in the Friesian Islands and in

TABLE 4.4

Visitors to the Dutch and Belgian coasts in 1969

	Domestic visitor-nights '000	Foreign visitor-nights '000	Hotel beds available	Camping places available
Belgium	12 274	2 296	34 710	35 916
Netherlands	5 260	654	3 385	58 800

Zeeland. The island of Texel, however, has the third largest number of hotels of any Dutch district in addition to possessing the most well-developed camping facilities in the Netherlands. In Belgium the distribution of hotels and camping sites is less clear, but the provision of hotels is much more important in the larger towns, for example, Ostend, Knokke, Blankenberghe and De Panne, than in the more rural districts, where camp sites abound. The leading camping districts, Bredene and Lombardsijde, lie between the towns of Ostend and Blankenberghe and Ostend and Nieuwpoort respectively. Additionally the character of resorts ranges from the sophisticated (Scheveningen and Knokke) to the quiet (Castricum and De Panne).

(iii) *Inland areas* Because there is little space in the Benelux countries for extensive tracts of waste land, regions where agriculture has been less intensively practised have traditionally supported recreational activity. The importance of such areas as the Ardennes, the Oesling of Luxembourg and the sandy heathlands of the Belgian Kempen and the Dutch Veluwe for tourism can be seen from Fig. 4.6. New developments, however, are increasing the importance of the inland tourist areas. An extremely rapid growth is being experienced in the demand for specialised activities such

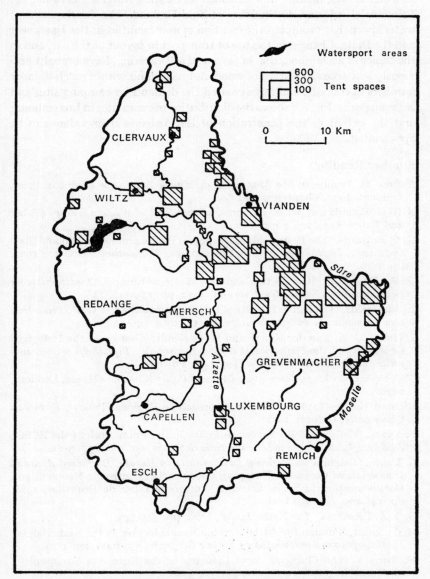

Fig. 4.8 The distribution of camp sites in Luxembourg in 1972

as water sports, making new demands on existing water areas round the Friesian Islands and on the lakes of Zuid-Holland. The development of water sports has prompted the creation of new facilities in the Ijsselmeer and the Delta. Changes in the use of transport in favour of the car, and in the choice of accommodation in favour of self-catering, have brought previously less accessible areas of wood and heathland within reach of large numbers of tourists, and have created the demand for camping sites and caravan parks. Fig. 4.8 shows the distribution of camp sites in Luxembourg and the extent of the penetration of the Ardenne river valley can be appreciated.

Further Reading

Audrey M. Lambert, *The Making of the Dutch Landscape* (Seminar Press, London), 1971, Chapters 7 and 8.

N. J. G. Pounds and W. N. Parker, *Coal and Steel in Western Europe* (Faber and Faber, London), 1957.

K. C. Edwards, 'The Historical Geography of the Luxembourg Iron and Steel Industry', *Institute of British Geographers, Transactions* No. 29, 1961, pp. 1-16.

G. A. Hoekveld, 'The Netherlands in Western Europe', *Tijdschrift voor Economische en Sociale Geografie*, 63, 1972, pp. 129-148.

J. Winsemius, 'The Dutch Industrial Development since the War', *Tijdschrift voor Economische en Sociale Geografie*, 54, 1963, pp. 52-58.

J. Hauer, G. A. Van der Knaap and M. de Smidt, 'Changes in the Industrial Geography of the Netherlands during the 1960's', *Tijdschrift voor Economische en Sociale Geografie*, 62, 1971, pp. 139-156.

Christopher Flockton, *Community Regional Policy* (Chatham House, London), 1970.

Richard Norton-Taylor, 'Flexible Approach to Regional Policy', *European Community*, October 1971.

F. Vinck, 'Methods of Reconversion Policy in the Framework of the ECSC', *Tijdschrift voor Economische en Sociale Geografie*, 60, 1969, pp. 3-11.

L. Davin, 'Belgium' in *Regional Disequilibria in Europe. Backward Areas in Industrialised Countries*, European Coordination Centre for Research and Documentation in Social Sciences, Université Libre de Bruxelles, 1968, pp. 141-209. (French text.)

G. J. A. Riesthuis, 'The Netherlands', *Ibid.*, pp. 325-349.

M. de Smidt, 'Foreign Industrial Establishments located in the Netherlands', *Tijdschrift voor Economische en Sociale Geografie*, 57, 1966, pp. 1-19.

K. Warren, 'The Changing Steel Industry of the European Community', *Economic Geography*, 45, 1969, pp. 314-332.

Audrey M. Lambert, 'Dutch Steelmaking: Past, Present and Future', *Geography*, 56, 1971, pp. 241-243.

E. Wever, 'Pernis-Botlek-Europoort. Un Complexe à Base de Pétrole', *Tijdschrift voor Economische en Sociale Geografie*, 57, 1966, pp. 131-140.

Chapter 5

TRANSPORT IN BENELUX

The economic development of the Benelux countries has to a large extent been dependent upon their ability to import materials and export the products of both factory and farm. The establishment of the Dutch *trafieken* and the Belgian industries processing colonial products was a result of efficient transport links as much as any other consideration, and the good use to which the rivers of the Low Countries were put at an early date materially affected the expansion of the Dutch and Belgian economies. The continuing importance of transport is evident both in the inclusion of the two major ports of Benelux, Rotterdam and Antwerp, in the growth areas of the Netherlands and Belgium, and in the increasing use of the Delta for industrial activity based on imported materials. That Rotterdam-Europoort is the largest port in the world is itself testimony to the importance of ocean transport in the Netherlands, and helps to explain why some 44 tons of goods per inhabitant were moved in Benelux in 1970, compared with 39 tons in West Germany and 34 tons in France.

Not all forms of transport are suited to the movement of passengers and goods over all distances. For example, although aircraft and trams are both used for passenger traffic, the former is a long-distance and the latter a short-distance method of transport. Since the characteristics of each form of transport are related to the distances over which it is employed, it is useful to examine transport on the basis of three scales of distance: the intercontinental, the intra-European and the urban or regional scales.

Transport at the intercontinental scale

At this scale the movement of passengers is restricted to air and sea transport, but during the last two decades competition between the two has been decided in favour of the former. Lacking the speed of the aircraft, passenger liners have been reduced in number and those remaining have increasingly been used to exploit an advantage they do possess over aircraft, that is, their value as mobile hotels. Regular trans-oceanic sailings have now been virtually abandoned by the Royal Netherlands Lloyd and Holland-Amerika companies, and Amsterdam, and to a lesser extent Rotterdam and Antwerp, have achieved some importance as international holiday cruise ports.

153

Air transport handles the greater part of intercontinental passenger movements to and from Benelux, and both Belgium and the Netherlands have acquired an importance in international air traffic out of proportion to their size. Both possess major international airports, at Schiphol, south of Amsterdam, and at Melsbroek, east of Brussels, which are respectively sixth and ninth busiest in the world in terms of international passengers handled. The problem of finding a suitable area within reasonable distance of the major conurbations for the location of an airport is acute in the densely settled Low Countries. Amsterdam was fortunate in that the reclaimed Haarlemmermeer polder was available for the construction of the centrally placed Schiphol airport, but Melsbroek had no such advantage. Both sites are in the process of expansion, but in neither has the problem of transport between airport and city centre been successfully resolved, although a railway line between The Hague and Amsterdam via Schiphol is expected to be operating by 1976. Both countries also possess major international airlines, Sabena in Belgium and KLM in the Netherlands, the latter being the oldest national airline in continuous operation. The size of the countries involved has precluded the development of a large home market for air transport, and part of the original impetus in both cases was the need for air routes to colonial territories. Their present position as international carriers is therefore maintained against fierce world competition.

Until very recently sea transport held a monopoly of intercontinental freight traffic. Chapter 6 will consider in detail the location, trade and hinterlands of the Benelux ports, but in general terms there have recently been three major interconnected changes in sea transport. The Benelux countries have been in the forefront of these changes, and have been profoundly affected by their results. Firstly, the realisation of the economies of scale in ship construction, movement and cargo handling has led to a growth in the size of vessel, with repercussions upon the growth of particular ports and on the magnitude and distribution of trade flows. Secondly, further economies have been reaped by the introduction of specialised ships, both in the dry and in the liquid bulk trades, giving rise to the need for specialised handling facilities. Finally, containerisation, with which could be included such techniques as palletisation, 'lighter-aboard-ship' (LASH) and roll-on/roll-off (RORO), has similarly affected both the direction and character of trade, and the nature and function of ports. These three trends have encouraged the emergence of a hierarchy of ports, ranging from the large specialised port such as Rotterdam-Europoort, to the small general cargo port such as Harlingen or Nieuwpoort, largely confined to the handling of transhipped cargoes for larger terminals.

The monopoly of long-distance sea transport has been modified in recent years by competition from air and land transport. Air freight has been growing in both Belgium and the Netherlands faster than the expansion in air transport generally, and the extension plan for Schiphol airport includes special handling facilities for what is regarded as an important future development. However, the relative costs of air and sea transport place severe limitations on the type of cargo carried. It is likely, therefore, that air freight will remain a small part of total freight movements, but useful in Benelux for products with a high value in relation to their weight, or those of a perishable nature. The movement of freight at the intercontinental scale may not always be the province of ocean and air transport, for negotiations are proceeding for the establishment of a Netherlands-Japan container route via the Trans-Siberian Railway, which compares favourably in time (35 days), but not cost per ton, with ocean transport.

Transport at the intra-European scale

(i) *Passenger transport* The competition for the carriage of passengers within Europe is principally between air, rail, road and North Sea/Channel ferry transport. Both Sabena and KLM maintain an intra-European network, but these are primarily feeder and distributor services for intercontinental flights rather than profitable enterprises in themselves. For distances below about 600 km, surface transport has shown itself capable of competing with air transport for the carriage of passengers on the basis of cost, and often even of time, except where short sea crossings intervene.

The development since 1955 of the Trans-European Express (TEE) network of fast passenger train services between the major West European cities has re-emphasised the positional advantages of the Low Countries. No less than 9 of the total 18 TEE services run through Benelux, and 7 terminate or originate there, with Brussels and Amsterdam being the third and fifth most well-served cities in this respect in Europe. The importance of the Rhine route as a means of access to Central and Southern Europe, and the use of Belgium for transit routes between Northern and South-Western date from the Middle Ages. Similarly, the Europabus long-distance coach service, financed by the larger European railways companies, makes good use of the central position of the Low Countries and maintains strong links with North Sea and Channel ferry ports and Eastern, Alpine and Mediterranean Europe. The TEE and Europabus networks are shown on Fig. 5.1.

The rapid rise in road passenger transport in Benelux is a result of the high level of private car ownership in all three countries. In addition the increasing use of the motor car for holiday travel has led to demands upon the Low Countries for transit facilities, in particular at the short sea

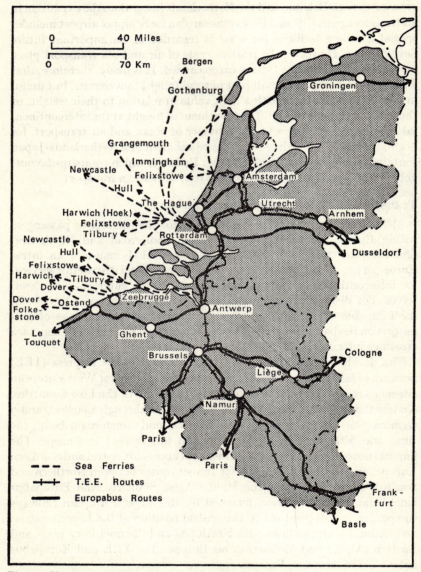

Fig. 5.1 Short-sea crossings, trans-Europe and express railway routes and Europabus services in Benelux

crossing ports. The designation of roads as E routes is an expression of this demand. For example the road improvements made as part of the Dutch Delta Plan together with the road over the *afsluitdijk* have enabled the E10 to link Scandinavia with the French, Belgian and Dutch North Sea and Channel ports. The E36 links the Rhineland motorway system of West Germany with the Dutch coast and the E5 provides a direct route from the Belgian coast to the Central Rhineland and Alpine Europe. In addition it must be remembered that increasing recreational demands and the high level of car ownership in neighbouring countries place large parts of Benelux within day-trip distance of many French and German cities. Thus in 1970 25 million foreign day-trippers made use of the Dutch road network. To accommodate these visitors, domestic car owners and the growth of freight haulage by road, a comprehensive motorway network is being built. The Netherlands has 28 km of motorway per 1 000 sq km, and is well ahead of the rest of Europe; Belgium with 16 km per 1 000 sq km is only marginally behind West Germany with 18 km. The Benelux motorway is shown in Fig. 5.2.

The configuration of the coastlines of Belgium and the Netherlands in relation to the other states of North-West Europe and the offshore island of Great Britain, makes the short sea crossing traffic over the North Sea and the Channel of importance to both countries (Fig. 5.1). The revenue earned from this traffic is a valuable invisible export, and the local tourist trade is greatly encouraged. Of the two countries Belgium lies in the most advantageous position, being on a direct line between the British Isles and Alpine Europe. In addition the narrowing of the North Sea southwards gives the Belgians an advantage over the Dutch, and the Dover-Ostend crossing, although approximately twice as long as the shortest Channel crossing, can also provide an alternative Great Britain-Mediterranean route, especially during the crowded summer months. A monopoly of the Ostend traffic is held by the state-owned Belgian Marine company. The growing pressure upon this route, caused by the steadily increasing tourist demand, led to the proposals by the private European Ferries firm for a new car ferry service. Local opposition at Ostend caused this to be located instead at Zeebrugge.

The Dutch are in a much less favourable position for exploiting the potential of the short sea crossing traffic. The additional distance between the Dutch and British coasts causes only through traffic from Britain to North Germany, Poland, the USSR and possibly Scandinavia to be routed through the Netherlands. Indeed the shortest route to much of the Southern Netherlands is via the Belgian rather than the Dutch ferry ports, and only fare agreements between the respective railway companies prevent this from being fully utilised.

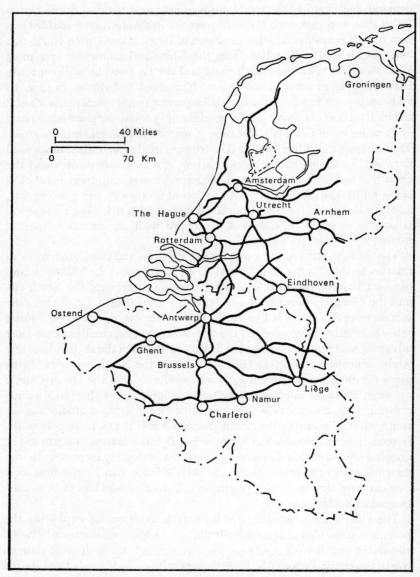

Fig. 5.2 The Benelux motorway network

The Dutch government-owned Zeeland Steamship Company, which until recently shared a near monopoly of the British traffic with British Railways, originally located its principal terminal at Vlissingen in Zeeland, thus minimising the length of the sea crossing. The length and difficulty of communication from this relatively isolated area to the cities of the West and Central Netherlands encouraged a move in the 1930s to the seaward end of the New Waterway at Hoek van Holland, where the bulk of this traffic is now handled. A substantial enlargement of this terminal with improved car-handling facilities is planned, and the new Rijnpoort, inland of Hoek, should be in operation by 1974. In recent years the position of the Netherlands in relation to the sea routes to the North of England, North Germany and Scandinavia has increasingly been realised, and ferry connections with Hull, Immingham and Gothenburg have been developed, occasionally with Amsterdam rather than Hoek as the Dutch terminal.

TABLE 5.1

Share of domestic freight traffic between transport media, 1971

	Road	Rail	Water
Belgium	44%	29%	27%
Netherlands	55%	7·5%	37·5%

(ii) *Freight transport* The growth in the carriage of passengers, especially passengers accompanying motor vehicles, over the North Sea should not conceal a similar growth in the short sea freight traffic. Roll-on/roll-off, trailer and container services are expanding between the English terminals at Harwich, Immingham and Hull and the Benelux ports, in particular Zeebrugge and Hoek/Europoort. In addition short sea crossing air services offer an alternative, if more expensive, service to both freight and passengers from Britain to Ostend and Zestienhoven (Rotterdam) for both scheduled and chartered aircraft.

In respect of freight traffic the dominant function of the domestic transport systems in Benelux at the intra-European scale is to connect the North Sea ports with a principally German and French industrial hinterland. Four transport media are employed for this purpose: road, rail, water and pipeline transport, and the way in which the first three share the movement of freight traffic within Belgium and the Netherlands is shown in Table 5.1. Perhaps the most distinctive feature of this breakdown within the context of Western Europe is the importance of water transport. In most countries, such as France where inland waterways carry only 10% of the freight traffic, water transport has been found to be too slow, and many of the canals too small, to remain an effective competitor with road and rail transport. The low-lying nature of the Netherlands and Northern Belgium and the presence of major river systems are conducive to the development of inland waterways. Many of the rivers have been canalised and some large canals, such as the Albert, Juliana and the Amsterdam-Rhine Canals, have been built in the recent past. In addition, some of the older canals, particularly in Belgium, have been, or are in the process of being modernised to allow the passage of 1 350-ton barges. The presence of the Ruhr and other West German industrial districts adjacent to the Rhine has substantially assisted the growth of water transport in the Netherlands, and more than half the total tonnage of the Rhine barge fleet operates under the Dutch flag. On the other hand, the absence of a direct link between Belgium and the Rhine helps to explain the smaller part waterways play in Belgium. Prior to the construction of trunk roads and the use of large lorries, water transport held an even larger share of goods traffic. In 1957, for example, waterways carried no less than 64% of all Dutch freight traffic.

Inland waterways have responded to the competition provided by other methods of transport by specialising in the carriage of bulky goods with a low value in relation to their weight, for example, sand, gravel, ores, coal and petroleum products. The development of oil and chemical pipelines, noted in the last chapter, has reduced the flow of oil along the Rhine and its distributaries, but inland waterways still represent an inexpensive method of supplying depots and tank farms. Economies of scale have been obtained by the introduction of push-boats which propel four 1 500-ton barges lashed together, enabling a load of 6 000 tons to be moved as a single unit. Radar is employed on the Rhine and associated waterways, allowing traffic to move at night. The most fundamental change has been the attempt to establish a comprehensive basic network capable of handling the standard EEC barge of 1 350 tons. In this way industrial areas and ports are linked by a system of barges whose capacity is large enough to justify very low freight rates, a critical issue in the case of materials of low value. The Neder Rijn, Lek, Waal and the lower Maas in the Netherlands have long been capable of accommodating 2 000-ton barges by virtue of the sheer size of these rivers, and the New Waterway and North Sea Canals are ship canals. The Belgian system, by contrast, has required much reconstruction to bring it to the necessary standard, but the basic network, comprising the Scheldt in the west, the Albert Canal and the Meuse in the east and the canals between Antwerp and Charleroi via Brussels in the centre, can now cope with 1 350 ton-barges. Of particular interest is the barge-lift installed at Ronquières on the Charleroi-Brussels Canal raising 1 350-ton barges 68 metres in tanks moving up an incline. The canalisation of the Mosel, completed in 1964, has been of considerable value to the Luxembourg iron and steel industry. Two major canals are projected: the Antwerp-Rhine or Benelux Canal which will link Antwerp with Rotterdam, and the Maas-Rhine Canal through Limburg. The former seems almost certain to be built, but the future of the latter is less sure. The Benelux 1 350-ton canal system is illustrated in Fig. 5.3.

The existence of a viable inland waterway network has limited the rôle of the railways for freight transport in both Belgium and the Netherlands, as Table 5.1 suggests. Only in Wallonie and in Luxembourg does the railway play an important rôle in supplying industry with sources of energy and raw materials, and in the distribution of products. With competition on the one hand from waterways and pipelines for bulk traffic, and from road haulage for smaller loads on the other, railways are struggling to maintain their share of traffic by such measures as the containerisation of cargoes, the use of unit trains hauling a single commodity to a single destination and the integration of facilities with other transport media, for example the running of 'piggy-back trains' in conjunction with motor-rail services.

The convenience of local collection and delivery by road has led to the steady growth in the proportion of intra-European trade being carried by road vehicles. The Dutch in particular have developed a profitable carrying trade by road within the EEC, and sharp clashes of policy have occurred between the Dutch, who at present handle over half of the total frontier-crossing road freight within the Community, and the Germans, among others, who wish to regulate such traffic for the benefit of their national road carriers, or other nationally owned transport media. The growth of the European trunk road network, the increasing realisation of the economies of larger vehicles and the simplification of frontier formalities under the *Transport International Routier* (TIR) regulations, are encouraging a further growth of this type of intra-European transport. At present the amount of freight carried by road is increasing by an annual 7% in the Netherlands and 6% in Belgium.

Transport at the urban scale

The movement of large numbers of people over short distances within city-regions, where space is limited and demand is concentrated into short periods of time, is best effected by underground railways, trams and buses. Unfortunately the use of these most efficient methods of urban transport is dropping sharply, a situation largely due to the increase in the private ownership of the motor car. In this respect an important difference within Benelux is noticeable. Belgium adopted the ideal of individual car ownership much earlier than the Netherlands which has

L

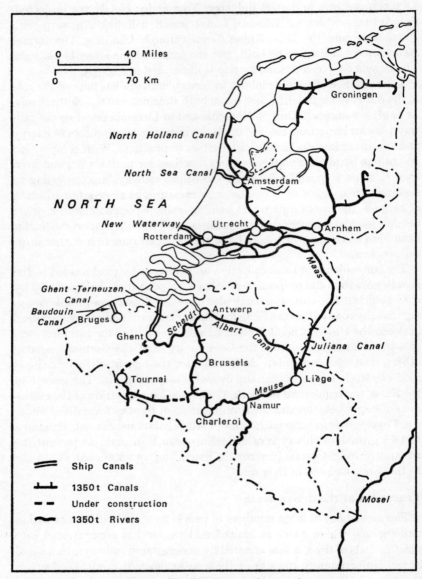

Fig. 5.3 The Benelux canal network

lagged behind the rest of Western Europe for many years. Much of Dutch physical planning, including the Second Structure Plan of 1966, was based on the assumption of low motor car ownership. The recent rapid increase in car ownership, however, appears to be raising the Netherlands towards parity with its neighbours and may pose a serious threat to the realisation of these plans. The policies available to the Benelux countries fall into three categories, although a combination of all three has been implemented in practice.

(i) *Making provision for the motor car* Redesigning Benelux cities for the increasing demands of the car has proved difficult. The morphology of many cities is medieval in origin with streets too narrow for modern roads, street plans ill-suited to dense vehicular flows and little land available for the provision of car parks. In addition many cities have an intricate network of waterways running around and through them, with a consequent channelling of traffic at narrow bridging points. Admittedly the maintenance of fortifications until relatively late into the modern period did allow land to be released upon their demolition for inner ring roads and parking spaces, as at Antwerp and Utrecht, but this was a fortuitous addition to space unlikely to be repeated. The provision of large road interchanges on the edge of the built-up areas, as for example the junction of the E10 and E5 outside The Hague, or the E3, E10 and E39 east of Antwerp, takes up valuable residential, agricultural and sometimes recreational land. It is increasingly evident, however, that further demands for land of this sort to accommodate additional increases in traffic cannot be allowed without endangering the urban-rural balance in the regions concerned. Much of the growth in motor car ownership in Britain and the United States has been associated with the creation of widespread suburban developments on the peripheries of urban centres. Such developments would threaten many of the basic tenets of urban planning in Benelux and encourage the coalescence of the urban areas of the Western Netherlands and Central Belgium into a single megalopolitan unit.

(ii) *Making provision for alternative individual transport* The Dutch tradition of cycling has been encouraged by both the prevailing gentle gradients and the relatively short distances within city-regions, and can be considered both a cause and an effect of the low level of car ownership. More recently the 'moped' has become an ubiquitous feature of both Dutch and Belgian towns, to some extent providing an alternative to the motor car in cities. The trend, however, is moving away from these alternatives, and although 10 million Dutchmen own 12 million cycles, fewer are actually used. This decline has been recognised by the planners and attempts have been made to counteract it by establishing separate bicycle circulation and parking systems within cities.

(iii) *The development of public transport* Much attention has been given in Benelux to the expansion of public transport as an alternative to the use of individual transport in cities. Urban tramways have been retained in many cities such as Brussels, Antwerp, Amsterdam, The Hague and Rotterdam, and they have been extensively modernised to form an integral part of the urban transport system. The savings in space and manpower obtained by the use of one-man operated, large, often articulated vehicles with a capacity of up to 300 passengers have been appreciated. Efficient working is maintained by operating on a reserved track as far as possible, as in the centre of Rotterdam, by traffic priority systems, and by extensive underground working, as in Brussels, where the system is known as the 'pre-metro'. Underground railways offer additional advantages of capacity and speed, but they need very large traffic flows to justify their costs of construction. The high density commuter traffic crossing the Maas in Rotterdam led to the opening of a short 6-km metro line in 1969, and this may later be extended to the growing residential suburbs south of the city. The Amsterdam tramways, which in 1970 carried some 260 million passengers, will be supplemented by an underground railway in 1974, and Brussels has a similar metro scheme at the planning stage.

Such rapid transit systems are, however, only economic to operate in the central areas of large cities. Smaller urban areas and the suburbs of the large cities must depend for public transport upon bus systems. The efficiency of these will in turn depend on the location of the route network and the ease of interchange between the different forms of transport. The solution adopted by Breda in Noord-Brabant, a town of 120 000 inhabitants, is a radial network of fixed-fare bus routes with a series of interchanges between buses and trains. There are also car parking facilities at some bus interchanges to encourage parking on the periphery. Amsterdam has chosen to use trams in the central area and buses in the suburbs where the flows are lighter. As Fig. 5.4 indicates, the principal interchanges between bus and tram routes are located about 4 km from the city centre. Some bus services do penetrate the city centre, and there is one tram route which extends to the outer suburb of Osdorp, where a large housing estate has been built, but these are exceptions to the general pattern.

Railways are important in the movement of passengers over distances between 20 and 100 km within the city region. In Belgium in particular relatively long-distance rail commuting has been encouraged by the policy of charging low fares. The Dutch 'inter-city' system links 40 of the principal urban areas with a fast, frequent service. Fig. 5.5 shows the pattern of railway commuting into the city of Utrecht and indicates the way in which future urban expansion will be accompanied by matching railway development. Both the Belgian and Dutch railways fail to make a commercial profit from the operation of these services, but the national governments appreciate the necessity for their retention and even extension. The Dutch 'inter-city' services link the separate nodes of the Dutch metropolitan area, and thus offer a direct alternative to the use of the motor car in the region of the greatest pressure on land. Over the period 1968-1975 Dutch railways expect to construct 6 new suburban lines, open 75 new suburban stations and to treble car parking facilities at stations in the Western Netherlands. It remains to be seen, however, whether the

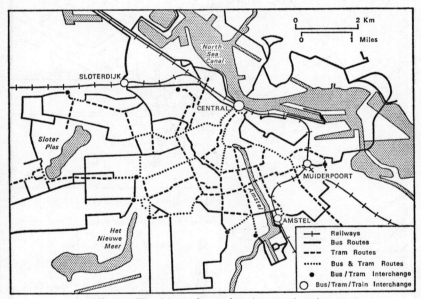

Fig. 5.4 The Amsterdam urban transport system

alternatives to the use of the private car in cities are sufficiently attractive to limit the increase in road traffic, which is capable of destroying the character of Benelux cities and of fundamentally altering the nature of the Benelux metropolitan regions.

European transport integration

The movement, albeit sporadic, of the EEC towards further economic integration, together with the forthcoming enlargement of the Community, are increasing the need for the integration of transport within Western Europe. This trend has a particular significance for Benelux because of its central position within the West European transport networks, and it was at the insistence of the Dutch that transport was specifically included in the Treaty of Rome, and that an 'action programme' for transport co-ordination was initiated in 1962.

The increasing standardisation of vehicles and equipment, especially for road, rail and inland waterway traffic, together with the adoption of a common legal framework for the movement of goods and passengers, will enable Benelux to extend its rôle as a carrier within and without the

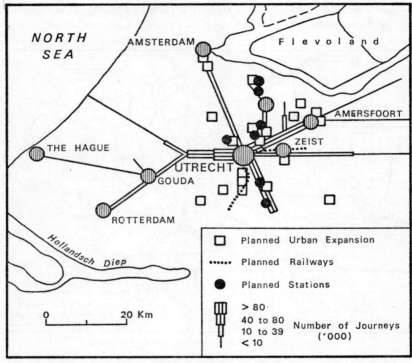

Fig. 5.5 Rail commuting in the Utrecht region in October 1969

EEC. In particular there are plans for the integration of freight services within the Community, which would include a European rail container system with three large terminals in Benelux, and a coordination of the EEC road freight and air freight networks. Licences for inter-state road freight are granted on a national quota system in accordance with the importance of member states in this traffic. The relatively large number of such licences granted to the Benelux countries, shown in Table 5.2, is an indication of their importance in this sphere and explains the concern of Benelux governments with this aspect of Community affairs.

Finally it is being increasingly realised that the problems of transport within the Benelux metropolitan region are not different from similar problems in other European cities. It is also evident that in many respects a single urban area is emerging in North-West Europe, and therefore a coordination of the transport policies of the Dutch and Belgian city regions with the Ruhr and the towns of Northern France is necessary.

TABLE 5.2

Interstate road freight licences, 1968

	Licence quota	Licences per million population
West Germany	286	5·2
France	286	5·9
Italy	194	4·0
Belgium	161	17·7
Netherlands	240	21·2
Luxembourg	33	110·0

Further Reading

Brian T. Bayliss, *European Transport* (Kenneth Mason, London), 1965.

G. L. Willemse, 'Netherlands Railways Reshape for the 1970's', *Modern Railways*, April 1969, pp. 205-207.

H. Kiestra, 'The Development of Commuting in the Western Part of the Netherlands, 1947-1960', *Tijdschrift voor Economische en Sociale Geografie*, 58, 1967, p. 67. Summary in English of an article in Dutch.

D. R. Parry, 'Public Transport and Commuting in the Utrecht Region', *The South Hampshire Geographer*, No. 4, 1971, pp. 7-13.

Nigel S. Despicht, *The Transport Policies of the European Communities*, (P.E.P., London), 1969.

Various authors, 'Transport and the EEC', *European Community*, January 1972, pp. 13-20.

Nigel Despicht, 'Transport', in Richard Mayne (Ed), *Europe Tomorrow*, (Fontana, London), 1972, pp. 164-202.

Chapter 6

THE PORTS OF BENELUX

Trade rather than the possession of raw materials was the basis of early Flemish and Dutch prosperity, and the establishment of great ports was part of the process by which this trade was effected. The development of an industrial economy in Western Europe in the 19th century greatly added to the international exchange of raw materials and goods, causing established ports to expand. Both Belgium and the Netherlands had colonial empires, Belgium was an important industrial nation and was involved in international trade on that count, and both countries were channels for the international commerce of adjacent industrial nations such as Germany, France and Luxembourg. The 20th century has witnessed great increases in the import of raw materials, and the greatest impact on the development of ports has been the switch from coal to oil as the basis of energy in Western Europe. This has been accompanied by the advent of the supertanker, vessels so large that only a few ports are now able to handle them.

It is more than a distinguished commercial tradition and a position on the coast of North-West Europe that have caused the Low Countries to possess in Rotterdam-Europoort the largest port in the world, and in Antwerp the second largest port in Western Europe. Site considerations have proved to be increasingly critical as the size of ships has increased, and both Rotterdam and Antwerp have been able to capitalise on their sites on two of Western Europe's major rivers, the Rhine and the Scheldt respectively. Amsterdam, facing the shallow Zuider Zee which was restricted to small craft after the construction of the *afsluitdijk*, does not enjoy similar site advantages, and has not been able to develop at the same speed. It must be emphasised, however, that it is rare for the advantages bestowed by nature to be sufficient in themselves, and much ingenuity has had to be exercised to adapt the physical environment to the changing needs of port complexes. Thus of the five largest Benelux ports, three (Rotterdam, Amsterdam and Ghent) are entirely dependent on canals for access to the sea, in three cases (Amsterdam, Ghent and Zeebrugge) shipping has to negotiate lock gates, and only Antwerp has unimpeded access to the sea. Recently, however, even the Scheldt has been found too shallow and sinuous for modern shipping, and since 1967

168

the largest vessels using the port pass through a canal joining the Scheldt near the Dutch frontier at Zandvliet. A further important physical consideration is the use to which rivers can be put in establishing connections with the hinterland of a port. The Scheldt is of small significance in this respect, but the Rhine links Rotterdam with the Ruhr, the towns of the middle Rhineland and with Switzerland. The less direct waterway links between Amsterdam and the Rhine is one of the reasons for its slow growth relative to that of Rotterdam.

No less than other towns, ports make an important contribution to the regional economy, and as such are part of national planning policies. Thus the Amsterdam port authorities argue that they receive insufficient support from the Dutch government which prefers to develop Rotterdam. In Belgium the cultural problem must be considered, for investment in Antwerp is closely watched by the Walloons who are anxious to develop Charleroi and Liège rather than the Flemish port. Rivalries between ports has existed for centuries, and ports may receive the support of governments. In the inter-war years the Belgian and Dutch governments backed measures, such as discriminatory railway freight rates, introduced to attract traffic to their own ports. The inauguration of the EEC has helped to reduce the competition between the Dutch and Belgian ports, and there are indications that it may be possible to develop the ports of the Rhine-Scheldt estuary based on a single, rather than two, nationally biased plans.

In this chapter the major ports are considered in turn, but certain common themes can be distinguished. In the face of the use of increasingly large ships, new docks have been constructed seaward of the old port. These new harbours form a linear strip along the ship canal which characteristically in Benelux links the port with deepwater, and extend beyond the suburbs of the port. Europoort-Rotterdam has come to link a series of towns between the North Sea and Rotterdam, 25 km to the east. Since the Second World War, the principal Benelux ports have not merely been expanded as transshipment points, but also as industrial complexes based on oil refining, chemical and petrochemical production. At the same time crude oil has come to be the leading commodity handled. We now turn to the examination of the three large ports in the chronological order of their growth. A brief consideration of the minor ports is made, and a final synthesis looks at the future of the Benelux ports.

6.1 THE PORT OF ANTWERP

The establishment of Antwerp on the right bank of the Scheldt some 88 km from the sea was a result of a combination of factors. The place-name itself, derived from '*aan der werfen*' (at the wharves), testifies to the original function of the settlement, the site of which provided suitably firm land for the construction of quays, and which was sufficiently far from the sea to offer sheltered moorings. At this point the river was narrow enough for early traffic to be controlled by Steen castle, built by the legendary Brabo the Giant, who obtained revenue by levying tolls on shipping. The sailing ship was the most efficient method of transport in medieval times, and a port sited some distance inland was attractive because onward, costly land haulage was reduced. The depth of the channel was not especially important in the era of sail, and until the appearance of the supertanker in the early 1960s the 12.20 metres of water available at high tide was sufficient for the largest vessels. Even at low tide there is an 8-metre channel, and the resulting amplitude of 4 metres is quite sufficient to set up a tidal scour which keeps the channel clear. Below Antwerp there are shoals caused by the slackening of the speed of the river, reducing the minimum depth to 5 metres at low tide. However, in 1894 training walls were set up to increase the scouring effect, and a depth of 6·50 metres is now ensured at low tide.

Expansion of the docks and composition of traffic

Such were the outstanding physical advantages of the port that Napoleon ordered that the port be reopened to navigation in 1803. New quays were constructed and two non-tidal basins, Bonaparte and Willem, were opened to the north of the city walls in 1811 and 1813 respectively. The two docks were strategic creations and from an economic standpoint they were premature. It was not until the founding of the Belgian state in 1830, giving rise to the need for a national port, and the opening up of the Walloon coalfield, that further dock expansion could be justified. Between 1860 and 1873 four docks, Kattendijk, Hout, Kempisch and Asia, were opened, and trade was assisted by the purchase from the Dutch in 1863 of the right to levy tolls on shipping using the Scheldt, and by the establishment of a colonial empire in Africa. Two docks, Lefèbvre and Amerika, were completed in 1887, but the first of the large-scale docks was Albert (1914), which was linked to Leopold and Hansa, and in turn the Scheldt 10 km below the city in 1928. Four years later No. 4 dock to the south of Leopold Dock was completed. Apart from the two small barge docks constructed in association with the Albert Canal, opened in 1940, subsequent expansion has been on an impressive scale, and work has proceeded virtually continuously since the end of the Second World War. Petroleum Dock (1951) and No. 5 Dock (1960) were dug from the remaining land between Hansa Dock and the Scheldt, implying that further expansion would have to be downstream. This was the basis of the tenyear plan, 1956-1966, which envisaged a 10-km-long Kanaal Dock running parallel to the Scheldt from the entrance of Petroleum Dock to locks at

Zandvliet to the north. Two new docks were to be constructed at the southern end of the canal, and one of these, Churchill Dock, was to be a specialist container dock. The scheme was completed in 1967 with the opening of the Zandvliet locks which are capable of handling 65 000-ton tankers. The whole project doubled the port area, which now covers 10 000 ha, increased the length of quays from 59 to 95 km and cost £88 millions. The extent to which the port has been extended in a north-westerly direction is evident in Fig. 6.1.

In line with this extensive programme of dock building, the tonnage of goods handled by the port has steadily increased during the last three decades. From a total of 34 million tons in 1938, the tonnage handled rose to 81 million in 1970 and even though traffic fell off to 67 million tons in 1972 the figure emphasises Antwerp's position as the main Belgian port, for the next largest port, Ghent, handled only 13 million tons. For many years imports and exports were almost precisely balanced, reflecting the importance of Belgium as an exporter of manufactured and semi-finshed goods. During the 1960s, however, imports have come to predominate over exports, accounting for two-thirds of the total traffic, as the sheer volume of bulk commodities such as oil and ores have steadily risen. Since 1951 crude oil has been the leading commodity, and in 1972 accounted for almost half of the total tonnage of imports, a situation common to many other ports in North-West Europe capable of accommodating the larger oil tankers. Since the opening of the 20-million-ton capacity pipeline from Rotterdam in 1971, however, crude oil imports have declined causing the fall in traffic experienced since 1970 and it is likely that the share of oil in the traffic of the port will continue to dwindle in favour of Rotterdam, where tankers of 250 000 tons can berth. Ores, timber, grain and 'colonial' produce make up much of the remaining imports.

The most important item of export is metal goods; about 60% of the total export traffic in steel products loaded in continental North Sea ports passes through Antwerp. The strength of the Belgian and Luxembourg iron and steel industry in relation to domestic demand has resulted in a strong export trade. Since Antwerp is closer than any national port for many French and West German steelmakers, the specialist handling facilities and frequent sailings make the port very attractive. The multi-plicity of destinations served is also conducive to the use of the port by other general cargo shippers. A wide range of manufactured goods, in-cluding chemicals, plastics, petroleum products, glass and textiles, accounts for most other exports. In spite of the greater volume of traffic at Rotterdam, Antwerp was the leading general cargo port in Western Europe until 1967, when it was superseded by Rotterdam. The port has an excellent record of labour relations, and a 1970 report on productivity

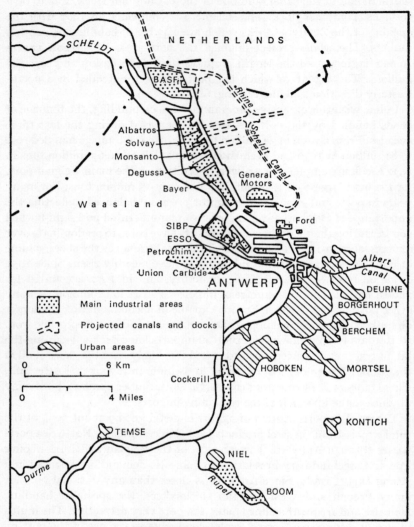

Fig. 6.1 The port of Antwerp

found that a gang of Antwerp dockers could move 24·8 tons per hour, compared with 18·4 tons at Dunkirk and 14·8 tons at Rotterdam. General cargo carries a higher revenue per ton than oil and other bulk goods, and this goes some way to offset the inability of the port to handle really large vessels. The speed with which the Churchill container dock was brought into operation, coupled with the initial problems faced by London's container dock at Tilbury, have made Antwerp the West European base for many container shippers. Fortunately container vessels are normally less than 30 000 tons, and their size presents no problem.

Links with the hinterland

In contrast to Rotterdam, the hinterland of Antwerp is more national than international. This is not entirely surprising in the light of the attenuated nature of the Scheldt compared with the Rhine. The centrality of Antwerp within Flanders and Brabant in the 16th century depended essentially upon the ease with which traffic could be channelled along the Scheldt and its tributaries, the Leie, Senne and Dender. The central position of the modern port within Belgium has been developed largely by means of a canal network which has only weak links with France and the Netherlands, and none at all with West Germany. National self-interest has contributed to this isolationist position, for proposals by the Dutch to improve the Maas in the border area between the two countries were rejected by the Belgians in the 1930s on the grounds that Rotterdam would be the principal beneficiary. The Dutch reacted by building the Juliana Canal along the eastern bank of the river within their own territory, completing the work in 1936. The Belgians linked Antwerp with the Meuse by means of the Albert Canal, leaving the small capacity lock on the old Liège-Maastricht canal at Lanaye as an effective barrier to international movement.

Slightly more than half the goods moved through the port in 1970 were carried by barge, and improvements have been made to many of the waterways, such as the Scheldt itself, the Antwerp-Brussels and the Charleroi-Brussels Canals, enabling them to take 1 350-ton barges. The most important waterway, however, is the Albert Canal, capable of handling 2 000-ton barges, and carrying one-third of all freight moved on Belgian inland waterways. When it is completed, the 2 000-ton Antwerp-Rhine Canal (Figs. 6.1 and 6.4) will allow the port to increase its share of West German river traffic, which is at present limited because of the navigational hazards presented by the Wester Schelde (the Scheldt estuary) in gaining access to the Zuid-Beveland Canal. The Belgians have long been negotiating for this canal, most of which lies in the Netherlands, and which clearly will take some traffic formerly handled by Dutch ports, but agreement had to wait upon the more cooperative climate of the 1960s. When it is opened the Belgians will cease the payment of 'Rhine premiums' to traffic using the old route, and they will be required to supply a quantity of fresh water equal to the volume of salt water passing from the Scheldt into the fresh-water Delta. This water will come from Wallonie and benefit Antwerp, a decision ratified after the inevitable squabble.

Railways play a more active rôle in linking the port with its hinterland than they do in the other Benelux ports, and over 1 200 km of track exist within the harbour area. The importance of this method of transport is a direct result of the poor international connections forged by the waterway network, obliging freight to and from areas outside Belgium to move by rail. In 1970 one-fifth of the total freight entered or left the port by rail, a figure which has doubled since 1958, and extensive marshalling yards have been installed in the new harbour areas. Road traffic has also increased in importance and two Euroroutes intersect here, the Paris-Rotterdam (E10) and the Lisbon-Stockholm (E3). The completion of the six-lane Kennedy tunnel under the Scheldt has alleviated one of the major Belgian road bottlenecks, and has greatly increased the centrality of the port within the European road network. One-tenth of the port's freight was moved by road in 1970.

The industry of the port

The emergence of Antwerp as a major industrial region during the last two decades is a result of two principal factors. Firstly, bulk commodities have a low value per ton and by processing such imports at the dockside their value is raised prior to onwards transmission. The growth of oil refineries and chemical plants at ports is a direct result of this. Secondly, the port has a particularly favourable economic environment. The efficiency of the Antwerp docker has been mentioned, the port and municipal authorities have made the harbour area attractive by tax exemptions, special interest rates and the offer of freehold land, and firms benefit from the existence of modern port equipment and from the existence of many other firms in the locality. One specific advantage Antwerp has over the Dutch ports is the low level of public awareness of atmospheric pollution. In 1969 the French chemical firm Progil was refused permission to set up in Amsterdam on environmental grounds, but was welcomed by Antwerp despite protests from Dutch villagers close to the plant.

Until the 20th century, industry in the port was associated with the colonial trade. Sugar refining, flour milling, biscuit and chocolate manufacture, tobacco production and the processing of vegetable oils into soap and margarine are located in the ring of suburbs just beyond the 19th century walls between Hoboken in the south and Merksem in the north. To this list should be added the cutting and mounting of diamonds, in which trade Antwerp now surpasses Amsterdam. The industry is localised in the old Jewish quarter of the city, De Pelikaan.

The recently established industry, on the other hand, is space-extensive and clusters in the harbour area, covering a huge area between the old docks and the Dutch frontier. Oil refining, the basic activity, is represented by five plants, only one of which, the International Oil Refinery with an annual capacity of 1·7 million tons, is sited to the south of the city. From south to north the others are: Raffinerie Belge des Pétroles (5 million tons per annum), Esso (4·7 million tons), SIBP (15·5 million tons) and Albatross (2·7 million tons), opened in 1968. These refineries supply materials for the petrochemical industry whose largest representatives are Petrochim and Union Carbide. Both these plants are outside the dock area on the west bank of the Scheldt for they receive their feedstock by pipe and have a more flexible site requirement than the oil refineries. There are five smaller petrochemical plants in the harbour area. The third sector in this great upsurge of economic activity is the chemical industry. There are five important, internationally owned plants, the largest of which, BASF, has a 455-ha site between the Zandvliet locks and the Dutch frontier, a site almost twice the size of the next largest in the port area. Other large concerns in the chemical sector include Bayer, Degussa, Monsanto and Solvay. Although not such an extravagant consumer of land, the engineering industry is a large employer of labour in the port area. The leading factories are the General Motors assembly and the Ford tractor plants, emphasising the point that the port has been successful in attracting a range of growth industries to its fold. During the 10-year expansion programme, private investment, mostly foreign, reached £900 millions and there are signs that there is more to come. Older established industries such as shipbuilding and ship repair and non-ferrous metal refining are located upstream at Hoboken and Temse. The diversity of Antwerp's industrial production contrasts strongly with that of Rotterdam whose dependence on oil refining and chemicals is more marked. The functions which in the Netherlands are divided between Rotterdam and Amsterdam are combined in Belgium in the single port of Antwerp.

The future expansion of the port

There is no shortage of firms wishing to establish themselves in Antwerp, and the Belgians are equally anxious to accommodate them. There are, however, several problems attached to further expansion. The first is that land on the eastern bank of the Scheldt is exhausted, and for the 7 000 ha of land on the opposite bank to be fully exploited, a dock building programme will have to be initiated. It is in fact planned to construct a dock system with access to the Wester Schelde by means of a ship canal passing through Dutch territory with sea locks at Baalhoek in Zeeuws-Vlaanderen. These locks will be capable of handling 125 000-ton vessels, but not supertankers. Despite protracted negotiations no agreement had been reached by 1970, and the Belgians went ahead with a smaller, 80 000-ton lock at Kallo, downstream of the Petrochim plant. The second difficulty is the navigational hazard of the shoals and the sharp bend in the estuary at Bath in Dutch waters. The removal of the 'Bath bend' is proposed by the construction of a ship canal west of the river, enabling ships to by-pass the 'bend', and making the port accessible to larger ships than at present. Thirdly, it is clear that the cost of dredging and other works necessary to allow supertankers access to the port is unjustifiable. It is therefore accepted that oil from these vessels will have to come via the pipeline from Rotterdam, and that although the tonnage of oil handled by the port may decline, oil refinery capacity can continue to increase. Should the Belgians cooperate in the development of the Dutch Delta, it may prove possible to expand Antwerp downstream on both banks of the river within the Netherlands. The economic and political climate of the EEC makes cooperation more realistic than competition, and the development of a truly international port is an exciting prospect.

6.2   THE PORT OF AMSTERDAM

The original settlement of Amsterdam sprang from the need for a transhipment point between inland and sea transport following the construction of a dam across the lower reaches of the River Amstel which flows into the Ij. Unlike Antwerp, whose site was obviously suitable for shipping, there was nothing to distinguish the port of Amsterdam from a score of other small ports, such as Edam and Medemblik, fringing the Zuider Zee, until the 16th century. The growth of the port depended more on human endeavour than on suitable site considerations. Many other ports in the locality benefited from the sheltered waters of the Zuider Zee, and from the navigational problems set by the sandbanks of the Rhine delts, plaguing such ports as Dordrecht. It was the position of the city in the United Provinces and the amazing rise in the commercial fortunes of the Dutch in the 16th and 17th centuries, coupled with the closure of the Scheldt in 1585 to blight the prospects of Antwerp, that gave rise to the growth of the port.

The first quays were built on the south bank of the Ij between the dam and the Zuider Zee in the quarter known as Zeedijk. The accumulation of sands and clays, however, began to cause problems in the 18th century, making navigation hazardous and limiting the draught of vessels. This was partly alleviated by unloading some cargo off Texel at the entrance to the Zuider Zee, or by using camels or pontoons to raise vessels above the level of the sea bed. The cost and delay occasioned by this solution, and the increasing size of vessel, prompted the construction of the North Holland Canal between Amsterdam and Den Helder between 1818 and 1825. The canal did not allow ships drawing more than 5 metres of water to reach Amsterdam, and since it was 80 km in length, it was no quicker than the circuitous route through the Zuider Zee. The northerly line pursued by the canal was necessitated by the inability of contemporary engineers to devise a method of safely breaching the coastal sand dunes. These technical problems were later overcome and the North Sea Canal was opened in 1876. This ship canal was of substantial dimensions, having a width of 125 metres and a depth of 9·6 metres, sufficient for the new iron-hulled steamships to reach Amsterdam. Successively enlarged to its present depth of 15 metres and width of 235 metres, the canal has locks at the seaward entrance at Ijmuiden capable of accommodating ships of 85 000 tons. The Oranje locks at the eastern extremity seal the Ij from the Ijsselmeer, although vessels using this entrance are restricted to 2 000 tons by the capacity of the *afsluitdijk* locks. Thus in 1876 Amsterdam turned its back on the Zuider Zee and became a North Sea port in spite of its poor location. Antwerp had a much better site, but it was not linked to the Rhine, as was Amsterdam by the Merwede Canal, completed in 1812.

Port industry in the 19th century was not the voracious consumer of land that it is today, and this change of direction in approach to the port did not result in a shift in the centre of gravity. Quays and warehouses were built on the south side of the Ij estuary to the west of the Oranje locks, and it was not until the inter-war period that there was substantial expansion along the Ij, west of the original dam. This development, which included the Petroleumhaven, has been continued since the Second World War in Westhaven and Amerikahaven, approximately half-way between the Oranje locks and Ijmuiden. The northern bank of the Ij has never been the scene of large-scale wharf-building, and is used by industrial premises, some of whom have their own quays. Reference to Fig. 6.2 shows that the projected expansion of the port envisages an extension of quay space on the south bank of the ship canal. South bank sites have much easier access to centres of population in the Western Netherlands, but nevertheless the 1970 development plan considers that land north of the canal will have to be brought into use in the 1980s. Inevitably the Amsterdam harbour area will reach Ijmuiden and Velsen, and the port will have become a linear strip between the Ijsselmeer and the North Sea. In its dependence on a canal incapable of dealing with the largest vessels afloat, Amsterdam is similar to Antwerp, but if it chooses, Amsterdam can expand the outer harbour at Ijmuiden to provide a deep-sea port unhindered by the depth and width resistrictions of locks and canals. Such a development would

M

prove particularly attractive to expensive container vessels which require a fast turn-round to justify their existence, and it would have an advantage over Antwerp's Churchill Dock for this traffic.

The composition of traffic and links with the hinterland

Although the volume of traffic handled by Amsterdam has steadily risen from 14 million tons in 1956 to a 1969 total of 29 million tons, its share of the total Dutch trade has gradually diminished because of the much more rapid growth of Rotterdam. Like most of the North Sea ports, Amsterdam is primarily concerned with imports, which represent three-

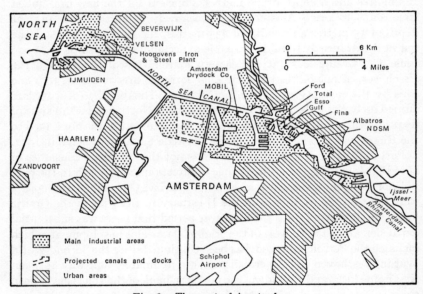

Fig. 6.2 The port of Amsterdam

quarters of all goods handled. However, Amsterdam differs from the great majority of West European ports, especially Rotterdam, in that the largest items of freight are mineral ores and scrap metals, which together account for a third of total imports. There are two reasons for this. Firstly, Amsterdam has but one medium-sized oil refinery with a capacity of 4 million tons a year, and even this was not opened until 1968. The inability of the port to accept supertankers, and the short distance separating the port from Rotterdam have caused the Mobil plant to be fed by pipeline from this port. Consequently crude oil imports, so important at Antwerp and Rotterdam, are insignificant. Secondly, the Hoogovens iron and steel-works at Velsen is fed exclusively by foreign ores and receives substantial scrap supplies by sea. Neither Antwerp nor Rotterdam possesses a similar plant, although both import ores and scrap for onward transmission. After mineral ores and scrap, the most important imports are agricultural produce and fuels. Outgoing cargoes are principally processed foodstuffs and metal and chemical products.

A disturbing feature of port trade during the last half decade has been the absence of growth in general cargo and container traffic. The Amsterdam container berth in Westhaven was the first to be built in the Netherlands in 1966, but competition from Rotterdam, Antwerp and Zeebrugge has been severe. In 1969 Amsterdam handled 198 000 tons of container goods, but the figures for Antwerp and Rotterdam were 1 196 000 and 2 043 000 tons respectively. Several shipping lines, including Container Marine Lines, which was the first company to use the Westhaven terminal, have left the port, and it seems likely that the operators who remain may begin to suffer from diseconomies of scale. In contrast to the difficulties besetting general cargo traffic has been the growth of passenger traffic. The building of a new passenger terminal has encouraged short sea crossing routes to England, Scandinavia and Northern Germany, and has placed Amsterdam on a major cruise circuit in Northern Europe. The attractions of a leading European tourist city, together with the facilities at the new terminal, compensate for the passage through the Ijmuiden locks and the North Sea Canal. The seaborne passenger trade of the port increased from 24 000 in 1962 to 153 000 in 1970.

The hinterland of Amsterdam is more restricted than the other two major Benelux ports, and this is an important factor in its slow growth. Compared with Rotterdam and its largely West German hinterland, Amsterdam can be considered as a Dutch rather than an international port. Until 1952 when the 2 000-ton capacity Amsterdam-Rhine Canal opened, giving a direct link with the Waal at Tiel, the port had to rely upon the decrepit Merwede canal for links with the Rhine-Ruhr industrial region, and it is not surprising that Rotterdam took most of the trade. The new canal has helped to secure some of the Rhine traffic, but although it is to be enlarged to accept the largest push-barge convoys by 1974, it is no substitute for the more direct Rhine link possessed by Rotterdam. The latter port has built up such an enormous lead, and such are the external economies stemming from the very wide range of services offered, that it will be very difficult for Amsterdam to capture much traffic from its rival.

The greater part of Amsterdam's trade originates in, or is destined for locations in Northern and Central Netherlands. Inland waterways have always been the principal means of distribution both to the west and south via the Haarlemmermeer ring canal and the Rijn-Schie Canal, and to the east and north-east via the Ijsselmeer. The advent of the railway contributed little to the extension of the hinterland of the port, and although the road over the *afsluitdijk* and the Amsterdam-Kampen road over the new Flevoland polders have improved access to the northern and eastern provinces, they have served to emphasise the port's national rather than international significance.

The industry of the port

As the headquarters of both the East and West India Companies, Amsterdam became the site of colonial product processing industries, and such activities as chocolate and soap making, tobacco processing, sugar refining, timber milling and diamond cutting became important. As in Antwerp these industries are associated with the older parts of the city, although the principal sawmills are adjacent to the timber wharves and storage areas of Houthaven to the west of the city. The shipbuilding, ship repair and marine engineering industries are well represented in the port, and they present an excellent example of areal specialisation for they are clustered on the north bank of the Ij between Zaandam and the Oranje locks. The largest shipyards are Nederlandse Dok en Scheepsbouw (NDSM) and Amsterdamse Droogdok, which also has a yard west of Westhaven, and the marine engineering firms of Stork and Werkspoor have achieved international renown with their diesel engines. Other engineering plants include Ford at Hembrug on the North Sea Canal, Fiat at Diemen, the Fokker aircraft company at Schiphol airport to the south, and railway engineering at Haarlem and Beverwijk. The Mobil oil refinery is located at Amerikahaven, but unusually it is not associated with a petrochemical complex. Both Mobil and the port authorities had expected the appearance of this industry, as had occurred at Antwerp and Rotterdam, but they were disappointed. Now it seems that Amsterdammers have become so pollution conscious that the petrochemical industry may never develop at all. The case of the Progil company, which chose Westhaven but which eventually established itself at Antwerp, has already been cited. The references to Total, Esso, Gulf and Fina in Fig. 6.2 refer to tankfarms rather than manufacturing plants. The chemical industry does exist in the port, but the plants are generally small; one medium-sized works, the Albatros superphosphate plant, is shown in Fig. 6.2. The largest single plant is the Hoogovens iron and steel plant at the western end of the canal. It is responsible for the importance of iron ore, coal, scrap iron, coke-oven by-products and finished steel in the traffic of the port. Its presence at the seaward end of the canal emphasises the value of sites adjacent to tidewater, and the characteristic manner in which many Benelux ports are developing along the line of ship canals.

Even before the construction of the North Sea Canal it was impossible to consider Amsterdam other than as part of a larger port complex. In particular the series of small ports and industrial towns stretching up the River Zaan to the north-west must be included. Since the building of Ijmuiden in the 1890s, the relationship between Amsterdam, Ijmuiden, Haarlem and the small industrial towns of Velsen and Beverwijk has become progressively more intimate until it is reasonable to conceive of a single port of Ijmond rather than a number of discrete centres. No political recognition of this emerging form is as yet forthcoming, and no plan for the integrated development of an Ijmond with its 1·5 million inhabitants has been mooted.

6.3 THE PORT OF ROTTERDAM

A large number of ports existed among the shifting distributaries of the Rhine-Maas-Scheldt delta from the middle of the 13th century, all of which had local functions as fishing and commercial ports for the Central Netherlands. Among these was Rotterdam, established at a dam at the mouth of the small River Rotte, first mentioned in 1283. The decline in prosperity of the ports of Flanders in the 15th century, and the eclipse of Antwerp in the 16th century, led to the growth in importance of the delta ports, as the centres of entrepôt activity migrated northwards from the Spanish-occupied Southern Netherlands. Even during this period of growth, however, it was Dordrecht rather than Rotterdam which was the foremost southern port serving the province of Holland.

The disadvantage of the location of Rotterdam in relation to the sea became critical during the latter half of the 18th and first half of the 19th centuries. The direct distance between the town and the sand dune coast is only 30 km, but it could rise to a travelled distance of 150 km through the continually shifting channels of the delta, and in the 1820s it sometimes took 32 days to reach the North Sea. The cutting of the Voornsche Canal in 1829 was an attempt to create a more direct route via the Haringvliet estuary, but soon after completion it was incapable of accommodating the largest ocean-going vessels. A solution to this progressive strangulation of the port was proposed by Pieter Caland in 1866. This involved a direct cut through the dunes to the sea, using the 1·75-metre tidal range at Hoek to help scour this open waterway. Completed in 1872 and deepened in 1885, this New Waterway, which can today take ships of 17-metre draught or 150 000 tons and whose western section can handle 250 000 ton ships, is the basis of the modern port of Rotterdam. The New Waterway enabled Rotterdam to exploit its position at the mouth of the Rhine at the time when the industrial expansion of the Ruhr necessitated an outlet to the North Sea. Even after the completion of the Dortmund-Ems Canal in 1899, Rotterdam was still 80 km nearer by barge to Duisburg than was

Emden. In addition the superior width and depth of the Rhine allowed the use of larger barges, and shipment costs were proportionately lower. High-grade ores, mine props, grain and general cargoes were imported for the Ruhr in exchange for coal and steel products. The port rapidly became a transit point for the Ruhr, and even in the 1930s, when the Netherlands herself was industrialising, three-quarters of the goods handled by the port originated in, or were destined for the Ruhr.

The expansion of the port and the composition of its traffic

As in the case of Antwerp and Amsterdam, the direction of the expansion of the port has been towards the open sea, in this case along the line of

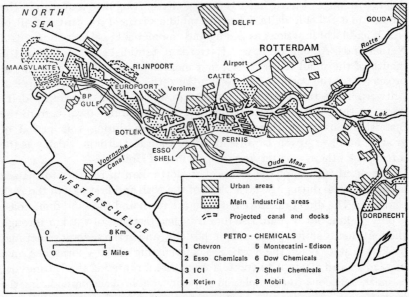

Fig. 6.3 The port of Rotterdam. Oil refineries are named in capital letters

the New Waterway (Fig. 6.3). The ease with which the land to seaward of the port can be excavated has been a major factor in its expansion, and such areas as the island of Rozenburg, with a relatively sparse population engaged in arable farming, have been transformed into docks and industrial complexes within a decade. The extension of the port towards the sea has not, however, caused the port authorities to cease the construction of docks once the sea has been reached, for the shallow offshore waters of Maasvlakte (the Maas-flats) have been reclaimed, and the westward march of the port has continued.

The oldest set of docks is located in the historic core of the city, between the cathedral, town hall and stock exchange, and is fed by the Rotte itself. These docks, called Leuvehaven, are now used exclusively by barge traffic, and have a capacity of 40% of the total international Rhine barge fleet. Expansion on to the south bank of the Maas occurred between 1878-1879 when the Binnenhaven was constructed on the seaward side of the Maas bridge. This is used for general merchandise. The rapid growth of trade in the last quarter of the 19th century, consequent upon the increasing demands of the Ruhr, is reflected in the construction of a succession of docks on both banks dating from this period: Rijnhaven (1894), Maashaven (1905), Waalhaven (1909), Isselhaven (1910) and Lekhaven (1913). Waalhaven and Merwehaven were completed in 1931 and 1932 respectively. The latter, now converted to container traffic, was the last substantial dock development possible on the north bank at Rotterdam owing to the presence of the towns of Schiedam, Vlaardingen and Maasluis. Subsequent expansion has occurred on the south bank on the islands of Ijsselmonde and Rozenburg. The first of the petroleum harbours that today are such an important part of the port was built in 1929 at Pernis, on Ijsselmonde, and the first refinery was opened here by Shell in 1936.

The Second World War left Rotterdam with one-third of its quays destroyed and much of its pre-war trade lost. Plans for post-war Rotterdam included a second petroleum harbour, which with remarkable foresight was constructed to accommodate 65 000-ton tankers although ships of this size did not then exist, with 1 500 ha available for the erection of refineries. This was established at Botlek on Rozenburg between 1950 and 1959. The economic prosperity of Western Europe over the last two decades, and the capitalisation by the port of its position in relation to the trade of the EEC, prompted the most ambitious expansion project in the history of the port. The specific impetus for the Europoort scheme, embarked upon in 1958, came from the decision by a group of oil companies to build a crude oil pipeline to the Ruhr, and to import the oil in 90 000-ton tankers which were above the capacity of Botlek to handle. Botlek could have been improved to deal with these ships, but since most of the industrial sites had already been leased, the port chose to develop 3 750 ha on the western part of Rozenburg. The harbour and approaches were dredged to take 100 000-ton tankers, but the increase in size of these ships began to accelerate in the 1960s at a truly remarkable speed, and in 1966 it was decided to deepen Europoort for 250 000-ton vessels, drawing 19 metres of water. This meant that an 11-km channel had to be dredged in the North Sea to allow these huge ships access to the New Waterway. The entrance to the latter is guarded by two breakwaters, and the area between the southern breakwater and the shore—Maasvlakte—is being reclaimed to provide an additional 2 100 ha for docks and industrial land. Coupled with these events is the contruction of two new canals parallel to the New Waterway, the Caland Ship Canal and the Hartel Barge Canal. The next stage will be to dredge a channel to allow 500 000-ton tankers drawing 27 metres of water access to Maasvlakte.

The determination of the port authorities to press ahead with dredging and new harbour works has had the effect of removing the competition provided by many other West European ports when the size of tanker did not exceed 10 000 tons. No other port in Western Europe can now compete with Rotterdam for the traffic generated by the largest tankers, and as these have become more numerous, the port has expanded increasingly rapidly in relation to Antwerp, Amsterdam, Hamburg and Le Havre. If Antwerp is the prime port of Belgium, then Rotterdam holds this position in Western Europe.

Rotterdam has been the world's busiest port since 1965, when it superseded New York, and in 1972 270 million tons of freight passed through the port. If it is assumed that it continues to be the only port in Western Europe capable of taking really large vessels, Rotterdam is expected to grow at a quite meteoric rate. It is thought that by 1980 the tonnage handled will be 430 millions, of which oil will represent two-thirds, and that at the end of the century the figure will stand at 830 million tons. Oil reserves in the world may not rise to this kind of demand, and nuclear energy may be the principal source of electric power by the end of the century, but by any standards growth of this magnitude is formidable. Clearly vast new port areas will have to be excavated.

The port is predominantly concerned with imports, which total more than three times the weight of exports. Oil accounts for more than half the total tonnage handled, and other bulk materials account for a further quarter. General cargo amounts to one-tenth of the total tonnage moving through the port, and its share of the traffic of the port is declining; the ratio of bulk to general cargo was 3 to 1 in 1939, but it is now 10 to 1. The economies of scale obtained from the use of large bulk carriers are very much greater than those to be had from large general cargo vessels, with the consequence that general cargo ships have not exhibited marked increases in size. They have thus been able to continue frequenting the smaller ports, and the larger ports have not been able to establish a monopoly of this traffic. In order to obtain economies of handling, general cargo is increasingly being packed into containers and transshipped at specialised quays. In Rotterdam the Beneluxhaven at Europoort has been developed for this purpose, and in 1972 almost 520 000 containers passed through the port. It is anticipated that by 1975 the figure will be 800 000 and plans are being made to allow 1 million to be handled by 1980.

Links with the hinterland

Rotterdam has three distinct hinterlands. Firstly, at the regional level, it is the principal port of the Randstad, having a third of the Dutch population living within 100 km. It is linked by road and rail to the more important cities of the Western Netherlands, and the canalisation of the Hollandse Ijssel and the Vaartsche Rijn to take 1 350-ton barges offers water transport links with the centre of Randstad and with Utrecht respectively. The Amsterdam-Rhine Canal provides a high capacity barge link with Amsterdam. The establishment of industry on sites adjacent to the New Waterway is increasing the tendency for a large part of the hinterland of the port to be Rotterdam itself.

Secondly, the port has an international hinterland, the growth of which has raised the status of the port from a regional outlet to its present premier position. Some 150 million people live within 500 km of Rotterdam, and it is water transport links that have enabled this hinterland to be tapped. The dependence of Rotterdam on these links can be attributed to several factors, the most important of which is the Rhine. The alignment of the river through North-West Europe, and its ice-free nature, have always presented enormous possibilities, despite the hazards to navigation in the Delta, the variations in flow and the difficulties of the gorge section. The bulk, non-perishable nature of so much of the traffic of the port, well suited to shipment by water transport, underlines the value of barge links with the hinterland. Additionally, by its very efforts to improve port facilities and to regulate river traffic, the port authority has increased its dependence on inland waterways as a means of transport.

Between 60% and 70% of incoming cargoes are discharged from ship to barge, and some 77% of all through-goods traffic in the Netherlands goes by water. The Rhine plays a central rôle in this trade, for half of the total traffic on the river throughout its entire length originates or terminates at Rotterdam. Unfortunately upstream cargoes are about eight times the weight of those moving in the opposite direction, necessitating the movement of laden barges against the current and the return of empty barges with the stream. Upstream cargoes are largely mineral ores, refined petroleum products and cereals, while the much smaller downstream cargoes are principally coal, fertilisers, metals and building materials. The hinterland of the Maas is tapped by the river itself and by the Juliana Canal, although at present the hinterland effectively ceases at the Belgian border. The advent of crude oil pipelines has meant that there has been a decline in the shipment of refined products from the Rotterdam refineries because the crude oil is refined at inland locations. Barge traffic in oil may have dwindled, but the oil hinterland of the port has not substantially changed.

The third hinterland of the port is a composite one comprising that of the other West European ports, including those in Scandinavia, which receive re-exported goods from Rotterdam. It is inevitable that the increasing size of bulk carriers, and the difficulty of docking these vessels in small ports, will cause a growing tonnage of goods to be brought to Rotterdam in very large ships and then transferred to smaller vessels for onward movement. The construction of crude oil pipelines to the ports of Antwerp and Amsterdam are examples of this trend. In 1969 rather more than one-third of the total tonnage handled was re-exported.

The industry of the port

Given the huge tonnage of bulk materials coming into the port and the advantages of processing them *in situ*, coupled with the availability of land, the growth of an important industrial complex might be regarded as inevitable. However this would have been impossible without the decision by the port authority to create an 'integrated port', that is, one in which the expansion of dock areas is paralleled by the establishment of industrial sites. The consequence is that the 19th-century port, then effectively a port for the Ruhr, has become an industrial complex in its own right, the largest in the Netherlands, forming a continuous industrial strip from Maasvlakte 50 km eastwards as far as Dordrecht. It is only surpassed in physical size in Benelux by the Haine-Sambre-Meuse coal-field district, and there is no doubt that, at least in Benelux, the major port areas are to the second half of the 20th century what the coalfields were to the 19th.

The tradition of the processing of raw materials, especially of colonial foodstuffs, is of long standing, but the present scale of industrial activity dates from the conscious decision of the Netherlands to industrialise after the Second World War. The development of industries directly related to the import of bulk materials has been greatly assisted by the preference given to these industries in national planning policy, which tries to direct activities which do not require access to deepwater to the peripheral areas of the country. The basis of industrial activity is oil refining, which supplies the raw materials for the second great industry, petrochemical manufacture. The oil industry was the first to recognise the value of the port in respect of Western Europe, and in 1901 the Royal Dutch company established its West European distribution centre here. The same firm, now Royal Dutch Shell, built the first oil refinery at Pernis with a capacity of 0·7 million tons a year, and it is from these small beginnings that Rotterdam has risen to be one of the largest oil

refining complexes in the world. In 1970 five refineries were in operation
with a total capacity of 64 million tons. Their location is shown on Fig.
6.3, and the capacities of the individual plants are: Shell Pernis—24·5,
Esso Botlek—16·0, Gulf Europoort—4·9, BP Europoort—5·8 and
Caltex Pernis—12·9 million tons per annum. Closely linked to the oil
refineries are the petrochemical plants, and as their number and range of
products increase, the area becomes increasingly attractive to other
chemical companies who use these products as raw materials. It was
agglomeration economies such as these that gave rise to the great
industrial areas of the last century, and the principle is still no less valid.
The major petrochemical plants are shown in Fig. 6.3.

For the most part other industrial activity in the port is smaller in
scale and is concentrated in the older parts of the harbour. The Unilever
soap and margarine works are at Vlaardingen and Feijnoord respectively,
and there are distilleries at Schiedam. Ship building and repairing is a
traditional occupation of many of the riverside towns such as Sliedrecht,
Werkendam and Gorinchem, which engage in the building and maintenance of the coasting and Rhine shipping fleets. Of special importance is
the construction of ocean-going tugs, and of recent, off-shore drilling rigs.
Larger ships of up to 100 000 tons are built in the yards between
Vlaardingen and Rotterdam, the largest yard belonging to the Verolme
company at Botlek. Dutch experience and expertise have resulted in
a considerable export of a wide variety of marine engineering products
not only for ships, but for many aspects of water control, such as lock
gates, bridges, floating cranes, water pumps and caissons. The Alblasserwaard region in particular has acquired a world-wide reputation for
producing both the equipment and the labour for dock construction and
reclamation schemes.

It is not surprising that because so much of the industry in Rijnmond,
the new 'Rhine-mouth' administrative area, is technically advanced,
that the area should be prospering. It was estimated in 1968 that the
net economic growth of Rijnmond was between 6% and 8½% per year,
compared with the national average of 4%-5%. Employment is increasing at 1·8% each year, against the national figure of 1·2%, and it is
anticipated that the number of jobs will have increased by 50% between
1967 and 1990. However, labour is becoming increasingly scarce, more
expensive and militant, and even though much labour is now recruited
in Noord-Brabant, involving workmen in 2-3-hour journeys, it is con-
ceivable that labour problems may slow down the speed of expansion.
The concentration of industry, especially petrochemicals, in the port has
raised the problem of atmospheric pollution, and it is disturbing to find
that some of the towns along the New Waterway have emergency

evacuation plans to be put into effect if this menace becomes a real threat to health.

The problems of the expansion of Rotterdam

Rotterdam faces a number of problems in consequence of its recent rapid growth. Having reached the limit of possible expansion westwards along the line of the New Waterway, future growth must be largely southwards into the Delta islands of Zuid-Holland and Zeeland. The isolation of the northern part of the Delta is being ended by the completion of the road links over the Haringvliet and Brielsemeer dams and by means of the Volkerak bridge. The expansion of Rotterdam southwards on to the islands of Voorne and Putten for both residential and industrial is now practical. Oostvoorne, Brielle and Spijkenisse can already be regarded as satellite towns, while Hellevoetsluis on the Haringvliet is expected to develop in the same way. It is anticipated that an overspill population of 250 000 will be accommodated in the Delta area by 1980.

The Maas has always been a limiting factor in the southward expansion of Rotterdam. The first two bridges, one road and one rail, were built between 1870 and 1878, and were sufficient until the expansion of the port and residential areas south of the river in the inter-war period. The need for navigation freedom prevented the construction of further bridges downstream, and the Maas tunnel, slightly more than 1 km in length, was opened in 1942. The maximum capacity of this tunnel was calculated to be 17 million vehicles per year, but by 1962 some 24 million vehicles per year were passing through it, and the bottleneck was inhibiting further southward expansion. To counter this the Brienenoord bridge was built east of Rotterdam to carry the E10 motorway between the Randstad and the south, and a second tunnel, the Benelux tunnel, was constructed at Schiedam. The opening of the Rotterdam metro in 1969 was a response to the continued build-up of north-south traffic, and if it is extended to Voorne the growth of settlements as far south as Hellevoetsluis will be assisted. The development of the port and the population of the city outside the local authority boundaries has created administrative and planning problems, but these have been minimised by the establishment of the Rijnmond authority. Some 28 *gemeenten* along the New Waterway and on the islands of Ijsselmonde, Voorne and Putten have surrendered some of their powers to this authority, and the organisation of the port and the associated population can, as a result, be more efficiently achieved. However, the future expansion of the port is likely to require further changes, for the anticipated ten-fold increase in land requirements between 1970 and 1980 will be sought in the Delta rather than by off-shore reclamation. The construction of the Antwerp-Rhine Canal and the proposals to develop major port areas at Kreekrak and Scheldhaven in the Delta are clear indications of the shift in focus from the linear port astride the New Waterway to a polynuclear 'super-port' or 'Deltaport' comprising several separate ports. As Fig. 6.4 suggests, this new port might well include the Belgian ports of Antwerp, Ghent and Zeebrugge, giving Benelux a huge central port and industrial core.

Fig. 6.4 The ports of the Rhine-Maas-Scheldt estuary indicating the way in which expansion is creating the concept of a Deltaport. The port symbols are not pro-portionately sized

6.4 THE MINOR PORTS

Many hundred lesser ports exist on the sea coast, rivers and inland water-ways of Benelux, and some of these, such as Zeebrugge, Ghent, Terneuzen and Vlissingen play an important part in the economic life of their respective regions. Moreover, there are signs that some of these ports, especially those adjacent to the Delta, may expand rapidly in the next two decades.

Ghent

The port of Ghent, the fourth largest in Benelux, is linked with the sea by the 35-km-long Terneuzen-Ghent Canal, opened in 1827 and several times subsequently deepened to take 60 000-ton vessels. Not only is the ship canal longer than those serving other Benelux ports, but it also passes through the Netherlands, with the consequence that improvements involve both the Dutch and the Belgians. Since it is the latter who benefit most from new engineering works, the Dutch are reluctant to cooperate in modernisation. Improvements to the Belgian sector are valueless without similar changes in the Netherlands, and in order to ensure that the most recent programme, completed in 1968, went ahead, the Belgians met 80% of the cost of the work carried out on the Dutch section of the canal. The existence of Benelux and the EEC certainly facilitated joint ventures such as this.

The port handled 13 million tons of traffic in 1972, the import of mineral ores accounting for one-third of the total, reflecting the presence of the SIDMAR iron and steel plant at Zelzate to the north of the city. Despite its distance from the sea, new docks have been built, and approval is being sought for the construction of a container dock. It is hoped that the projected dock area at Rodenhuize, shown to the north of the Texaco refinery in Fig. 6.5, will lead to further industrialisation of the port area. Although some of these proposals are perhaps optimistic at present, further growth will certainly take place, for the area is aided by government subsidies and benefits from the buoyant economic climate of Flanders. Apart from the oil refineries operated by Shell and Texaco, and the SIDMAR plant, firms such as Bowater-Philips, Bell Telephone, Volvo and Johns Manville have plants alongside the canal, and they represent an important growth sector. It is possible that canal-side expansion in Belgium will eventually meet up with that in the Netherlands where the port of Terneuzen is now the site of establishments belonging to Philips and Dow Chemicals.

Although the three Belgian ports of Zeebrugge, Ghent and Antwerp are linked by the Wester Schelde and the North Sea, suggestions have been made to construct a 125 000-ton-capacity canal between them. This would be enormously costly, but it can be argued that such a canal would lead to additional growth both at the ports concerned and along the canal itself, at the same time providing Antwerp with a more efficient outlet to the sea than she at present possesses.

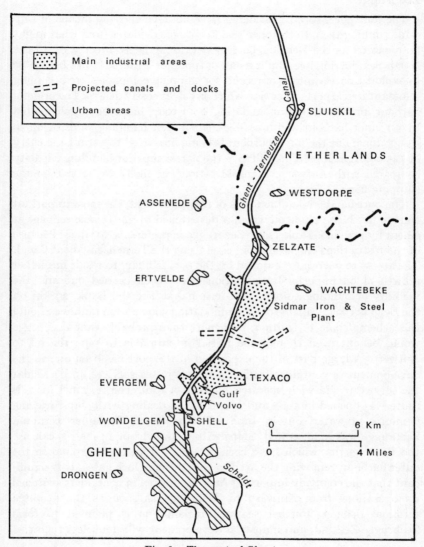

Fig. 6.5 The port of Ghent

Zeebrugge

The four ports so far considered have all developed by means of ship canals linking them to the open sea. Zeebrugge deviates from what might be regarded as the Benelux port model, for it faces directly on to the North Sea, having been built as an outport for Bruges. It has been able to exploit this advantage of recent, for shipping companies are becoming reluctant to use ports, access to which involves costly delays. The original harbour, protected by a mole dating from 1907, has been supplemented by an inner harbour and a sea-lock capable of handling ships of up to 55 000 tons, but the inner harbour is being improved to permit the entry of 125 000-ton ships. This will give the port a superior handling capacity compared with Antwerp, a consideration not likely to be lost on the shipping firms.

The port handled 8 million tons of freight in 1972, the most important commodity being crude oil which is despatched to the Texaco refinery at Ghent by pipeline. Tankers use Zeebrugge in preference to Ghent because of the restrictions on the size of vessel using the Terneuzen-Ghent Canal. The access to deepwater enjoyed by the port is likely to result in further growth of oil imports. Investigations have been carried out into the viability of building a floating oil-terminal at Thorton Bank, 26 km off the Belgian coast, capable of accommodating 500 000-ton tankers. Should this scheme come to fruition, it is more than probable that Zeebrugge would benefit even though the initial intention is to pipe the oil to Antwerp. A large part of the expansion of the port has been due to the development of container traffic on the short sea services, in particular the service to Harwich operated by British Rail. The terminal for this route was opened in 1968 and is capable of dealing with ships drawing 6 metres of water, but in June 1971 the Ocean Container Terminal Zeebrugge was inaugurated. Ships with a draught of 14 metres can use the three berths, which have been constructed on made ground in the outer harbour, removing the need to pass through lock gates, It is significant that the company importing Australian wool in containers switched its operations from Antwerp to Zeebrugge as soon as the deep-sea terminal opened. Further seaward reclamation is planned to form Zeebrugge-Zeestad, and industrial development will doubtless follow.

Delfzijl

The Dutch port of Delfzijl on the west bank of the Dollart estuary has been expanded as part of regional development policy, which aims at stimulating the backward regional economy. The port handled 4 million tons of freight in 1970, the chief items of trade being agricultural products, timber and fuels. Since the establishment of the aluminium smelter adjacent to the port, imports of alumina have built up. The 20-km Eems Canal links Delfzijl with the regional capital of Groningen, and together with the Eemshaven extension of Delfzijl to the north, forms an axis of development to which manufacturing industry is being attracted.

There are many other Benelux ports whose total trade may be well below those mentioned above, but which specialise in the handling of particular commodities. Ijmuiden, whose iron ore trade serves the local blast furnaces is such a case, and the Dutch NATO naval base at Den Helder and the Belgian naval base at Ostend are other examples. Fishing ports also fall into this category. The traditional dispersal of small fishing ports around the Benelux coast and partially enclosed seas was a response to the small size of the vessels used, and the small-scale marketing and distribution systems. The growing sophistication of shipboard equipment has now increased the range of the ships and concentrated investment into fewer, more complex vessels, and marketing is increasingly operating at the national scale. Fishing has therefore become concentrated on the few ports possessing the necessary marketing and processing facilities. In Belgium, Nieuwpoort and Ostend handle most of the Belgian catches, while the much larger Dutch catches are landed for the most part at Ijmuiden and Scheveningen.

6.5 THE FUTURE OF THE BENELUX PORTS

The future of the Benelux ports must be viewed in the context of the rapid and far-reaching changes facing maritime trade throughout Western Europe. By 1992 it is estimated that the seaborne trade of the enlarged 9-member EEC will have more than doubled in volume, and demand for harbour facilities will have increased accordingly. Changes in shipping technology leading to larger and more specialised vessels are radically changing the nature and distribution of ports. A growing volume of traffic is being handled by fewer, but larger and better equipped ports which, as they expand, creep inexorably towards the North Sea. A favourable position in respect of deepwater is sufficient to induce the growth of new port areas, and Zeebrugge, Vlissingen, Kreekrak and Scheldhaven are examples of the trend. The advantages of ports as industrial areas is likely to continue and the development of ports in Benelux will occupy an increasingly large share of national investment.

These changes are leading to a growing spirit of cooperation in place of the traditional competition, and this is best exemplified in the proposals for the Delta region. The expansion of Rotterdam southwards and of Antwerp north-westwards into the Wester Schelde has given a community of interest in the region to the two ports. The Antwerp-Rhine

N

Canal, to be called significantly the Benelux Canal, will link the two ports with a 2 000-ton capacity waterway through the Volkerak locks, Zeeuwsmeer, Eendracht and the Zuid-Beveland isthmus. This, coupled with the new Zoomweg motorway connection and the proposed fixed link crossing of the Wester Schelde, will encourage trade between the two great Benelux ports across the Delta. Port and industrial developments within the Delta, such as those proposed for Kreekrak and Scheldehaven, will help create a single, inter-connected port region, and it is a short step from this to the emergence of a 'Deltaport'.

Further Reading

James Bird, 'Seaports and the European Economic Community', *Geographical Journal*, 133, 1967, pp. 302-327.

Jean Chardonnet, *Métropoles Economiques* (Armand Colin, Paris), 1959. Chapters on Antwerp and Amsterdam.

E. Wever, 'Pernis-Botlek-Europoort. Un Complexe à Base de Pétrole?', *Tijdschrift voor Economische en Sociale Geografie*, 57, 1966, 131-140. (In English.)

D.P.I.O. Stornebrink, 'Location Tendencies in the New Rotterdam Waterway Port Area', *Tijdschrift Koninklijk Nederlands Aardrijkundig Genotschaap*, 77, 1960, pp. 332-340.

M.C. Verburg, 'The Gent-Terneuzen Developmental Axis in the Perspective of the E.E.C.', *Tijdschrift voor Economische en Sociale Geografie*, 1964, 55, pp. 143-150.

F. Posthuma, 'Port Modernisation. The Lessons of Rotterdam-Europoort', *Progress*, No. 1, 1968, pp. 143-151.

Chapter 7

REGIONAL DEVELOPMENT IN BENELUX

With the exception of the introductory chapter, where physical regions are examined, there has been no attempt to consider the geography of the regions of the three Benelux countries, rather the approach has been systematic. However, differences between regions are an important consideration for the geographer and cannot be neglected. This chapter seeks to examine regional differentiation, largely from a socio-economic standpoint, and to look at the effects of regional policy and possible future trends. It would be possible to consider developments in every region in Benelux, but this would necessarily be a lengthy process and, since many areas have the same problems, somewhat repetitive. The approach is therefore to construct a typology of regions and to select examples from each category of region.

Many countries of the world possess areas in which economic growth is developing increasingly rapidly, and in which the population is expanding at a rate faster than the national average. Such growth regions represent the first category of region, and appear in Benelux as the Western Netherlands or Randstad, and the Brussels-Antwerp axial belt. The Grand Duchy of Luxembourg is also included here for the country is so small that it may be regarded as a growth area in its entirety. Because of their obvious importance, all three regions of growth are examined. Such is the speed of technological advancement that some areas find it very difficult to adapt sufficiently quickly to the decline of what is often a narrow economic base. The plight of such regions is often made worse by the very success of the growth areas, to which there is usually a migration of people and resources. Governments react to these problems by encouraging the restructuring of the socio-economic base of such regions, which in Benelux comprise the Walloon coalfield, Belgian and Dutch Limburg, Tournaisis and Oost-Vlaanderen in Belgium, central and eastern Noord-Brabant and the Twente district of the Netherlands. The first three of these 'restructuring' regions are selected for study. Finally, because of their distance from growth areas and proximity to international frontiers and coastlines, peripheral regions have long exhibited slow growth and relatively low standards of living. In many ways these peripheral regions exhibit the same problems as the restructuring regions, but they are

195

normally rooted in agriculture rather than in declining manufacturing
and have not known prosperity over the last two to three centuries. Like
the restructuring regions, the peripheral regions have been in receipt of
government aid. There are three such areas in Benelux: West-Vlaanderen,
the Northern Netherlands and the Ardennes. The first two are discussed
in this chapter.

A. The Growth Areas of Benelux

7.1 THE WESTERN NETHERLANDS OR RANDSTAD

A single prime city, which dominates the economic life of the nation and
gathers to itself all the national central place functions, has not developed in the Netherlands. No Dutch city can imitate the rôle of
Copenhagen, Vienna, Brussels, London or Paris within their respective
countries. Instead economic, political and social life has become strongly
focused upon an area of the Western Netherlands, within which a
number of cities compete for primacy. The legal capital, the seat of
government, the leading port, the ecclesiastical capital and the foremost
education centre are all located in different cities within the Western
Netherlands. The idea of the Randstad or 'rim-city' links these separate
cities into a conceptual unit whose physical size and number of inhabitants
allow it to be compared with the other major metropolitan regions of
Western Europe, and allow it to be treated as a unit for planning purposes, although it has no legal existence.

The polycentric nature of the Randstad, as opposed to the unicentric
development of Brussels or Paris, can be attributed to the slow growth of
the Dutch cities until well into the modern period, despite their early
foundation. As late as 1850 the combined population of the four largest
Dutch cities of Amsterdam, The Hague, Rotterdam and Utrecht was less
than half a million. As a result Randstad lacks the areas of slum housing
which characterise many European cities whose growth began earlier.
The 1850 map shows few signs of the coalescence of the urban nuclei to
form urban zones, and it is impossible for another 50 years to detect the
beginning of the near-continuous rim of urban settlement around an open
heart which is at the root of the Randstad concept.

The three provinces of Noord- and Zuid-Holland and Utrecht, which
are effectively the Randstad, have an average population density three
times as high as the remainder of the country, and produce almost two-
thirds of the national product on less than a quarter of the national land
area. The prime region attracts service industries with a national market,
including both public and private office development. As it is itself the
largest single market in the country, and the principal source of labour,

much secondary industry is also attracted to the region. A peculiarity of the Dutch prime region compared with many other primate cities is that it contains the major national port, Rotterdam-Europoort, which is the largest port in the world and an important growth point within Randstad. Industries seeking port locations are thus added to those seeking market locations, thereby increasing demands on land and labour in this relatively small region.

Pressure on resources consequent upon the demands of industry is augmented by residential demands. The concentration of employment opportunities in the West and the higher wages typical of the area account for the traditional immigration of population from the peripheral regions. Of even greater importance is the natural increase of the already existing numerous population which is expected to increase by half a million between 1970 and 1980. An indication of the speed of the growth of the population between 1960 and 1969 can be obtained from Fig. 7.1. In addition, increasing material prosperity is leading to substantially greater demands from the same population. The bourgeois ideal of the two-storey single nuclear family dwelling with a private garden is within the financial reach of an increasing proportion of Dutchmen. Similarly mass motor car ownership not only makes demands for its own accommodation, but also encourages a low density suburbanisation which again increases demands upon land resources. The need for recreational space within the Western Netherlands also poses problems. An increasingly affluent, mobile and leisured population both within and without the Netherlands requires that an increasing proportion of woods, heaths, beaches and lakes is reserved for recreational use. The 1966 Structure Plan proposed that as much as half of the total area of the three provinces including Randstad be designated for some recreational use (Fig. 7.2), which in turn increases the scarcity of land for industrial and residential purposes.

The delimitation of Randstad

The existence of a horseshoe-shaped conurbation measuring some 100 km from north to south and 80 km from east to west, open towards the south-east, was noted by the Dutch planners in 1960. The criteria adopted included population densities between 500 and 2 000 persons per square kilometre and near contiguity of the built-up area. The conurbation was not entirely urban for some regions of intensive agriculture were included, such as the flower and bulb district between Hillegom and Lisse and parts of the market gardening regions of Delftland and Westland. This conurbation, Randstad, was divided into two sectors. The northern part was centred on Amsterdam and may be considered as a linear zone stretching some 20-30 km from north-west to south-east on either side of the city. The extension of Amsterdam north-westwards into the Zaanstreek was of long standing, and the building of the railway to Haarlem and the seaside resort of Zandvoort, together with the cutting

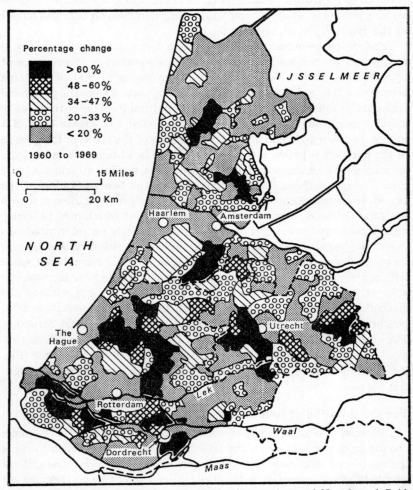

Fig. 7.1 Population changes by *gemeente* in the provinces of Noord- and Zuid-Holland and Utrecht, 1960-1969

of the North Sea Canal to Ijmuiden, had encouraged the emergence of an urban axis from the North Sea to the Ijsselmeer at Amsterdam. South-east of Amsterdam the sandy heathlands of the Gooi ridge have been progressively drawn into the orbit of the city, first as a location for the secluded retreats of 18th-century merchants and later as an area of middle-class commuter housing. The towns of Naarden, Bussum, Blaricum and Laren have expanded rapidly in recent years and have coalesced to form the municipality of Het Gooi. The continuation of the

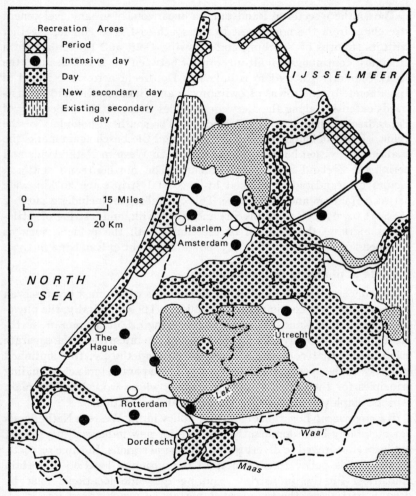

Fig. 7.2 Proposed recreation areas in the Western Netherlands

Gooi ridge south-eastwards, known as the Utrechtse Heuvelrug, has provided a line of expansion through Hilversum to Utrecht. Utrecht forms the southern boundary of the northern part of the Randstad, and the expansion of this city prior to 1960 has been largely north-westwards along the Vecht valley, or northwards along the Heuvelrug rather than south across the Kromme Rijn on to the inter-riverine islands. To the east, the Geldersche Vallei and the Veluwe beyond mark the traditional frontier between the heartland of the Western Netherlands and the periphery.

The southern sector of Randstad is a linear zone of urban development stretching from the north-west to the south-east. The Hague, together with its suburbs of Voorburg and Rijswijk, Delft and Rotterdam form an almost continuously built-up corridor between the North Sea and the Maas. Similarly Rotterdam is linked to Dordrecht across the island of Ijsselmonde by the towns of Zwijndrecht and Barendrecht, and an eastwards extension along the Merwede includes the riverside settlements of Papendrecht, Sliedrecht and Gorinchem. The southern boundary of the defined Randstad along the Hollandsdiep and Biesbosch again marks the traditional division between the metropolitan Western Netherlands and peripheral Zeeland and Noord-Brabant. The northern and southern sectors of Randstad are linked by a coastal strip some 20 km wide between Haarlem and The Hague. This coastal region includes a number of resort towns such as Zandvoort and Noordwijk, and a string of settlements marking the junction of the dunes with the polders, such as Bloemendaal and Leiden. Fig. 7.3 shows the extent of Randstad in 1960.

Aspects of planning in Randstad

The concept of the Randstad has three facets which must be preserved if the concept is to continue to have validity. These are firstly, the physical separation of Randstad from neighbouring urban clusters in North-West Europe; secondly, the maintenance of the integrity of the separate urban nodes that comprise the urban rim; and thirdly, the continued existence of the open heart in the centre. These parameters act as guiding principles for the Dutch Planning Service, whose work has four main aspects: employment, housing, transport and recreation.

(i) *Employment* Location of industry policy in the Western Netherlands has inevitably been dominantly negative for new industrial investment has been encouraged to divert to the peripheral regions. In three respects, however, this policy runs counter to the optimum location of certain industries. Firstly, industries requiring quayside locations must be sited in port areas, the two most important of which are in Randstad, and this has caused the policy to be relaxed. The growth of the Rijnmond and Ijmond industrial complexes has not been substantially impeded in point of fact, although there are misgivings about the size of these industrial areas. Secondly, the existence in the West of a large part of the domestic market renders it attractive for the consumer goods industries and for manufacturers of components for the diversified local industrial market. The recent establishment of the Singer domestic appliance company outside Utrecht, despite government pressure to locate in a development region, is an example of many such moves. Thirdly, the fast growing service sector of the economy requires locations close to the centres of political and administrative power. The Dutch Planning Service has had some success, especially in the public sector, in both dispersing these functions among the Randstad cities and also in establishing new locations outside the West. The location in the West of the two principal tourist reception areas, the coast and the historic cities, is an additional exacerbation, especially where the coast, historic city and major commercial centre coincide, as they do in The Hague-Scheveningen.

(ii) *Housing* Increases in population and in living standards have led to a substantial increase in the demand for residential land within the West. In an area short of land, low-density housing development would cause an encroachment into the open heart and green belts, but fortunately, since multi-storey dwellings close to the city-centre have long been the rule in the Netherlands, high-density housing areas have been favoured. As a result most Randstad cities are characterised by a girdle of high rise flats around their peripheries with more than 20 houses per hectare. The Amsterdam Extension Plan, formulated in 1935 and substantially revised since then, was responsible for the creation of four *tuindorpen* or satellite towns, principally of medium to high-rise flats, just within the *gemeente* boundary. In some cases existing settlements outside the urban area have been deliberately expanded to become in practice new towns, such as Hellevoetsluis for Rotterdam, Hoogvliet and Spijkenisse for Pernis and Botlek. Further similar projects are envisaged, for example, Jutphas for Utrecht and the Zuid-Flevoland polder towns for Amsterdam. Although low-density suburbanisation is officially discouraged it nevertheless occurs on a considerable scale in some areas, which have attracted a middle-class commuter population well able to afford the high land values. Examples include the Gooi to the east of Amsterdam and the towns of Zeist, Bilthoven and Doorn which have developed along railway routes to the north-east of Utrecht.

(iii) *Transport* A polycentric conurbation arranged around the rim of an open heart clearly has different transport requirements from a concentric urban form. In a unicentric city most transport flows are likely to radiate from residential and minor commercial and industrial areas on the periphery to the principal source of employment and commercial services in the centre. In the Dutch case, however, as a result of both the location of the urban nuclei in relation to each other and the dispersal

of central place functions through many centres, there is a complex
pattern of linkages between all the Randstad settlements. The successful
maintenance of both the independence of the individual centres will
largely depend upon the efficiency of these transport links. The problem
is complicated by the coincidence of scales of movement within the same
region. Randstad transport systems must accommodate local, inter-
urban, national and international traffic. Locally, buses are used as the
main public service. On the regional scale reliance has been placed on
passenger railways and main roads. The 'inter-city' rail service was
inaugurated in 1967 to provide fast and relatively cheap passenger transport between the Randstad towns. At the national and international
scale the transport system consists of inland waterways, a network of
pipelines between the ports and their hinterlands and an increasingly
comprehensive motorway net which integrates Randstad within the
European motorway system.

(iv) *Recreation* It has been recognised by Dutch planners that the
quality of life of the inhabitants of the Randstad towns depends in part
on the satisfaction of their needs for recreation. This is no small task for
it is estimated that between 40% and 60% of the Randstad population
leaves the towns in search of recreation on a summer Sunday. There is a
demand for the provision of parks within the urban cores, a demand
made more intense by the high densities of housing already mentioned.
Public land is used to replace the private garden and urban parks have
been given a high priority. It has been laid down that there should be
125 square metres of parkland for each city-dweller, and that the average
distance between home and park should be 3·2 km. Also provided are
extensive areas of allotments with attached summer houses to serve the
flat dwellers of Rotterdam. The 960-ha Amsterdamse Bos, or Wood,
performs a vital function for the inhabitants of the city. Day recreational
demands are met by the siting of high-capacity recreational developments
at appropriate distances from urban centres. In the southern sector of
Randstad, for example, day recreational facilities have been created
on the Zuid-Holland lakes, the rivers and in the northern part of the
Delta. Beyond this zone specific developments are sited on the coast,
as in the Biesbosch, the Plassengebied and the Grevelingen estuary. The
day recreation areas outlined in the 1966 Structure Plan are shown in
Fig. 7.2.

The dune coast of Holland presents a special problem in that a variety
of types of recreational demand is concentrated upon it. These conflict
both with each other and with other land-uses. The dunes are a major
aquifer for Haarlem and Amsterdam and act as reservoirs for water
pumped from the Rhine. Additionally they are important military train-

ing zones and their flora and landscape are subject to conservational measures, not least because they form an 84-km-long natural defence against the sea. The reconciliation of these demands necessitates a careful channelling of visitors along specified routes to particular sites and a clear designation of priority among competing uses for each part of the area. As a result only some 15% of the area of the dunes is open to public access and access to a further 40% is restricted. Access to the sea is limited by linking each resort individually to a main road running parallel to the coast but at least 5 km from it. Those resorts with the best transport links with the cities have been developed for day recreation. These include Zandvoort, Scheveningen and Hoek which serve Amsterdam, The Hague and Rotterdam respectively.

The expansion of Randstad

The outward expansion of the urban rim has been initiated by the pressure on space evident in each of the aspects considered above. Dispersion and relocation policies for both secondary industry and services are encouraging a centrifugal movement, while increasing personal mobility is enlarging the commuting hinterlands of the urban centres. The improvement in transport which are in the process of implementation not only improve movement in the Western Netherlands, but also increase its accessibility, making the immediate periphery more attractive for industrial, residential and recreational use. The planning response to this expansion has been to channel it along particular corridors rather than attempt a policy of containment. The principal corridors of expansion may be treated separately.

(i) *Noord-Holland* The traditional isolation of the Noord-Holland peninsula was removed with the completion of the *afsluitdijk* road in 1932, and it is possible to expand northwards into a region which is no longer a cul-de-sac. There are two axes of growth: north from Velsen along the coast towards Alkmaar, and north from Amsterdam adjacent to the Ijsselmeer. The future reclamation of the Markerwaard polder provides additional possibilities for growth.

(ii) *Flevoland* The draining of the two Flevoland polders presented Amsterdam with the opportunity of creating a major corridor of expansion eastwards as far as the new Ijsselmeer capital of Lelystad, which is under construction at the junction of the Flevoland and Markerwaard polders. Transport along this axis will be effected by the 2 000-ton capacity Oostvaarterdiep which connects the peripheral polder canals with the Ijsselmeer, and the R10 motorway opened in 1970, linking Amsterdam with the Noord-Oost polder via Lelystad. It is proposed that industrial and commercial developments be confined to a zone 5 km wide and 25 km long between the Ijmeer and Lelystad, with initial growth being confined to the Zuid-Flevoland polder and to the Lelystad area, where an industrial estate is being laid out. Eventually this zone will be paralleled by another on the Markerwaard polder when it is drained. An

Fig. 7.3 Randstad and its probable expansion (R = Rotterdam, A = Amsterdam)

'inland coast' for recreational use has already been established and in 1971 there were 16 camp sites, 17 yacht harbours and 37 000 ha of recreational land in existence.

(iii) *The Arnhem-Nijmegen axis* The eastern edge of the Randstad has suffered considerably from the growth of commuter settlements and the roads radiating from Utrecht to Hilversum, Amersfoort and Veenendaal exhibit many large stretches of continuous residential development. The area is also in demand for recreational purposes for the Utrecht lakes west of Hilversum provide scarce water sport facilities. The towns in the each of the 'rim-city' are themselves expanding. Utrecht is housing some 50 000 overspill population to the south at Jutphas, Ijsselstein and Vreeswijk. The growth of Arnhem has caused towns on the southern edge of the Veluwe such as Rheden, Ede, Oosterbeek and Wageningen effectively to become suburbs of Arnhem. The eastwards expansion of Randstad is creating an axis of growth between Utrecht and Arnhem, and this has been encouraged by the construction of the main Randstad-West Germany motorway, the E9, along the corridor between the Lek to the south and the Veluwe and Heuvelrug to the north. As a consequence settlements such as Veenendaal and Rhenen have expanded as employment and residential centres. Similarly to the east Winterswijk is being drawn into the economic orbit of Arnhem. Nijmegen on the Waal occupies a similar site to Arnhem on the Lek, and the two are separated by only 10 km of the Betuwe. Fortunately, Nijmegen has not yet experienced the same rapid growth as Arnhem. The West German border only 4 km from Nijmegen marks the limit of eastward movement.

(iv) *The Noord-Brabant axis* The string of towns that grew up at the junction of the Kempen heaths and the Noord-Brabant polders have grown rapidly and have developed as industrial centres of some importance. From west to east these are Bergen-op-Zoom, Roosendaal, Breda, Tilburg and Eindhoven, with extensions to Hertogenbosch in the north-east and Helmond in the south-east. It is estimated that between 1970 and 1980 the province of Noord-Brabant will increase by 410 000 and by a further 480 000 in the following decade. The 1965 provincial development plan mooted a policy of 'dispersed concentration' and its implementation has resulted in the creation of an almost continuous zone of low-density housing and scattered industrial estates, interrupted by green buffer zones, stretching for 120 km from the Delta to within 15 km of the West German frontier (Fig. 7.4). The expansion of Randstad from Zuid-Holland into Noord-Brabant has been encouraged by the completion of the Volkerak bridge, which has removed the bottleneck caused by the Moerdijk bridge, and by the opening of the Zoomweg motorway between Rotterdam and Bergen-op-Zoom. Two examples illustrate the ferment of change taking place in the small towns of west Noord-Brabant. The towns of Willemstad and Dinteloord are expected to double their population as a result of the new Oranjestad development, and secondly, the 150-ha industrial estate which is being laid out along the River Mark at Moerdijk will give rise to an increase in the population of the town from 10 000 to 16 000 by 1980. It is therefore increasingly possible to conceive of a single Noord-Brabant growth axis, the Brabantse Stedenrij, rather than a series of separate nodes, and to see this axis linked with Zuid-Holland as a south-eastward extension of the Randstad.

(v) *The Delta* Until recently the existence of the Rhine-Maas-Scheldt delta effectively contained the southward expansion of the Randstad. The execution of the Delta Plan has removed this constraint by bridging the estuaries, and has opened up the possibility of using what was previously an underutilised region for relieving the pressure on the Western

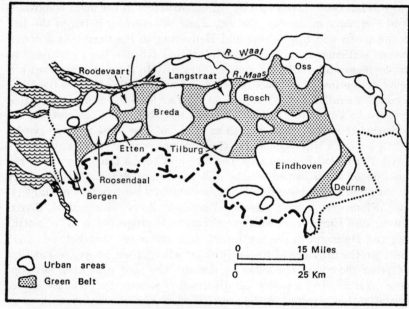

Fig. 7.4 Proposed urban agglomerations in Noord-Brabant

Netherlands. The earlier isolation has preserved a region which, by national standards, is scantily populated, and yet whose labour force is traditionally underemployed. It is planned that the Delta will provide relief for the central metropolitan area in four respects. Firstly, land can be made available for industrial sites, especially for industries requiring deepwater facilities. The Wester Schelde estuary in the south and the Zuid-Holland islands in the north will be capable of becoming extensions of Antwerp and Rotterdam respectively. Indeed the aluminium smelter and oil refineries at Vlissingen suggest that this is already taking place. Secondly, the region will be able to provide space for residential growth and it is thought that Zeeland's present population of 260 000 will double in the next 30 years. Towns such as Vlissingen, Middelburg and Goes have been experiencing rapid growth since the mid-1960s. Thirdly, the completion of the estuary enclosing dams, in particular those across the Brouwershavengat and the Oosterschelde, and the Volkerak sluices, will create a freshwater lake, the Zeeuwsmeer, conveniently situated in respect of the centres of demand for water in the Western Netherlands. Fourthly, the large, sheltered water surfaces will prove attractive for recreational purposes.

The results of the expansion of Randstad

As a result of the extensions described, the view of the Dutch metropolitan region as a circular rim-city must be modified, for it is now beginning to resemble two parallel linear urban zones 150 km in length between the North Sea and the West German frontier, separated by a 20-40-km-wide buffer. The anticipated form the new conurbation will have taken by 1980 is illustrated in Fig. 7.3. The open heart of the Randstad has become a series of 'open corridors'. The earlier open heart has been reduced largely to the lakes area of the Plassengebied, but has been given access to the coast between Zandvoort and Katwijk, since the flower district of Hillegom-Lisse is now classified as 'open' rather than urban. Further corridors link Zeeland through the Biesbosch with the riverine islands between the Lek and the Waal, and Limburg and north-eastern Noord-Brabant are reached through a 10-km gap between the north and south wings west of Nijmegen. Large areas outside of, rather than between the wings of the new conurbation are being preserved from large-scale urban development, and have important recreational functions. They include extensive areas in Zeeland, the Kempen, the Veluwe, the Ijsselmeer peripheral polder canals, or *randmeeren*, and the Waddenzee, if its proposed use as a National Park is approved.

The implementation of the planning proposals is not carried out without difficulty for at present there is no Randstad planning authority. The separate provincial plans are coordinated only at the national level, where it has been suggested that more attention is paid to the problems of the peripheral regions than to Randstad. This vital coordination tends to be conducted in very general terms with little detailed planning. There is, for example, no supra-provincial authority capable of creating new towns, or rationalising the population overspill between the three western provinces. Attempts at coordinated district plans or *streek-plannen* have not been notably successful, especially where they operate across provincial boundaries, and the Rijnmond authority has been the only large-scale attempt in this direction. Planners also face the problem of the slow coalescence of the Lower Rhine area in West Germany with the Dutch metropolitan region, and at a more localised level it is proving increasingly difficult to maintain the open areas in the face of urban expansion. Despite these shortcomings, it cannot be denied that a series of compromises is being maintained more successfully in Randstad than in many other countries with similar problems.

7.2 THE BRUSSELS-ANTWERP AXIAL BELT

To a large extent it is inevitable that the area of a country containing both the capital city and a great international port should be the most rapidly expanding region in that country. This hypothesis is particularly relevant in the case of nations such as Belgium whose economy is especially reliant on international trade effected for the most part by sea. The distance between the centres of Brussels and Antwerp is only 40 km, with the result that the process of suburbanisation, which has accelerated sharply in the last two decades, has all but caused the two cities to merge, engulfing Mechelen which lies between them. In addition Brussels has exhibited a marked southward spread in the direction of Charleroi, Namur and even Liège, suggesting that in the not too distant future all the most important Belgian cities will be encompassed within the central axial belt.

A number of indices may be used to identify the limits of this axial zone. Some of these provide data at the provincial level and thus do not offer a rigorous delimitation of the growth area, although they do indicate that Brabant and Antwerp together form the economic core of the country. Thus these two provinces have 47% of the Belgian working population, 42% of employment in manufacturing, 38% of the total population, and between them they generated 45% of the gross national product in 1970. In each case Brabant had the larger share: 30% of the working population, 23% of employment in manufacturing, 22% of the total population and 28% of the gross national product. In both provinces the level of unemployment is not only lower than the national figure of 3%, but also the lowest in the entire country; the rate for Brabant is 1·2% and for Antwerp 2%. If population growth is used as a delimiting criterion, we find that although both Brabant (+9·4%) and Antwerp (+6·9%) grew at a faster rate than the national average (+5.3%) between 1960 and 1970, the situation is complicated by the high fertility exhibited by the province of Limburg (+12·9%). Limburg, of course, is by no means a growth region. The use of population data at the level of the *arrondissement* is open to the same objection. Over the same period the Brabant *arrondissements* of Nivelles and Leuven grew 15·8% and 10·7% respectively, and the Antwerp *arrondissements* of Turnhout, Antwerp and Mechelen grew 11·5%, 6·0% and 4·5% respectively. But Maaseik, Hasselt and Tongeren, in the province of Limburg, increased their population respectively by 16%, 13% and 18%. Additionally it is doubtful whether Turnhout, the *arrondissement* most distant from the city of Antwerp, is a truly prosperous area, rather it belongs to the problem region of the Kempen to the east.

A more precise indication of the attraction of particular areas can be obtained by the use of migration data, for these isolate regions where employment prospects are good from areas of high fertility. Limburg, for all its population growth, suffers from consistent emigration—a reflection of local employment prospects. In 1970 Brabant had a favourable net migration balance with all the other Belgian provinces, including Antwerp, the largest gains being at the expense of Hainaut, Oost-Vlaanderen, Liège and West-Vlaanderen. Antwerp was not nearly so attractive, for not only were there only four provinces with which Antwerp had a favourable balance, but also the gains were relatively small. This was in part because the Walloons from the coalfield areas are most reluctant to move to Flanders. A generalised picture may be obtained from migration data at the provincial level, but they are also available for *arrondissements*, allowing a more realistic growth area to be built up. This is mapped in Fig. 7.5 and is based on contiguous *arrondissements* which returned a net immigration balance of more than 500 over the four years 1967-1970. The map indicates that a number of areas outside Brabant and Antwerp, that is, Namur, Huy and Waremme, are part of the axial belt, and that Turnhout, although within the province of Antwerp, is excluded. This confirms what is apparent from the figures quoted above, that it is the southern part of the belt, influenced by the city of Brussels, which is the core of the growth area. Indeed, Halle-Vilvoorde and Nivelles returned immigration balances of 15 640 and 13 463 respectively between 1967 and 1970, approximately five times greater than the figure for the Antwerp *arrondissement*. The southwards extension of the axial zone appears to be proceeding vigorously, for Namur had a slightly higher migration balance than did Antwerp itself, and Huy fell only marginally behin Mechelen. Although Namur, Huy and Waremme include former coalmining areas, for the most part they bear few scars of the industrial revolution, and readily fit the image of the new ebullient growth axis. However, since these *arrondissements* do traverse the coalfield they are considered subsequently with the Walloon coalfield. Brussels-Capital itself represents a hollow centre, for it exhibits emigration on a very large scale, a result of the construction of offices and administrative blocks in the old city, the desire to live in suburbia and to a smaller degree, the construction of the rail link between the Nord

o

and Midi railway stations, which caused the loss of 17 ha of residential land.

The causes of the growth of the axial belt

The development of the Belgian growth area, a north-south axis in a country where most divisions are east-west, is a function of the expan-

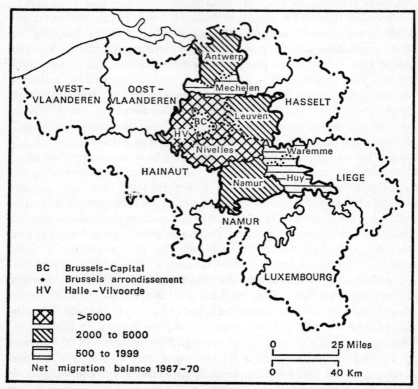

Fig. 7.5 The Brussels-Antwerp Axial Belt delimited on the basis of the net migration balance, 1967-1970

sion of prosperity in the two largest cities in the country. Greater Brussels has a population of 1·3 millions and Antwerp 0·7 millions, compared with 0·4 millions for Liège, the third city. Antwerp has grown as a port because of the importance of foreign trade to Belgium, its location in respect of the major industrial areas of the EEC, the availability of large tracts of land for the construction of docks and industrial sites, the decision of foreign firms to build plants at the larger ports of the EEC and the willingness of the port authority to meet the requirements of new industry. The details of the evolution of the city and its rapid industrial-isation during the last two decades have been traced in Chapter 6.

Capital cities normally attract to them important manufacturing and tertiary activities, and Brussels is no exception. The decision by Duke Wenceslas and Duchesse Jeanne to abandon their seat at Leuven, where their rule was meeting with increasing hostility from the burghers of the town, at the end of the 14th century, and to establish themselves at Coudenberg castle overlooking the crossing point on the River Senne, is the root cause of the rise in the fortunes of the town. Prior to this it was no more important than many of its neighbours and was smaller than Leuven. The political leadership of the town was confirmed by Philip the Good and once again by its selection as capital of the independent Belgium in 1830. Consequently the court, parliament and the civil service are established in the city, as are foreign diplomatic missions, including the EEC Commission. These activities generate considerable demand for goods and services since those employed in them command high incomes. For example, there are 6 000 officials employed by the EEC Commission, and a middle administrative grade salary in £8 000. Banks and insurance companies seek out the capital city in most countries, and two-thirds of Belgian employment in these sectors is in Brussels. The city also houses the stock exchange and a wide range of commodity markets, collectively known as the *bourses du mercredi* or Wednesday markets, in addition to fruit and vegetable markets. The tertiary employment sector receives further impetus from the 450 offices opened in the city by the multi-national corporations who have begun operations in Belgium since the Second World War. The attractions of Brussels as the capital of the EEC seem to be gathering force for the early 1970s have witnessed an upsurge in office building, largely because of the expected increase in demand for premises following the larger membership of the EEC. It is estimated that between 1972 and 1976 some 241 540 square metres or offices will be constructed in the Quartier Léopold, 130 060 square metres in the Quartier Louise and some 102 190 square metres in the confines of the old city. It is not surprising that tertiary employ-ment should be better developed in the capital than elsewhere in Belgium; 68% of the total employment in Brussels-Capitale is in the tertiary sector, and that the figure for Brabant is as high as 55% suggests the influence of the city upon the city region. The service sector is less im-portant in the province of Antwerp, where it accounts for 41% of the total employment, although the figure for the city itself is 55%. Since tertiary incomes are higher than those in manufacturing, and since the former sector is so important in Brussels, it is predictable that *per capita* income in the city should be the highest in Belgium. Brussels is actually the most prosperous region within the EEC. At the end of 1972, assuming the average EEC income to be 100, Brussels, returned an index of 150 compared with 148 for Paris, 108 for Western Netherlands, 99 for Flanders and 90 for Wallonie. The south-eastern region of Britain had an index of 109.

As a consequence of its size, importance and central location within Belgium, Brussels is well served by railway lines and trunk roads. It lies on the E5 between Ostend and Liège, on the E10 between Antwerp and Mons and on the E40 from Luxembourg. Although it is not central to Belgium, Antwerp benefits from the configuration of the coastline which causes traffic between Paris and Rotterdam to pass through the city. The E39 provides a link with the Ruhr via Liège. Road and rail services allow the easy movement of goods, but they also permit commuting on a substantial scale. There is a daily influx of 160 000 commuters into Brussels from all parts of Belgium save the Ardennes, and some 36 000 travel to Antwerp, making a valuable contribution to the economy of both areas. The Willebroek Canal links Brussels with the Scheldt, enabling 2 000-ton barges to reach the city, but more importantly in the 1970s, the Belgian national airport is at Melsbroek, to the east of the city, providing employment for 10 000. Brussels is also the national centre of communications, for the national radio station is at Veltem and the television station at Wavre.

Finally, the expansion of manufacturing industry is an essential component of growth in the axial belt. The wealth of the capital was conducive to the establishment of industries producing a wide variety of luxury goods, and the continued growth of the city, and of these industries, coupled with the high wages typical of the city, have for many years provided an attractive goal for migrants. To a less extent this has also been true of Antwerp. The employment opportunities in Brussels and Antwerp may be regarded as the 'pull' factor in migration, but also important is the employment situation in other areas of Belgium. The decline of the textile industries of Oost- and West-Vlaanderen and the contraction of coalmining and other coalfield industries in the Kempen and Wallonie, have caused the 'push' factors influencing migration to be very strong. Thus the increase in population in the growth area is at least as much a function of decline in the peripheral regions as of prosperity in the centre.

Industrial activity in the axial belt

The most striking characteristic of the industries of the axial belt is perhaps the most predictable, that they are almost entirely growth industries. Of the once important Brussels textile industry nothing remains, for although Brussels lace is sold it is no longer made in the city. Most of the old-established industries which continue are those, such as jewellery, haute couture and leather goods, for which demand shows no signs of abating. Naturally there are some exceptions. For example the diamond cutting industry is at present rationalising and becoming increasingly mechanised, bringing hardship to rural areas such as Nijlen and Berlaar in eastern Mechelen, and temporary unemployment in the Antwerp suburbs of Deurne and Borgerhout. Another exception is the iron and steel plant south of Brussels at Clabecq with blast furnaces and oxygen steel-making capacity. Its very location is unusual for it is neither on a coalfield, ironfield, nor on the coast, and yet output continues to increase. The brick-making industry concentrated on the River Rupel, a right bank tributary of the Scheldt, based on local clays, is another traditional industry. Apart from instances such as these the industries of the axial belt are essentially neotechnic. The great majority of plants that have been opened since 1945 are medium-sized in respect of their workforce, and of the 376 plants at present on industrial estates in Brabant and Antwerp excluding Turnhout, only 33 employ more than 500. It is a commentary on the difference in the industrial activity that has grown up in the two provinces that 22 of the 33 large firms are in or adjacent to the city of Antwerp, and a further 6 are immediately to the south around the town of Mechelen. Plants in Brabant may be smaller, and for the most part engaged in lighter industries, than those in Antwerp, but they have a very much wider range of products, and this diversification is a feature of the industrial structure of the province and of Brussels in particular.

In common with many other capital cities in Western Europe—London, Paris and Dublin are good examples—Brussels is the most important industrial region in the country, with 19% of the Belgian manufacturing labour force. Four principal sectors may be recognised. Firstly, the city has a virtual monopoly of many of the activities typical of prime cities: printing and publishing, jewellery, haute couture and the clothing trades. Secondly, there is a well-diversified metal-working and engineering sector producing such high value goods as scientific instruments, electronic equipment (Philips and IBM) and motor vehicles (Renault, Citroen and VW). The third sector is the chemical industry. Unlike Antwerp, which is largely concerned with the early stages of the industry, in Brussels the emphasis is very much on the final preparation of products for the consumer market, and there are a number of plants making soap, cosmetics, perfumes and pharmaceuticals. Finally, there is an important food processing industry manufacturing goods such as chocolate, sweets, beer and confectionery. Even though much of the capital's industry is footloose and not tied to particular sites, a degree of localisation does seem to have taken place. The heavier industries, concerned with metal-working, paper-making, carbochemicals and steel production are aligned along the north-south axis of the River Senne, with its Willebroek and Léopold Canals, between Vilvoorde in the north and Halle and Clabecq in the south. This axis gives rise to the industrial suburbs of Vilvoorde, Koekelberg, Molenbeek, Anderlecht and Forest. The factories of the *industries de grande ville* are in the centre of the city, but elsewhere regional specialisation is often the result of one particularly large plant or activity dominating the local employment situation. This is the case with iron and steel-making at Clabecq, the manufacture of special steels at Court St. Etienne, man-made fibres at Tubize, paper-making at Genval and quarrying at Quenast.

Industrial employment occupies a larger share of total employment in Antwerp than it does in Brussels, but even so much of Antwerp's manufacturing is linked with the port and is more specialised than that in the capital. The importance of the port is reflected in the province's 33% share of the national transport product. The three leading manufacturing sectors are metal-working, chemicals and food processing, each respon-sible for 41%, 13% and 12% of the industrial workforce respectively. Metal-working includes the three electro-smelters at Hoboken based on imported ores, three shipyards each employing 2 500 workers and the various vehicle plants, the largest of which, General Motors, has a labour force of 7 000. The early stages of the chemical industry are very well represented in Antwerp docks, and this cluster is responsible for almost half the value-added by chemical manufacture in Belgium. Agfa-Gevaert at Mortsel adds some element of diversification to the basic chemical industry of the area. Food processing in the city is largely based on imported materials. To the south of the city flanking the Scheldt, Rupel and the Willebroek Canal as far as the town of Willebroek are cement works, smaller shipyards, brickworks and a number of engin-eering plants. There is a cluster of vehicle assembly plants at Mechelen.

Predictably, much of the expansion in manufacturing has been achieved outside the framework of governmental regional policy, and Fig. 7.6 shows that, apart from western Halle-Vilvoorde, it is only where the Kempenland abuts into the axial belt in eastern Antwerp, Mechelen and north-eastern Leuven that development areas appear. Of the 46 industrial estates shown on the map, only 6 lie within the assisted areas, and of these only Heist, Aarschot, Landen and Tienen are national estates, that is, they are entirely funded by the central government. Moreover, all four are modestly sized, with areas of 43, 45, 45 and 96 ha respectively, and between them they possess only four firms with more than 100 employees. The largest of these is a clothing firm employing 900

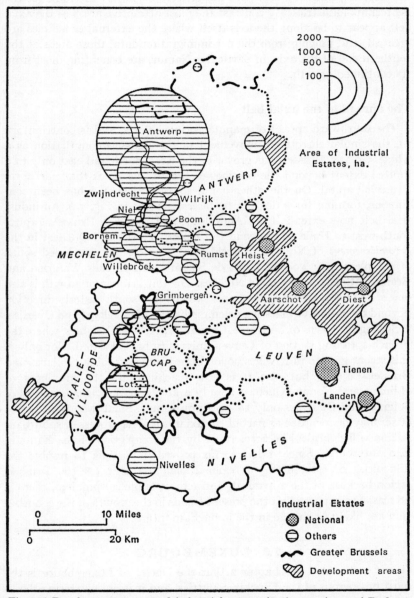

Fig. 7.6 Development areas and industrial estates in the provinces of Brabant and Antwerp, excluding Turnhout

at Aarschot, but even this does not strictly belong to the ranks of the neotechnic industries. By contrast the most attractive areas of the axial belt appear to be along the axis itself where the external economies are greatest, and judging from the net immigration data, those areas at the southern end of the axis, in particular Namur, are benefiting most from its continued growth.

The spread of the axial belt

The southward spread of manufacturing reflects, and is contributory to, the similar directional movement of the Brussels conurbation as a whole. Greater Brussels has grown to the west, north and east only to a limited extent beyond the confines of the 19 *communes* that now form Brussels-Capital. On the other hand, southward spread has been continuous, forming three distinct tentacles, evident in Fig. 7.6. An industrial belt now extends from Anderlecht and Forest in Brussels-Capital south-west to Halle and beyond to Clabecq, Tubize and Quenast in the *arrondissement* of Nivelles. A residential tentacle has developed south of the pleasantly wooded Forêt de Soignies and reaches Waterloo and Braine l'Alleud, once more in Nivelles. The third ribbon of growth is also one of residential development and extends in a south-easterly direction beyond the intensive market gardening district of Hoeilaart and Overijse, including the towns of La Hulpe, Genval, Wavre and Ottignies, where the French-speaking section of Leuven university has relocated. Not only is this recent growth in Nivelles beyond the Flemish-speaking collar round Brussels-Capital, but also it is now reaching into the provinces of Hainaut and Namur. Quenast is only 2 km from the *arrondissement* of Soignies and Ottignies only 10 km from Namur. Small wonder that the latter may be regarded as part of the axial belt. The process of suburbanisation will doubtless be accelerated by the completion of the E10 and E40 autoroutes. Since it has so far proved impossible to resolve the difficulties of establishing a regional planning unit for the Brussels region because of the apparently intractable language problem, there is no reason to suppose that the present trends in the growth of the conurbation are likely to change in the immediate future.

7.3 LUXEMBOURG

It has been noted in Chapter 2 that the Duchy of Luxembourg is the most prosperous of the Benelux countries, and it is not surprising therefore that the country should be classed as a growth area. There are several indications of economic success, for example, the virtual absence of unemployment, the lack of a regional problem and the high rate of immigration by foreign workers, but the question as to the cause of the prosperity remains. Since the Gilchrist-Thomas steel-making process ushered in the era of an iron and steel industry based on *minette* ore, this industry has been the basis of the economy of the country. However, the iron and steel industry, especially one located so far inland, has not been characterised by major growth, and indeed many steel producing areas in Western Europe are regions of indifferent economic health. That Luxembourg is an area of rapid growth is therefore due to the speed with which diversification away from iron and steel manufacture has been effected. Between 1958 and 1968 the contribution of the industry to the country's industrial production fell from 60% to 49%, and during the same period the industry's share of exports dropped from 86% to 69%. However, the proportion of the industrial labour force employed in the iron and steel industry has remained static at 48%, and this and the other figures clearly indicate that the activity is still central to the economy. It is no wonder that the government is anxious that foreign investment should continue to be attracted to the Duchy, and the generous incentives offered to new industry, inaugurated in 1962, still operate. Recent changes in the economy fall into two categories: those in manufacturing and those in the tertiary sector.

Changes in manufacturing

Apart from trying to achieve economies by operating in large units (see Chapter 4), the iron and steel industry has made other efforts to overcome its poor location. The larger of the two firms, ARBED, has developed a computer-controlled blast furnace at Esch-Belval, and at the same time it is endeavouring to diversify its range of steel products. In conjunction with an American firm, National Standard, ARBED has begun to manufacture steel wire for use in tyres at Dudelange, and in association with the Saar firm of Rochling is building a second steel wire plant at Volklingen in the Saar. With the aid of another American firm, the Continental Ore Corporation, ARBED is shortly to begin the manufacture of alloy steels at its Dommeldange plant, north of Luxembourg City. ARBED has a subsidiary engineering company, Paul Wurth, which has substantially diversified its interests during the last decade, and has recently added the construction of atomic reactors to its repertoire. The firm has important interests outside Luxembourg, very largely in steel-making, for example it has a holding in SIDMAR at Zelzate, but it also controls Felten and Guilleaume, the West German electrical engineering concern.

Important though they may be, these developments have been over-shadowed by the rapid expansion of neotechnic industry since 1962, accounting in large part for the current prosperity and laying a solid foundation for the future. Some 50 firms have established themselves in the Grand Duchy as a result of the 1962 development legislation, accounting for 40% of industrial growth and for one-fifth of the growth of the country's national income. In the process 6 000 new workplaces have been generated. American firms have been responsible for much of the expansion, and the leader has been Goodyear, the tyre manufacturer. This firm set up its first plant at Colmar in 1950, long before the era of government assistance, in order to produce tyres behind the Benelux tariff barrier, and thus to be able to compete with the Belgian firm of Englebert. During the 1960s Goodyear expanded its original plant, where employment rose from 400 in 1951 to 2 000 in 1971, and added two at Colmar, known as Luxembourg Industries and Luxmold, and a steel wire plant, Luxwire, at Bissen near Colmar. Goodyear now employs 3 000 and it is anticipated that this will have risen to 3 500 by 1975. The next largest firm is Monsanto, manufacturing man-made fibres at Echternach, followed by another chemical company, Du Pont, which began production of polyester foil in 1965, and is building a plant at Contern, east of Luxembourg City, for the manufacture of photographic materials. Goodyear, Monsanto and Du Pont are responsible for two-thirds of investment by the new industries, and it is noticeable that all three are in various branches of the chemical industry, so that for all its diversification, Luxembourg's industry is still largely restricted to two sectors. There are indications, however, that a third sector, engineering and metalworking, may become important during the 1970s. The engineering firm of Commercial Hydraulics at Diekirch and Cleveland Tramrail at Chervaux are respectively the fourth and fifth largest of the new firms, and General Motors has opened a heavy truck and scraper plant at Bascharage. Apart from the ARBED alloy steel plant at Dommeldange, a high grade metal foundry has been opened at Grevenmacher, and an aluminium fabricating plant is in operation at Troisvierges.

As Fig. 7.7 illustrates, very little of the employment arising from the developments of the last decade has been effected in the iron and steel region in the south, nor has Luxembourg City itself attracted many new firms. The dispersed nature of the new employment is quite marked and emphasises the absence of a regional problem in the country. By virtue of Goodyear's operations, Colmar has been the recipient of the largest number of new workplaces, followed by Echternach in the east, Wiltz, Diekirch and Chervaux in the Oesling to the north, and Contern to the east of the capital. The case of the Ardenne town of Wiltz is particularly interesting, for at one time the local leather industry employed almost the entire industrial population. The last large leather works closed in 1960

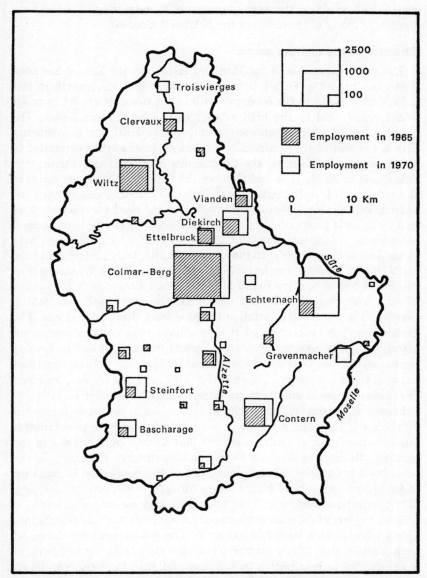

Fig. 7.7 Employment changes in industries established in Luxembourg, 1960-1970

and within the space of three years a range of new industries had been established, avoiding the unemployment and emigration that has been the fate of many of the towns of the Belgian Ardennes.

Changes in the tertiary sector

The rapid expansion of banking and finance in the Duchy has been noted in Chapter 4. Suffice it to mention here that the growth in this field is very useful to the economy both in the invisible export earnings which result, and in the high salaries earned by the employees. The country has benefited from membership of the EEC, for Luxembourg City is the seat of the Community's Court of Justice, the Secretariat of the European Parliament, the Community Statistical and Publication Office, and in April, June and October the Council of Ministers meets in the city instead of Brussels. Apart from the building programmes involved, long-term employment is created by the need for office workers and for a wide range of services such as hotels, taxis, restaurants and entertainment facilities. The tourist industry is exhibiting steady growth. Being unable to compete with the resorts of Spain, Italy, Belgium and the Netherlands, Luxembourg has tried to develop the distinctive scenery of the Petite Suisse country round Mullerthal and Echternach, the castles of such towns as Vianden and Chervaux, the many medieval-looking towns and the national reputation for good food, drink and service. The government has enacted legislation to improve the environment in an attempt to foster tourism, to protect ancient monuments and to develop recreation centres. The recently completed Holiday Inn, built on American lines and sited between Luxembourg City and its airport, received government support and there are plans for a second similar hotel.

In spite of the obvious prosperity of Luxembourg, the future is clouded by the acute shortage of labour. A low natural increase in population is often characteristic of problem regions, but Luxembourg has one of the lowest birth rates in Western Europe, although more than 90% of the population is Catholic. Already one-third of the population is made up of foreigners and 35% of births are to foreigners who account for 39% of the industrial workforce. Unemployment may be only 1%, but it is difficult to expand the economy without an adequate working population, unless more foreign labour is recruited. The government has favoured capital rather than labour intensive firms for some time, but unless there is substantial retionalisation in the iron and steel industry, continued growth can only be achieved by further immigration, and this may lead to problems of social integration.

B. The Restructuring Areas of Benelux
7.4 THE WALLOON COALFIELD

The Haine-Sambre-Meuse coalfield, spanning Belgium from the Borinage to Liège, is the only example in Benelux of a manufacturing region based on the classic principles of steam industrialism. The outcropping coal seams, the presence of local iron ore, glass sands, clay suitable for pottery and of navigable waterways, were utilised by the early industrialists to fashion a Black Country without parallel in mid-19th-century continental Europe. The collieries were producing three times the output of the Ruhr in 1850, and the discovery that much of the coal mined in the Borinage and the Centre was of prime coking quality emphasised the suitability of the area for iron-making. That the first Belgian coke-fired blast furnace was erected in 1823 and that the Ruhr should have to wait until 1849, when the Mulheim works was begun, is indicative of the lead the region set up. The traditional ingenuity of the Liège armourers, who had been producing a wide range of weapons from swords to pistols and artillery pieces since the Middle Ages, was harnessed to the manufacture of machinery of all kinds. Further regional specialisation included, for example, the concentration of glass-making at Charleroi, of pottery in the Borinage and zinc-refining along the Meuse valley between Huy and Liège, but coal was at the root of these activities, irrespective of location.

In common with many British coalfields, the Walloon field moved into the 20th century with a narrow economic base, although it was by no means so specialist as South Wales, Lancashire or North-East England. Protective measures introduced by the government in the 1930s helped the coal industry to withstand competition from the Ruhr, some collieries built coking plants and went into carbochemicals, and in particular there was diversification by the engineering industry. The Charleroi district, which had concentrated on heavy engineering with the manufacture of large forgings, boilers and railway rolling stock, added turbines and heavy duty electrical equipment to its range. In this it was aided by the establishment of Ateliers de Constructions Electriques de Charleroi (ACEC) at the behest of Leopold II at the turn of the century. As an outgrowth of the skills of the metalworkers of Liège, here there was a shift into lighter engineering, including such activities as the production of cars, motorcycles, aircraft, aircraft components and automatic weapons.

The established industries of the coalfield

The most important employer of labour in the region in the 1950s was coalmining, and it has been particularly unfortunate that this activity should prove to be the most uneconomic of all the coalfield industries. The contraction noted in Chapter 3 was delayed by the subsidies received from the Belgian government and the ECSC, and by the private ownership of the pits, but the retention of the existing capacity could not be justified after 1960. There has since been a steady fall in output and the labour force has dwindled from 111 000 in 1957 to 12 000 in 1970. The difficulty of finding work for the unemployed miners has been compounded by the largest reduction in manpower being effected in the Borinage and the Centre, where alternative employment is in shortest supply. In 1958 there were 22 000 coalmining jobs in the Borinage, and now there is only one pit remaining employing 1 500; employment in the Centre was 16 000 in 1958, but now the single pit in operation has work for only 1 000 men. Had it not been for the repatriation of Italian and other foreign miners and the registration of Flemish miners in their home employment exchanges, the problems of re-employment would have been worse than they were. As it was there were many angry scenes at the pits in the early 1960s before the miners came to accept their fate. There seems little future for the industry, and the task of providing alternative employment will continue in the 1970s. The high cost of coal has adversely affected the carbochemical industry and some coking plants have had to close. Carbonisation Centrale at Tertre in the Borinage, however, has kept open by switching to the use of petrochemicals as raw materials.

The second major industry, iron and steel production, is by no means faced with the same calamitous situation. Indeed, in terms of output the industry is expanding, although as we have seen in Chapter 4, it is disadvantageously located in comparison with the coastal iron and steel districts. Thus expansion has not been as rapid as at the SIDMAR and Hoogovens plants. Further, by means of rationalisation it has proved possible to decrease the labour force as production has risen, with the consequence that from a total of 52 000 workers in 1956, employment has fallen to 44 000. Oxygen and electric steel-making have been introduced at the larger existing works, a new steelworks has been built at Chertal near Liège, but some of the smaller, older works such as that at Gilly, Charleroi, have been forced to close. A number of specialist plants have been taken over by the large groups, and this should ensure their continuation; in the case of Usines à Tubes near Mons, recently acquired by Cockerill, the works provides useful diversification in an area which has never been strong in metal-working. The industry plans to invest 30 000 million francs (£250 millions) between 1970 and 1975, but it is not anticipated that more jobs will be forthcoming. Steel and metal products are an important part of Belgian exports, but it is significant that between 1957 and 1967 their share of exports fell from 49% to 28%. Since the coalfield is the main producer of these goods, the figures emphasise the difficulties the region is facing.

The coalfield possesses several other old-established industries, none of which is as important as coalmining or iron and steel, but which were once large employers of labour. The Borinage pottery and porcelain industry has been hard hit by the advent of plastics and has almost disappeared. In 1921 Charleroi boasted some 18 of the 21 Belgian glassworks, but now all but four of the coalfield works are closed. It is a commentary on the changing centre of gravity in Belgian economic activity that the largest glassworks is the Glaverbel plant at Mol in Kempenland. However, the historic works at Val St. Lambert near Liège, manufacturing high-quality glass is still in production, although it is now operated by the government. Of the once important zinc-refining industry in the

TABLE 7.1

Contraction of the labour force in the declining Walloon industries, 1959-1969

	Loss	%
Coalmining	69 000	−72
Leather and rubber goods	1 667	−29
Clothing	2 932	−21
Textiles	4 436	−18
Iron and steel	8 306	−9
Chemicals	757	−7

Liège district only two plants remain, at Flône and Prayon, and the Verviers wool textile industry is slowly contracting. The heavy machinery industry of Charleroi may not be contracting, but at best it must be described as stagnant. In Flanders heavy engineering is not well developed, and in its place are such growth industries as vehicle assembly. The heavy chemical industry producing soda, ammonia and fertilisers, is experiencing slow growth, but this compares unfavourably with the speed of expansion of similar plants at Antwerp. The Solvay works at Couillet is linked to the Benelux-West German ethylene grid, and by means such as this the Walloons optimistically hope '*maritimiser la Wallonie*' rather than to have '*maritimiser l'industrie belge*'. The loss of jobs in some of the declining coalfield industries is set out in Table 7.1.

Quite apart from its high cost compared with other sources of energy, coal can no longer draw industry to its source because of such factors as improvements in transport, the small proportion (*c.* 4%) of the cost of energy in total costs, and because oil, natural gas and electricity are more flexible. New industrial development has been particularly attracted to the Brussels-Antwerp axial belt, not only because of the advantages of this region, but also because of the depressing environment and outworn infrastructure of the coalfield. Outdated labour skills, workpeople with a reputation for being intransigent, poor housing, inadequate roads, atmospheric pollution particularly round Charleroi and Liège and a plethora of colliery spoil heaps in the somewhat constricted valleys of the Haine, Sambre and Meuse, can but repel new manufacturing and above all service industries.

Symptoms of the decline

Although the roots of the problems of the region are to be found in the absence of diversification in the first half of the 20th century, the backward nature of much of Flanders obscured the plight of the coalfield until the 1960s. With the exception of the Borinage with its very narrow economic base, unemployment rates in the coalfield were lower than that for the nation in 1959, but as Table 7.2 indicates, this situation began to change in the early 1960s, and the reverse is now the case. Between 1959

TABLE 7.2
Unemployment in the Walloon coalfield, 1959-1970

	1959	1964	1970
Mons	6·0%	5·0%	8·5%
Charleroi-La Louvière	1·7%	0·9%	3·3%
Namur	2·3%	1·4%	3·6%
Liège-Huy	3·8%	1·9%	7·7%
Verviers	3·6%	1·9%	4·7%
Belgium	5·5%	2·0%	3·2%

and 1970 the coalfield's share of national unemployment rose from 20% to 46%, emphasising the favourable situation in the old industrial region compared with that in Flanders at the beginning of the period. The present high unemployment rate on the coalfield must be viewed against the background of a declining working population, which diminished by 20% during the 1960s. This was a result of the low birth rate found on the coalfield, the early retirement of miners and other redundant workers, and perhaps most importantly, emigration to areas of better employment. It is fortunate that there is one French-speaking growth area in the country, that is, Brussels, for without this outlet the Walloons would have to remain in Wallonie since they would not be accepted in Flanders. During the four years 1967-1970 there was a net outflow of migrants to Brussels-Capitale from the three coalfield *arrondissements* of Charleroi, Mons and Liège of 2 524, 1 681 and 1 676 respectively. In addition, the proximity of the capital and the cheap rail fares encourage considerable commuting from the coalfield towns to Brussels, so that some 12 000 of the younger, more dynamic population of the Borinage who work in Brussels contribute to the growth of the capital rather than to the region in which they live. Employment in the Valenciennes district in France is better than in the Borinage, and 35 000 cross the frontier each day. Between 1959 and 1967, output *per capita* rose 3·2% in Wallonie as against 4·7% in Flanders, and electricity consumption, a useful index of prosperity, increased 155% in Flanders between 1953 and 1965, compared with a rise of only 69% in Wallonie. It is not surprising that foreign investment should be directed to the confidently expanding region between Brussels and Antwerp. The provinces of Hainaut and Liège received only 12% and 3% respectively of foreign investment in Belgium during the period 1959-1969.

It is not only the economic but also the social infrastructure of the region which is in a parlous condition. Because the population is falling there is not the demand for new housing characteristic of expanding areas. Thus three-quarters of the houses in existence in 1961 were built before 1914, and most of these had inadequate methods of heating water. Working-class housing is found juxtaposed with factories, waste land and spoil heaps, and towns like La Louvière in the Centre possess weakly developed urban functions, with the consequence that the quality of life is not as good as it would be in a well-diversified regional centre.

The reconversion of the region

Although the coalfield industrial region is still patently in decline, without financial assistance from the EEC, the Belgian government and local authorities, coupled with help from regional development organisations such as the Conseil Economique Wallon, the area would be fast becoming an industrial ruin. The 1959 regional development legislation was principally concerned with the absorption of structural unemployment in West- and Oost-Vlanderen, large areas in the western part of the Kempenland, together with a few areas in Wallonie, such as the coalmining districts of the Borinage and the Centre, and the Verviers textile district. At that time economic conditions in the Charleroi and Liège districts were not unsatisfactory, and predictably some two-thirds of the funds allocated went to the Flemish districts where there was much rural unemployment. It was not until the 1966 legislation came into operation that the larger part of the coalfield received government aid (Fig. 7.8). This time the assistance was greater than that assigned to the Flemish development areas. In 1969 the province of Hainaut received 4 784 million francs (£40 millions), but the following year the figure rose to 8 101 million francs (£67 millions), representing nearly half the total Belgian expenditure on regional support in that year. This figure is

P

exceptional for it is to some extent a result of the inflow of government
funds in connection with the expansion of oil refining and petrochemical
production in Féluy, but it is nevertheless indicative of the size of the
support measures that are being effected. Between 1959 and 1969 some
29 000 jobs were created in Hainaut and 17 000 in Liège, one-third and
one-quarter of the respective workplaces having been established in new
factories. Impressive though they are, these figures muse be seen in the
context of the loss of 69 000 jobs in mining alone and of expansion elsewhere. Over the same period 39 000 jobs were created in the province of

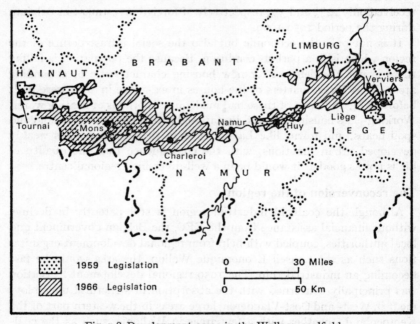

1959 Legislation

1966 Legislation

0   30 Miles

0   50 Km

Fig. 7.8 Development areas in the Walloon coalfield

Antwerp, and some of those—in the port area, for example—were not
influenced by central government aid. Even in Oost-Vlanderen some
30 000 workplaces were generated in these years, great impetus being
due to the establishment of the SIDMAR iron and steel plant.

New employment is encouraged not only by the financial incentives of
regional policy, outlined in Chapter 4, but also by the availability of
industrial estates equipped with public utilities, including in many cases
natural gas, and good access roads. The first estates were set up in those
areas benefiting from the 1959 legislation and ECSC conversion grants
available in areas of contracting coal production. The funds for these

estates, which are deemed to be of national importance, came from Brussels and from the ECSC. Some of the national estates, mapped in Figs. 7.9 and 7.10, are very large indeed. The two at Ghlin-Baudour, facing each other across the Nimy-Blaton canal, have a total area of 952 ha, the estate at Namur is 571 ha, and that at Hauts Sarts, Liège, is 550 ha. It is interesting to observe that two of the larger national estates, at Seneffe (305 ha) and Féluy (598 ha), are not located on the coalfield but to the north along the line of the Léopold (formerly Charleroi-Brussels) canal. Féluy is in fact half way between Brussels and Charleroi, and this has been an important advantage in persuading firms to patronise the estates. A second tier of estates, those of regional significance, receive 65% of their funds from the central government, the *inter-communales*, or municipal development associations, finding the remain-

TABLE 7.3
The size of plants established on the Walloon coalfield, 1959-1970

			Number of workers			
	1-10	11-50	51-200	201-500	500	Total
Borinage	2	13	16	4	4	39
Centre	1	10	13	3	2	29
Charleroi	2	5	4	2	1	14
Namur	—	8	2	1	—	11
Liège	6	16	20	5	5	52
	11	52	55	15	12	145

der. There are five *intercommunales* with estates on the coalfield. The Société Coopérative Intercommunale de Développement Economique et d'Aménagement du Territoire du Hainault Occidental (SIDEHO) operating in the western Borinage, and there are similar bodies in the Borinage-Centre, Charleroi, Namur and Liège districts. The regional estates are smaller than the national estates, the largest being at Dour-Elouges (203 ha) in the Borinage. The local estates, set up by the individual local authorities and private development companies, are not numerous outside Liège, where there is a cluster of seven, the largest of which, Chertal (185 ha), houses the Espérance-Longdoz (now Cockerill) steel mill. Predictably the big national estates have the greatest number of workers, and Ghlin-Baudour and Hauts Sarts each provide employment for more than 3 000.

As a direct result of financial inducements and the provision of industrial estates, some 145 new plants were established on or adjacent to the coalfield between 1959 and 1970. As Table 7.3 shows, 107 of these plants employ between 11 and 200 workers, and there are only a few large plants with more than 500 employees. The distribution of the plants is a function of the size of the industrial estates, itself related to the need to provide new employment, and of the size of the industrial regions. The Borinage is an example of the former principle, with four large firms, ICI at Peruwelz, Bell Telephone at Wasmes, Verlica Glass at Ghlin-Baudour and Salik Clothing at Quaregnon, and Liège of the latter. Liège has the largest number of new firms and has five large plants: Espérance-Longdoz at Chertal, Elphiac making power station equipment also at Chertal, MBLE manufacturing electric light bulbs at Hollogne, Owens Corning Fiberglass at Battice and Westinghouse at Awans. The Centre has benefited from the Seneffe and Féluy estates which have attracted British Leyland and the Petrochim petrochemical plant respectively. Charleroi has only one large plants, the American Caterpillar firm at Gosselies, producing earth-moving equipment.

A vital consideration for the future is the nature of the products of the new factories, for ideally firms manufacturing neotechnic goods are most likely to exhibit the fastest growth, and they are also most likely to be long lived. It is therefore comforting to see that there is a good spread of the new technological industries among recent entrants to the coalfield. Of the 27 largest firms in Table 7.3, five are in oil-based chemicals, four are in electronics, four produce transport equipment and components, three are concerned with aluminium fabrication and two are in precision engineering. Only the three clothing firms, the glassworks, the steel plant and the worsted combing mill could be said to be extensions of the staple industries of the coalfield. It is to be hoped that the new industries will be able to expand as rapidly as their counterparts in the Brussels-Antwerp axial belt, for this has not been the case with the older industries. Only paper production has exhibited a growth rate superior to that achieved by this industry in Flanders over the past decade.

It is possible that the regional specialisation that is beginning to occur will assist the newly established coalfield activities. The most obvious specialisation is the Chevron oil refinery and the Petrochim petrochemical complex at Féluy; it is probable that additional petrochemical plants will establish themselves in the locality. Also in the Centre-Charleroi district a cluster of transport equipment plants is evident. Apart from British Leyland at Seneffe, there are spark plug (Champion), brake lining, car accessory and earth-moving equipment plants in the region. The French aircraft firm of Dassault has a works at Gosselies, as does Fairey Aviation who are currently expanding their production lines to allow the assembly of Islander and Trislander aircraft. Gosselies also possesses a firm making aeronautical spare parts. Regional specialisation in the Liège district has taken the form of an extension of established technologies in engineering and metalworking into electronic products, nuclear power station equipment and aluminium fabrication. In a region which formerly manufactured vehicles and aircraft (and still does produce engines for the Belgian Air Force), it is not surprising to find a sprinkling of vehicle component firms, a branch of the Van Hool bus assembly firm and an aircraft component plant. If plans to build light aircraft and electronic equipment by Israel Aircraft Industries and the Beech Aircraft Corporation at Bierset airport materialise, Liège might come to rival Gosselies in respect of aircraft production.

In conclusion, if the renewal of unsatisfactory housing and the removal of unsightly spoil heaps is proceeding slowly, at least the transport infrastructure is being satisfactorily modernised. The Sambre between Monceau and Namur was opened to 1 350-ton barges in June 1969, so that with the completion of the impressive barge-lift at Ronquières on the Léopold canal the previous April, there is now a complete 1 350-ton canal network linking Antwerp, Liège, Charleroi, Brussels and Antwerp. The modernisation of the Scheldt has been greatly delayed by the need to complete the Ghent ring-canal in advance of the other works, but it is hoped that the two remaining sections between Peronnes and Tournai and Oudenaarde and Ghent will be opened in the mid-1970s. When the Canal du Centre between Mons and La Louvière is modernised the western 1 350-ton canal loop linking Antwerp, Brussels, La Louvière, Mons, Tournai, Ghent and Antwerp will have been achieved. The Namur-Liège railway line was finally electrified in 1970, creating an electric rail service between the Ruhr, Aachen, Liège, Charleroi and Paris via the Sambre valley. It is noticeable that this new railway link and, for the moment, the 1 350-ton barge network, avoid both the Centre and the Borinage. Perhaps it is just as well that most of the new industries rely on road transport and that the *Route de Wallonie*, the E41 motorway which traverses the coalfield, providing road links with the Ruhr and Paris, is virtually complete (Figs. 7.9 and 7.10). This will help to open up markets in France and West Germany, but since it will act similarly for French and German industry, it must be hoped that the new Wallonie will be able to hold its own. Meanwhile the region is by no means fully 'reconverted', as the unemployment data indicate, but if present trends in the Brussels-Antwerp axial belt continue, it would seem that within the next decade the Liège and Namur sectors of the coalfield will have become an integral part of the Belgian growth area.

7.5   THE DUTCH AND BELGIAN PROVINCES OF LIMBURG

Dutch and Belgian Limburg were separated by the arbitrary political contingencies of the 17th century, and the division was confirmed, al-

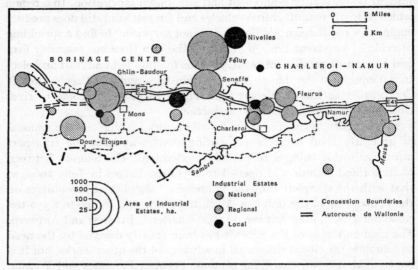

Fig. 7.9 Industrial estates in the Borinage, Centre and Charleroi coalfields

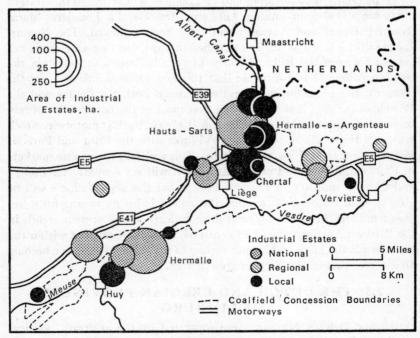

Fig. 7.10 Industrial estates in the Liège coalfield

though not without strenuous opposition from both sides of the frontier, in 1839. Despite their inclusion in separate states, it is convenient, in view of the similarity of the problems facing the two regions, to consider them together. Although both areas have peripheral locations within their respective states, and were throughout the 19th century overwhelmingly agrarian, they are included within the category of restructuring regions since the early years of the 20th century saw a radical switch into coalmining, an activity which in the 1970s is fraught with problems.

The Belgian province of Limburg is situated in the north-east of the country away from the main centres of Belgian political and economic power. The location of the Dutch province is even more eccentric when viewed from the Randstad. It is a salient thrust 50 km southwards, surrounded on three sides by foreign states, and connected to the 'mainland' by an isthmus which narrows to only 8 km. A feeling of cultural identity, encouraged by this isolation, exists strongly in both regions. This was reflected in the Belgian case by a staunch adherence to Flemish nationalism which underlay the economic grievances that culminated in the riots at Zwartberg in 1966. In the Dutch case the province of Limburg has agitated three times in the last 150 years for inclusion in a state other than the Netherlands, and was governed almost as a Dutch colony until its full legal integration into the Netherlands as late as 1869.

The coalmining industry

The existence of a coal basin stretching across both provinces from east to west in a band some 65 km long and 15 km wide has been known since the Middle Ages, and small-scale working for local needs has been carried on in the Dutch sector since the 12th century. The depth of the seams in Belgium and western Zuid-Limburg, coupled with the aquiferous sands and gravels which made shaft sinking very difficult and prohibitively costly, delayed large-scale mining until this century. The exploitation of the coalfield in areas devoid of large settlements necessitated the construction of communities as well as collieries. In Belgium, company estates, known as *swijnwijken*, as at Eisden and Zwartberg, were built. In the Netherlands small existing country towns and villages such as Kerkrade, Heerlen and Geleen mushroomed into colliery towns. In both types of settlement the newness and isolation bred distinctive self-contained communities reminiscent of the South Wales mining valleys, although the later timing of the development enabled the grosser despoilation of the landscape to be avoided.

An important difference between the two parts of the field can be found in the development of ancillary industries at the pithead. In

Belgium only a small proportion of the coal was used locally, most being exported by barge. In the Netherlands, however, because of the difficulties of transport northwards from Zuid-Limburg prior to the opening of the Juliana canal in 1936, and the greater degree of state planning, a far higher proportion of the coal won was processed *in situ*. Large coking plants were established at the Maurits and Emma pits and the by-product gas piped to the towns of Limburg, Noord-Brabant and the Ruhr. A substantial chemical industry developed, exemplified by the nitrogen fixation plant at Geleen, the production of naphtha at Beek and of methane south of Sittard. Between 1930 and 1960 the output of fertilisers increased ten-fold to reach 1 million tons a year, of which over half was exported, and much of the remainder was used on the Ijsselmeer polders. Four large power stations were constructed and feed power into a grid operating between the Western Netherlands, West Germany and Belgium.

The change in Dutch energy policy that reversed the expansion of the mid-1950s to a retraction a decade later was remarkable in both its abruptness and its completeness. In the ten immediate post-war years the principal problem affecting the Zuid-Limburg coal industry was its inability to expand fast enough to keep pace with demand. A labour shortage developed, foreign labour was attracted and a modernisation programme set in motion. In spite of this in 1964 the Dutch government took the decision to phase out coal production in Zuid-Limburg completely. On the other hand, the Belgians could not justify such action in respect of the Kempen. Their response can be attributed to their greater national commitment to coal, compared with the early post-war commitment of the Dutch to imported oil, and to the discovery of the huge natural gas field in Groningen in 1959. In addition, Zuid-Limburg was the sole Dutch example of a coal-dependent region and could thus receive the full attention of the central government. The Kempen had to compete for attention with the Walloon field whose need for assistance was more immediate.

The contraction of employment in coalmining can be detected in the Dutch field from 1958, and by 1966 only 35 000 jobs remained out of a previous maximum of 67 200. In Belgium a similar decline from 42 200 to 26 500 occurred between 1957 and 1968. This decline will continue to the point of extinction in the Dutch field, where the last colliery is scheduled for closure early in 1973. Employment in the Kempen was down to 19 000 in 1971. The effect of colliery closures in regions with few alternative employment opportunities was large-scale unemployment and much insecurity about the future of Limburg as an industrial area. This was particularly true of Zuid-Limburg where mining still provided 52%

of jobs in 1966, especially in the older field in the east round Heerlen, where few coal processing activities had developed, and where the mines were mostly privately owned. In the Kempen alternative employment was limited to activities such as non-ferrous metal refining, brick-making, clothing manufacture and glass production.

The restructuring of the region

The attraction of new industrial plant was hindered in Zuid-Limburg by the shortage of sites on the coalfield where a high density of population, reaching 1 264 per square kilometre in the old field, had left few extensive areas of flat land unoccupied. On the Belgian field land was more plentiful, but a major obstacle was the unattractive image of the coalfield environment and of its labour force held by industralists. On the credit side the coalfield could offer a large pool of labour accustomed to rates of pay below those found among industrial workers in the Western Netherlands or in the Brussels-Antwerp region, financial assistance from government funds, the provision of industrial estates, of retraining schemes and of copious information. A major attractive factor has been the reassertion of the centrality of the Middle-Maas region, not only within Benelux, but also within the EEC.

Transport is of critical importance to the industrial restructuring of the region. Canals were developed during the period of the coal economy (Fig. 7.11). The Juliana Canal of 2 500-ton barge capacity, running parallel with the Maas in the Dutch panhandle, was the principal coal outlet for the Dutch field; the coal port of Stein was the second busiest inland port in Western Europe in 1961. In Belgium the Albert Canal provided the link between Antwerp and Liège, and the northern part of the province was served by the Zuid-Willems canal. Paradoxically the Albert Canal has done little to aid the development of industry within Limburg, since its existence had made it more economic to move coal to the well-established plants at Liège and Charleroi than to construct canal-side plants in Limburg. Recent investment in the transport infrastructure of the region has concentrated largely on motorways which exploit its central position. The Boudouin motorway or Boudewijnweg (E39) has been completed between Antwerp and Liège, following the Albert Canal through Limburg as far as Hasselt. The planned Brussels-Aachen motorway cuts through the Kempen field and the Zuid-Limburg field, where it has already been completed. A major European north-south route, the E9, links Liège and Amsterdam, providing a spine road along the Maas the full length of the Dutch province. Between Liège and Maastricht, however, this road is not of motorway standard.

Industrial estates, financed partly by the state, by the ECSC and by the local municipalities have been set up in both provinces, and have proved attractive, especially to the medium- and small-sized firms. In the Netherlands four major estates have been established, with half the cost of the land and a quarter of the fixed costs being met by the

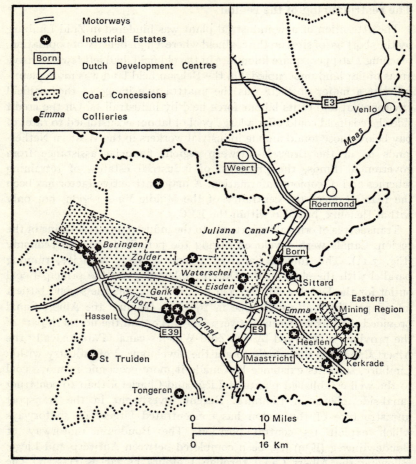

Fig. 7.11 The Belgian and Dutch provinces of Limburg

central government. These are at Roermond in the north, Buchten 7 km north-west of Sittard, Beitel south of Heerlen and at Kling. In Belgium national estates are located at Beringen, Houthalen, Mechelen aan de Maas and Genk, a regional estate at Lenaken and there are five estates of local importance. In addition to the planned estates, some large firms have opened plants in the region. Philips have located themselves at Hasselt in Belgium and at Sittard in the Netherlands. Siemens have a factory at Lanklaar in Belgium and there are automobile plants at Genk (Ford) and Born(DAF) on the Juliana Canal. The early diversification of the Dutch Staatsmijnen into chemical manufacture has provided a valuable growth sector in Zuid-Limburg, especially since it has proved technically possible simply to switch from coal as the raw material to oil, natural gas and ethylene, all of which are imported by pipe. In addition, DSM are to construct an oil refinery at Geleen. In Belgium the increasing use of the Albert Canal can be noticed, especially where firms desire the cheap movement of bulk commodities. Examples include the development of the chemical industry at Kwaadmechelen and Tessenderlo, the use of canal bank sites at Genk for paper, chemical and stainless steel plants at Genk.

TABLE 7.4

New employment in Belgian Limburg, 1960-1971

Engineering	22 506
Textiles and clothing	8 868
Food processing	1 912
Metal industries	1 837
Paper	722
Chemicals	434
Metallurgy	245

The result of this regional restructuring is that between 1960 and 1967 Belgian Limburg had an annual growth rate in excess of that for the country as a whole. Some 42 000 new jobs were created between 1960 and 1971, of which half were in the engineering industries. The attraction of the area within the EEC is reflected in the part played by foreign investment in this growth: 38% of the new employment was in West German plants, 30% in Dutch plants and 14% in United States' plants. However, mining is still an important activity in the Kempen field and the short-term problems of the region are likely to hinge upon decisions as to the level of coal production held to be desirable. In Zuid-Limburg, coal has almost gone, and it is to the great credit of the planners that this fundamental transition has been effected so smoothly.

C. The Peripheral Regions of Benelux
7.6 THE NORTHERN NETHERLANDS

Despite the considerable differences that exist between them, the three northern provinces of the Netherlands, Friesland, Groningen and

Drenthe, are usually considered as a single entity—the North—because of the sharp socio-economic distinctions between the region and the rest of the country. The problems facing the North are the most difficult that Dutch regional planning has had to face, and they may be demonstrated in a number of ways (Table 7.5).

Average incomes in the North are substantially below the national average, Friesland and Drenthe suffering more than Groningen in this respect. During the last two decades there has been a considerable net outward movement of people from the North, leaving the area with an unbalanced age and sex structure. A much higher proportion of the labour force is employed in agriculture than in the country as a whole, the proportion in Drenthe reaching a remarkably high level for an area

TABLE 7.5

Socio-economic characteristics of the Northern Netherlands, 1970

	Groningen	Friesland	Drenthe	Netherlands
Population density (1971), km²	227	156	141	388
Population in towns 50 000, %	31	17	—	47
Population in villages 2 000, %	37	51	54	22
Per capital income (1965), index numbers	93	83	84	100
Agricultural employment, %	16·4	22·7	27·3	10·7
Industrial employment, %	38·9	34·9	38·2	42·2
Commercial employment, %	24	21	15	23
Communist vote (1971), %	11·4	3·5	4·0	3·9
Gereformde church membership, %	15·0	21·2	13·1	6·9

within an advanced country. As a consequence employment in manufacturing and in the tertiary sector, with the exception of Groningen in the latter instance, is lower than the national average. Friesland is especially short of manufacturing industry, and Drenthe of service activities. Both the figures for manufacturing and also those for commerce and banking, however, conceal the lack of variety in the former and the local nature of the latter. The relatively low density of the population and the small size of the settlements have discouraged the construction of transport facilities, raised the *per capita* cost of public works schemes and have sometimes created problems of labour supply when industry is created. In particular the existence of only one major centre, Groningen, with a population of 170 000, known throughout the North simply as *de stad*, or the city, has hindered the development of service industries with big market thresholds, because of the low purchasing power in the North. Even Groningen cannot be considered as a major population centre by the standards of the remainder of the Netherlands, and of the other towns only Leeuwarden (90 000) has more than 30 000 inhabitants. As Table 7.5 indicates, more than half the population of Drenthe and Friesland live in settlements of less than 2 000 people. Since 1950 the unemployment rate in the North has been three times larger than the national figure, and this reflects the way in which industrialists see the economic potential of the area. Finally the area has several distinctive cultural and political characteristics. The strongest manifestation of these is the existence in Friesland of a separate national identity, supported by a distinct language. In addition, religious extremism is witnessed in the strength of the *gereformde* church. These cultural expressions illustrate not only the isolation of the North, but also the implicit problems of generating change.

It is difficult to ascribe the relative poverty of the North to any single influence, but in general terms most of the problems stem from the peripheral location of the region. A peripheral location within a state may be used to advantage if it combines centrality within a larger region, as is the case with Limburg, but the North abuts into the dominantly agricultural region of Lower Saxony in West Germany. The physical isolation of the North is a result of both distance from the Randstad and the barrier presented by the Zuider Zee and the Wadden Zee to the north and west, and by the sandy heathlands to the south and east. Transport improvements have not substantially altered this situation, for although the *afsluitdijk* road link was completed in 1932, and is now supplemented by the R6 road across Flevoland, a rail link has never been completed. The transport network in the North is less dense than in the rest of the country, whether considered in terms of inter-city rail routes, motorways or 1 350-ton canals. In addition the region has suffered more than proportionately from railway closures following the rationalisation of the Dutch railway system. The North can rarely generate sufficient traffic to support transport investment, and there is little incentive to develop through routes. All inland water routes, and most road and rail routes terminate within the region; even the E10 road, linking Groningen, Leeuwarden and the *afsluitdijk*, and the E35, which joins the north German coast and Randstad, are neither of them yet built to motorway standards.

In addition to its isolation, the poverty of the North has been traditionally related to the physical character of the region and its consequent effects upon agriculture. It is more revealing, however, to regard pedological differences as a cause of differentiation within the North rather than as an explanation of the distinction between this region and the Netherlands. The agricultural potential of the clay lands of coastal Groningen or the reclaimed Middelzee area of Friesland is theoretically as great as the Zuid-Holland polders, and has long supported a profitable agriculture. That these regions have not developed the intensive agriculture of Noord- and Zuid-Holland is due to the absence of a large local market and the distance from the market represented by the Western Netherlands. The sand and peat of the Drenthe plateau and the Zevenwouden area in eastern Friesland, on the other hand, are comparatively infertile and have never been capable of supporting as dense an agricultural population. A typical *zeeklei gemeente* such as Appingedam in Groningen has a population density of 448 per square kilometre, but *gemeenten* such as Opsterland in Friesland and Vledder in Drenthe, with sandy soils, return population densities of only 97 and 60 per square kilometre.

Some solutions to the problems

For over twenty years the central government has recognised its responsibility for correcting the regional imbalances of the North. All, or selected parts, of the region have been included in the various regional development policies instituted since 1949. The most optimistic proposals were contained in the second physical planning report of 1966 which postulated a two-fold increase in the population between 1965 and 2000, although without being explicit as to how this was to be achieved.

Agriculture is in the process of extensive restructuring and between 1950 and 1968 the labour force was halved. The North has been allocated priority in the government agricultural re-organisation schemes, and two-thirds of the cultivated area has been, or is in the process of being, affected by this *ruilverkaveling*, or land consolidation. By the year 2000 agriculture in the North will be a smaller, but in all probability, a more profitable industry, specialising increasingly in livestock farming on holdings large by the standards of both the Netherlands and the EEC.

In the last decade the North has become, somewhat unexpectedly, the main producer of energy in the Netherlands. The development of the Schoonebeck oilfield in south Drenthe and the Slochteren gasfield in Groningen (Fig. 7.12) has brought some benefits to the provinces, although less than was at one time anticipated. The oilfield directly employs about 1 000 workers and makes a royalty contribution within the province. Only small quantities of these products are in fact used within the region, and the cost advantage to an industrial firm of locating at the energy source is small. The publicity resulting from discoveries, however, brought the North to the attention of potential investors.

The North can offer an extensive array of financial inducements to industrial firms (Chapter 4), together with a pool of labour available at relatively low wages, access to natural gas at reduced rates in certain circumstances and land obtainable at a lower cost than in the West. Industrial development has been concentrated into a few centres and Delfzijl has emerged as the principal industrial growth point following the establishment of the aluminium smelter in 1966 and the DSM/AKZO methyl alcohol and salt processing plants. Emmen in southern Drenthe has shown a most remarkable growth, expanding in the post-war years

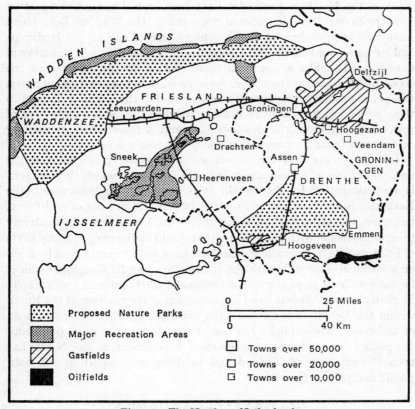

Fig. 7.12 The Northern Netherlands

from an agricultural village to a major centre of synthetic fibre manufacture with a projected population of 150 000 by 2000.

The low population density, the relative isolation that has preserved both landscapes and rural customs and the lack of industrial development can be seen as advantages in the development of the North as a recreation area. Distance from the main centres of recreation demand, however, encourages the growth of certain specific types of recreational activity whose impact on local income and employment is small. In practice the North has attracted land-extensive forms of holiday accommodation, particularly camp sites, for domestic rather than foreign visitors, recreational activities dependent on the water resources of the Friesian lakes, and second home developments for Randstad residents. Only in the Wadden Islands are the more profitable developments, catering for foreign tourists staying in hotels, to be found. Two extensive areas of the North in particular have been considered for designation as recreational areas of national importance, the Wadden Zee, where recreation is subordinated to the conservation of the unique landscape and its fauna, and the Drenthe plateau. In neither case will recreational developments make a significant contribution to the solution of the economic problems of the region. Some increase in the provision of hotels and pensions and other services is anticipated in the towns peripheral to these parks, but these benefits must be weighed against the imposition of restrictions on industrial development, and a fossilisation of existing communities that a conservation policy inevitably involves.

The contention that the seriousness of regional problems and the success of regional policies depends on the context in which they are set, is well illustrated by the North. It is demonstrable that within the Netherlands the North is relatively deprived and in need of assistance, but when viewed as part of Western Europe, it emerges as a relatively prosperous region with an economy that would be the envy of many parts of France or Italy. Regional policies that have until recently been justified on a national scale will, with the emergence of an EEC regional policy, be more difficult to justify in the context of the Community as a whole. Similarly an impediment to an improvement of the position of the North within the Netherlands has been the existence of other regions in need of assistance, whose plight has been more obvious, or more politically compelling. In particular, the greatest impediment of the North has been the existence of Zeeland and Limburg as competitors for both public and private finance.

7.7 WEST-VLAANDEREN

Like most peripheral regions, West-Vlaanderen is faced with a number of difficult problems which are rooted in the distance separating it from the mainstream of national economic life. These difficulties are compounded by the existence of national boundaries on three of the four provincial borders: France to the west, the North Sea coast to the north and a small common frontier with the Netherlands in the north-east. The province is thus very much a cul-de-sac, and indeed the western half of the region is known as Westhoek, or western corner, in Belgium. The political frontier is also responsible for separating towns such as Kortrijk and Menen from their natural focus, the Lille-Roubaix-Tourcoing conurbation in French Nord, with the consequence that their growth has been proportionately reduced. It is now accepted that interest in, and knowledge of regions decreases with increasing distance from the capital city or central region, and this is particularly true of West-Vlaanderen. The province is not blessed with important natural resources which might have helped to overcome its isolation, and until recently large parts of the province, especially in Westhoek, were predominantly agricultural. Some 10% of the working population is still employed in agriculture and fishing compared with the national figure of 6%. Throughout the 19th century, and for much of the 20th, the most important industry was textile manufacture, an activity that has been declining since the inter-war period, but until the 1960s little alternative employment was forthcoming to take its place. Far from registering a declining population, the province has a higher birth rate than the national average, and between 1960 and 1970 the population increased 6·3%, although the national mean was 5·6%. It is not surprising that unemployment is high and that average incomes are 13% lower than those for Belgium.

The 19th-century reaction to high rural population density was the development of industrial crops such as sugar beet, tobacco and flax which are labour-intensive, and also the expansion of the textile industry to make use of tradition skills and low rural wage rates. These strategies, however, were not entirely sufficient, and the industrialisation of the Lille region after mid-century led to some emigration, but more importantly, out-commuting to France. The latter process was aided by the construction of rural tramways, the lower price of consumer goods in Belgium and, after 1889, by the introduction of military conscription in France but not in Belgium. The practice reached enormous proportions in the Depression, when almost 100 000 workers commuted on either a daily or weekly basis to France. The French and Belgian governments took steps in the 1930s to control the movement of workers across the frontier, but as late as 1960 some 35 000, or 17% of the working population of West-Vlaanderen, were employed in France, more than the total working in the other regions of Belgium. Commuting to work in France was at best a palliative, for in times of recession it was always the Belgian workers who were laid off first, and the French were able to export some of their unemployment to Belgium. In the recession between 1950 and 1954, for example, the number of French employees in the Roubaix-Tourcoing textile industry fell 17%, but the decline in the number of Belgians employed there was 35%. The number of cross-frontier commuters, or *frontaliers*, has declined rapidly over the last decade as

Q

employment opportunities in West-Vlaanderen have improved, although it is ironic that the EEC allows much greater international mobility of labour than was previously the case. There are now only 10 000 *frontaliers*, almost all of them drawn from areas such as Menen, Wervik, Wevelgem, Ieper and Poperinge, lying within the sphere of influence of the Lille-Roubaix-Tourcoing-Armentières conurbation.

If the dependence on France for employment has decreased, the extent of out-commuting from the smaller centres in the province is an indication that the switch from an agrarian rural society to one based on manufacturing has not yet been achieved. Towns such as Tielt in the east of the province may be expected to rely on the neighbouring province for some employment, but others, notably Diksmuide, two-thirds of whose working population is employed outside West-Vlaanderen, still rely upon distant regions for a large part of their livelihood. The existence of seasonal migration in West-Vlaanderen after the practice has virtually died out elsewhere in Belgium is a comment on local employment opportunities, for it is a marginal activity and earnings from it merely supplement income from smallholdings. Traditional venues of seasonal employment are the hop-growing district of Aalst, west of Brussels, and the sugar beet regions of Brabant and Hesbaye. A further indication of the problems faced by many of the smaller towns is the low rate of female employment, suggesting that there is still considerable disguised unemployment. Veurne is a case in point, for here only 11% of the female population is employed, compared with 18%-20% in the large towns.

Perhaps the redeeming feature of West-Vlaanderen has been the 67 km of sandy beaches facing the North Sea and the attractions of the medieval town of Bruges. Over the last half century fishing ports and agricultural villages adjacent to the coast have been transformed by the development of tourist facilities, and Ostend in particular has become a substantial resort. Some two-thirds of nights spent in Belgium by tourists are attributable to the North Sea coast, and the absolute numbers are constantly increasing, adding a valuable increment to the regional income. The employment structure of the coastal area reflects the importance of the tourist industry, for only 30% is engaged in manufacture against some 64% in services; agriculture and fishing is a mere 5%. Unfortunately, however, much of the work is of a seasonal nature, and although summer earnings are high, there is nevertheless much unemployment in the off-season.

Faced with dwindling demand for agricultural workers, largely a result of mechanisation and rationalisation, with decline in the largest industry, textiles, and seasonal unemployment on the coast, the province experienced severe unemployment in the 1950s, reaching 15% in 1954. Since 23% of the workforce was employed outside the province, there were no less than 38% more workpeople than jobs. By 1960 unemployment had fallen to 9% and the numbers working in other provinces stood at 17%, but clearly there was ample justification for the inclusion of such areas as Veurne, Diksmuide, Poperinge, Ieper and Tielt within the framework of the 1959 regional policy legislation (Fig. 7.13). The 1966 statute went much further and gave assisted status to the whole of Westhoek, with the exception of the coastal strip, following its tourist activities. Some areas, for the most part those including the regional centres, received assistance from both Acts of Parliament. Only the coast, Bruges, Kortrijk and the Leie valley towns, and the eastern areas of the province were considered sufficiently healthy not to require development area status. In the summer of 1970, unemployment had fallen to 2%, although it must be borne in mind that this was at the height of the tourist season.

Regional policy legislation, coupled with the work of the Westvlaamse Ekonomishe Raad (the West-Vlaanderen Development Council), has made an excellent start to the restructuring of the provincial economy. Six industrial estates, funded by the national government, have been established, five of them in Westhoek; that at Ieper is the largest in West-Vlaanderen with an area of 273 ha. Some 16 estates of regional significance are operated by the Westvlaamse Intercommunale voor Economische Expansie en Reconversie (WIER), in some cases in conjunction with local authorities, and there are four estates of local importance. One of the latter, at Bredene near Ostend, is larger than many of the estates belonging to other levels of the estate hierarchy. As Fig. 7.13 indicates, some of the regional estates are not in the development areas, and this is in line with the policy of encouraging growth in the more favoured areas in addition to the regions of sluggish expansion. The result of this policy, and of the advantages possessed by ports capable of handling large tankers and bulk carriers, is that the Zeebrugge-Bruges axis along the line of the Boudewijn Canal has become a major growth point in the province. No less than 7 of the 15 largest plants to have been opened in West-Vlaanderen between 1960 and 1970 are to be found here, and they include such neotechnic manufacturing as telecommunication equipment, vehicle transmissions, bus assembly and the production of outboard motors, industrial alcohols and paints. There are plans for the construction of new sea locks between Zeebrugge and Heist, capable of handling 125 000-ton ships, and for the cutting of a canal to join the Baudouin canal inland of the present inner harbour. The land in the angle of the two canals and to the east of the Boudewijn Canal will be made available for industrial development, giving a total of 1 460 ha, creating an un-

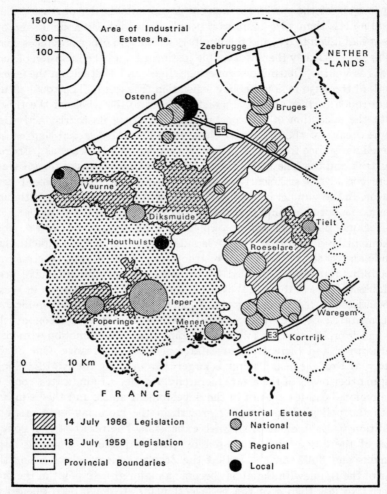

Fig. 7.13 Development areas and industrial estates in West-Vlaanderen

interrupted 12-km-long industrial zone between Zeebrugge and Bruges—
a veritable second Antwerp within Belgium.

Outside Zeebrugge-Bruges, large firms have been attracted to Westhoek
by cheap, particularly female labour and development area incentives.
The greatest expansion has been in the production of ready-made
clothes and underwear, and four large plants have been established in
Ieper alone. A number of smaller engineering works has been opened in

the last decade and it can be seen from Table 7.6 that the province is beginning to diversify out of textiles. It is to be hoped that the existence of the EEC will allow plants in Westhoek to market their goods in France as well as Belgium, and that the E3 motorway between Ghent, Kortrijk, Lille and Paris will assist this process.

TABLE 7.6

Industrial employment in West-Vlaanderen, 1970

Metalworking	25·5%	Wood/cork processing	8·5%
Textiles	19·5%	Food processing	5·0%
Construction	19·0%	Non-metallic minerals	4·0%
Clothing	9·0%		

Further Reading

R.H. Buchanan, 'Towards the Netherlands 2000: the Dutch National Plan', *Economic Geography*, 45, 1969, pp. 258-274.

G. L. Burke, *Greenheart Metropolis. Planning the Western Netherlands*, (Macmillan, London), 1966.

P. Hall, *World Cities* (Weidenfeld and Nicholson, London), 1966.

G. R. P. Lawrence, *Randstad Holland* (Oxford), 1973.

W. Steigenga, 'Randstad Holland: Concept in Evolution', *Tijdschrift voor Economische en Sociale Geografie*, 63, 1972, pp. 149-161.

R. E. Dickinson, *The West European City* (Routledge & Kegan Paul, London), 1961, pp. 142-183.

P. George and R. Sevrin, *Belgique, Pays-Bas, Luxembourg*, Magellan, Paris, 1967, pp. 94-107.

E. C. Vollans, 'Urban Development in Belgium since 1830', in R. P. Beckinsale and J. M. Houston (Eds.), *Urbanisation and its Problems* (Blackwell, Oxford), 1968, pp. 171-198.

Anon, 'Economic Problems in Belgium's Wallonia', *European Studies*, 11, 1971, pp. 1-4.

R. C. Riley, 'Recent Developments in the Belgian Borinage. An Area of Declining Coal Production in the E.C.S.C.', *Geography*, 1965, pp. 261-273. *The Times*, London, 31st May 1972.

P. Huyskens, 'Dutch Limburg: the Heart of Europe in Metamorphosis', *Progress*, 1970, pp. 107-115.

G. R. P. Lawrence, 'The Changing Face of South Limburg', *Geography*, 56, 1971, pp. 35-39.

R. H. Osborne and P. T. Wheeler, *Rural Studies in the N.E. Netherlands*, Geographical Field Group No. 14, Nottingham, 1969.

R. Tamsma, 'The Northern Netherlands: Large Problem Area in a Small Country, Small Problem Area in a Large Economic Community', *Tijdschrift voor Economische en Sociale Geografie*, 63, 1972, pp. 162-179.

G. R. P. Lawrence, *Randstad Holland* (Oxford), 1973.

Chapter 8

CONCLUSIONS

By way of conclusion a brief consideration will be given to some of the relationships of the Benelux countries to a wider world, and to aspects of internal change.

International relationships

(i) *Trade* Emphasis has been placed on the growing similarity in the economic development of the Benelux countries. The Netherlands is gradually diversifying from her specialisation in agricultural products, and Belgium and Luxembourg are widening the range of their formerly narrow industrial base. These trends are reflected in patterns of international trade, particularly imports. The structure of imports in both the Netherlands and the Belgo-Luxembourg Economic Union (BLEU) is now almost identical, with manufactured goods, machinery and transport equipment accounting for 46% and 50% respectively. Foods account for 12% of the value of imports in both countries, mineral fuels for 10%, in spite of the greater tonnage of crude oil imports into the Netherlands, and chemicals for 8%. Only in the case of crude materials is there an obvious discrepancy (BLEU 14% compared with 10% for the Netherlands), largely a result of the greater importance of imported ores and scrap in BLEU. The similarity between the two trading groups is less striking in terms of exports, for agricultural products are very much more important in the Netherlands (28%) than in BLEU (8%). The imbalance shows up in the export of manufactured goods, machinery and transport equipment, with these items taking a 66% share of exports from BLEU compared with only 39% from the Netherlands.

International trade data may also be used to stress the part played by Benelux within the EEC, especially as originally constituted. Table 8.1 shows that both BLEU and the Netherlands are very closely tied to the other members of the original Six. Some 54% of imports into and 64% of exports from BLEU involve original EEC countries, and the figures for the Netherlands resemble these closely: 54% and 57% respectively. If two other countries, the United Kingdom, now a member of the Community, and the USA are added, it can be seen that more than two-thirds of BLEU and Dutch international trade is accounted for by these nations.

246

CONCLUSIONS

The table indicates that both the United Kingdom and the USA are more important trading partners with the Benelux countries than Italy, although the latter is a founder member of the EEC. This emphasises the extent to which trade and business links operate at a truly international scale, rather than merely within the confines of the Community. The importance of trade with the USA must be regarded as unusual, for the effect of distance normally ensures that international trade is greatest when the distance separating countries is small. This hypothesis is true of the Benelux countries in respect of their trade with each other and with West Germany and France, but the USA is their next most important trading partner. Indeed, some 11% of Dutch imports originate from the

TABLE 8.1

Origin of Benelux imports and destination of Benelux exports,
1968 (% *value*)

	BLEU		Netherlands	
	Imports	Exports	Imports	Exports
BLEU	—	—	18%	14%
Netherlands	14%	21%	—	—
W. Germany	21%	21%	26%	28%
France	15%	18%	6%	10%
Italy	4%	4%	4%	5%
UK	7%	4%	5%	8%
USA	8%	9%	11%	5%
Total	69%	77%	70%	70%

USA, almost twice as high as the percentage from France. The explanation is to be found in the importance of the USA in world trading patterns, the extent of American investment in Benelux and the fact that ocean transport is relatively cheap, helping to reduce the problems set by distance.

Having established the extent to which other countries share the international trade of Benelux, it is useful to see how important this trade is to the countries concerned. Clearly trade with Benelux is likely to be only a small part of the trade of very much larger countries, and as Table 8.2 illustrates, this is the case with the USA. The Netherlands takes 4% of USA exports, more than that of Mexico and only just less than that of West Germany. However, despite the size of the two major industrial nations of the 'old' Community, West Germany and France, both BLEU and the Netherlands nevertheless manage to figure prominently in their trading relations. 10% of West German trade is with the Netherlands, although it is slightly less with BLEU, and again 10% of French trade involves BLEU. French trade with the Netherlands is, however, much less developed, and only accounts for 5% of France's exports. Predictably, both BLEU and the Netherlands have the greatest share in each other's trade, amounting to approximately 20% in both cases. British trade with Benelux does not account for a large proportion of the national total, largely due to the size of the UK and to her extensive trading links with other parts of the world. By virtue of their small size, the Benelux countries may not be a major international trading bloc, but they are an important and integral part of the Six, and their location between France and West Germany, and now the UK, places them very much at the centre of both the old and the new European Economic Community.

TABLE 8.2

The importance of trade with Benelux to Benelux's trading partners, 1968 (% *value*)

	Imports from BLEU	Exports to BLEU	Imports from Netherlands	Exports to Netherlands
BLEU	—	—	14%	21%
Netherlands	18%	14%	—	—
West Germany	8%	7%	11%	10%
France	10%	10%	6%	5%
Italy	3%	4%	4%	5%
UK	2%	4%	5%	4%
USA	2%	2%	1%	4%

(ii) *Other international links* Trade in commodities, however, is only one indicator of the international contacts of the Benelux countries. The exploitation of central position, especially in relation to the contiguous states of West Germany and France, shown in the account of trade flows, could also be demonstrated with reference to other aspects of international contact. In the foreign tourist industry, for example, more than half the total foreign visitors to each of the Benelux countries come from adjacent states. Similarly the importance of international capital flows and the early establishment of multi-national industrial corporations has already been mentioned, and the Dutch in particular, with such firms as Unilever, Shell, Philips and Hoogovens, have forged investment links with their near neighbours. The same theme is again noticeable in the provision by Benelux operators of international transport services, traditionally waterborne, but increasingly by road, and once more it is the French and the West German markets that are the most important.

(iii) *Participation in international institutions* The central position of Benelux and its rôle within Western Europe has been reflected institutionally by its involvement in international political and economic bodies. The creation in 1921 of BLEU itself, a comprehensive customs and financial union, was indicative of the outward-looking attitude of the two countries involved. The Union effectively stemmed from the small size of Luxembourg and her need to replace the trading links forged with Germany in the 19th century, and was agreed to with some reluctance by Belgium after negotiations between Luxembourg and France had failed. However it can now be seen as the modest beginning of the much larger enterprise of the European Community. The exigencies of war set in motion the London discussions between the Dutch and Belgian governments in exile. These led to the 1943 monetary agreement, the 1944 customs convention, and finally to the 1948 Benelux Union, ratified in 1958. Although in many ways merely a recognition of an already apparent convergence of interests, its significance both in formally ending the long standing competition of the two states and as the precursor to the EEC is clear.

All three Benelux countries were among the first to accept the concept of collective security as embodied in the League of Nations and later the United Nations, and were founder members of such organisations as the Organisation for European Economic Cooperation (OEEC), the Organisation for Economic Cooperation and Development (OECD), the Council of Europe and West European Union. All three states are committed to the NATO defence system, with a Dutchman currently holding the office of Secretary General. The experience of the Benelux Union and the realisation of the advantages to be gained by small trading states within a larger market, prejudiced the Benelux countries in favour of the establishment of a European Economic Community. Once this was under way it was the Benelux countries, and in particular the Netherlands, who consistently supported an enlargement of the Community to include Britain and other members of the European Free Trade Association (EFTA).

Changes within Benelux

During the last three decades there have been a great many changes within the three countries, but the most important of these may conveniently be grouped into the categories of economic and social activity.

(i) *Economic activity* Despite regional policy there has been a continued concentration of economic activity in the growth areas, although there can be no doubt that this concentration is not as great as it would have been in the absence of government action. The demise of coal in Belgium and the Netherlands in favour of oil and natural gas has removed the backbone of coalfield employment—mining, and no labour intensive activity has taken its place. Nor have the peripheral and other restructuring regions exhibited notable expansion. Unfortunately the industries most attracted to the growth areas are the neotechnic industries which are characterised by very rapid expansion, and these activities do not seem to be unduly influenced by the loss of financial support incurred by locating themselves outside the development areas. In both Belgium and the Netherlands the growth areas include the major port areas, and since estuaries and deepwater harbour installations have been the site of important industrial development in the last two decades, the possibility that this phenomenon might aid problem regions has been virtually precluded. Only Zeebrugge, Vlissingen and Delfzijl outside the principal port areas have benefited from the growth of industrial plants at break of bulk points.

There is evidence that the very success of the growth areas may well assist some of the less fortunate regions, for the 'spread effect' of expansion within the next decade is likely to see large areas of Gelderland and Noord-Brabant caught up within Randstad, and parts of the Walloon coalfield coming under the aegis of Brussels. By the same token the Dutch Delta may be transformed into a 'Deltapoort', Europoort having exhausted its land resources. In contrast with Belgium, where all kinds of industry are still welcome, both the Netherlands and Luxembourg have become acutely conscious of the pollution hazards peculiar to some industries. In Luxembourg the state is the restrictive force, but in the Netherlands it is both the state, municipalities and local opinion which have exercised sanctions against 'dirty' industries. Doubtless the Belgians will follow suit in due course. The realisation that manufacturing industry now employs fewer people than the service sector, which is expanding at the expense of the former, has caused great stress to be laid on the need to improve amenity, for the tertiary industries always seek out the most pleasant areas in which to locate themselves. It is probable that many of the declining Walloon coalfield areas will continue to decline unless their infrastructure is substantially modified. Diversification of their manufacturing industries may not be sufficient.

(ii) *Social activity* Until recently the Benelux countries were noted for the rigid stratification of their societies and the stability and conservative nature of their social and political institutions. A careful balance was maintained between groups, each of which recognised its rôle and fulfilled its responsibilities within the social framework. The all-pervading power of the church, the restricted rôle of women outside the home and the strength of the middle class all contributed to this stability. In the Netherlands the *verzuiling* or pillar principle justified a form of social *apartheid*, where each section of society, whether Catholic or Protestant, worker or bourgeois, townsman or countryman, maintained a remarkably separate existence but formed individual pillars on which the state was carefully balanced.

Perhaps the most important feature of modern Western society has been the recent rapid acceleration in the rate of social change, which because it is a continuous process often passes almost unnoticed. Although this phenomenon is common to Western Europe it is not surprising that the Benelux countries, with their central position and their traditional tolerant receptiveness, should be once again in the forefront of change. There seem to be three causes of these social changes. Firstly, the arrival of mass affluence has radically altered the pattern of consumption and society has become more materialistic. Secondly, increasing technological inventiveness and the shortening time lag between innovation and mass application has virtually solved the problems of poverty and drudgery, and made possible such feats of engineering as the Delta Plan. At the same time, however, problems of social adjustment stemming from new work relationships and an increase in leisure time have arisen. Thirdly, the lengthening journey to work and to leisure has created new suburban communities and a new man-land relationship in which amenity values have a prominent place.

The symptoms of social change are manifested in a number of directions. The nature of old problems, such as the Belgian nationality issue, has subtly altered, while new tensions, such as racial conflict, have come to the fore. The religious and political cleavage represented by the 'confessional' political parties that have governed in Belgium and the Netherlands for most of the century, is being challenged by new political alignments. In Belgium the two extreme federalist parties, the Flemish Volksunie and the Rassemblement Wallon have increased their representation, and in the Netherlands the Provo movement and its successor, the Kabouters (gnomes), have made considerable headway in proposing an alternative society that largely ignores the traditional issues and divisions.

The goals of the Benelux states are similarly being challenged. Economic growth as an end in itself is being modified by arguments that stress the quality of life and look to the enhancement of the natural and the man-made environment. The implementation of economic and social planning policies is meeting increasing resistance from those who place a high value on neighbourhood communities. Issues such as the continued industrial development of Rijnmond and the North Sea Canal zone of Amsterdam, the restructuring of the central areas of cities and the extension of the inter-city motorway system, although often envied abroad, are receiving increasing criticism within Benelux.

Although it is unrealistic to assign a date to a continuous process of change, it is possible to recognise 1966 as a watershed in public recognition of what was happening. In that year the riots at the Zwartberg colliery in Belgian Limburg and at the University of Leuven brought to a head the nationality dispute. At the same time these events highlighted regional economic grievances and resulted in major changes in Belgian regional development policy. 1966 saw the challenge to the Dutch facade of political compromise by the open defiance of the monarchy shown in Amsterdam at the wedding of Crown Princess Beatrix and Count von Amsberg, itself a break with tradition. The balance of political power held by the traditional political parties was questioned in 1966 by the election of the first Provo to the Amsterdam city council and by the foundation of the D66 party, representing new alignments in society.

Benelux is richer than ever before with an assured economic future within the enlarged European Community. Considerable success has been achieved in the distribution of the fruits of economic progress and an equitable society has largely been attained. At the same time, however, the old social order is rapidly changing and the traditional centres of power are no longer accepted without question, although no clear substitutes have yet been found. Amid these doubts and uncertainties two themes remain: the central position of the Benelux states within the new European Community, and the open nature of Benelux society which has always been able to put this centrality to good use.

Further Reading

F. Hugget, *The Modern Netherlands* (Pall Mall Press, London), 1971.

Vernon Mallinson, *Belgium* (Ernest Benn, London), 1970.

J. E. Meade, H. H. Liesner and S. J. Wells, *Case Studies in European Union: The Machanics of Integration* (Oxford), 1964.

Secretariat of the Benelux Economic Union, *What is the Significance of Benelux?*, 1965.

INDEX